Established 1858.

TRADE MARK.
THE STEEPLE, ST. NINIANS, NEAR STIRLING.

Industries of Stirling and District

.

INDUSTRIES OF
STIRLING AND DISTRICT

Originally published
Stirling, 1909

Stirling Council Library Service
1998

Published by
Stirling Council Library Service

ISBN 1 870542 37 1

Printed by
Cordfall Ltd, Glasgow
0141 332 4640

INDUSTRIES

OF

STIRLING AND DISTRICT

PROFUSELY ILLUSTRATED

With Introduction, Burgh and County Information, List of
Members of Public Boards, Officials, Statistics, &c.

STIRLING :

ENEAS MACKAY, 43 MURRAY PLACE.

JOHN JAMIESON, 40 CRAIGS.

———

1909.

STIRLING OBSERVER
PRESS
40 Craigs; Stirling

FOREWORD

Throughout 1908, the *Stirling Observer* ran a series of articles describing some of the businesses operating in Stirling and Stirlingshire during that period. These articles, with accompanying photographs, line drawings and advertisements were put together into book form and published as *Industries of Stirling and District* in 1909. As some of the firms were founded in the very early nineteenth century, the book provides a valuable insight into Stirling's business history for student, researcher and the general reader.

Of particular interest are the photographs of people at work – candle-makers, printers, brass-finishers, grocers, laundry-workers and mill workers – occupations either made obsolete by progress, or so changed by technological innovation as to be virtually unrecognisable today.

It must be borne in mind that the articles constituted the equivalent of today's advertising feature and thus written from the management point of view, they show each firm in a particularly positive light.

Inevitably, over the ninety years, changing consumer trends have dictated the demise of most of these erstwhile well-known firms. It is perhaps surprising therefore, but happily so, to note that there are still a few survivors, and Stirling Council Library Services acknowledge with gratitude financial assistance from the management of The Drummond Trust, 3 Pitt Terrace, Stirling, and of Grampian Engineering Co. Ltd, Causewayhead, Stirling. Thanks are also due to Fife and Central Scotland Chamber of Commerce for help with publishing costs. The text is exactly as it was published in 1909. Some of the illustrations however have been adjusted in size.

THE GRAMPIAN ENGINEERING CO. LTD
STRUCTURAL ENGINEERS

CAUSEWAYHEAD

STIRLING, FK9 5EL

TELEPHONE: 01786 450367

ESTABLISHED 1907

FAX: 01786 463701

CONTENTS.

Stirling from the River Forth.

TELEGRAMS: "VIRTUE, STIRLING." TELEPHONE No. 13.

VIRTUE & CO.,

General Ironmongers,

Cabinetmakers,

Upholsterers,

Removal Contractors,

Storers of Household
Effects,

14, 26, 30 MURRAY PLACE,
STIRLING.

SEE BUSINESS NOTICE—PAGES 141-148.

THE "MAIN" GAS COOKER

Is indispensable where

Good Cooking is required.

COOK BY GAS.

Cheaper, Cleaner, and more efficient than Coal.

The " MAIN " COOKER is the only Stove with all Interior Fittings Porcelain Enamelled.

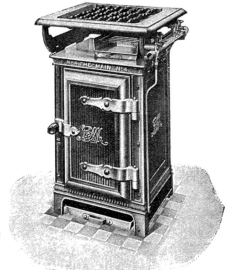

The "St. Mungo" Gas-Heated Steam Radiators.

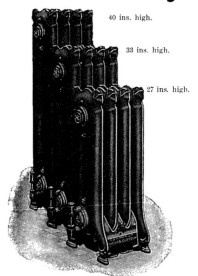

40 ins. high.

33 ins. high.

27 ins. high.

Invaluable for Heating Schools, Churches, Public Buildings, Corridors, Halls, Country Houses, Banks, and Counting Houses.

Cheapest and Best to Use.

Each Radiator is fitted with a new reliable type of Automatic Gas Regulation.

On Hire, at Moderate Rentals, from

Stirling Gas=Light Coy.
Showrooms—
MURRAY PLACE, STIRLING.

FOR HIGH-CLASS MOTOR CARRIAGES,

GEORGE OWEN,

Motor Car Merchant and Engineer,

69-81 PORT STREET,

▫ ▫ STIRLING. ▫ ▫

DISTRICT AGENCY FOR   ARGYLL, ARROL-JOHNSTON, HUMBER, VULCAN, ROVER, ADAMS, and other British Makers.————

OFFICIAL REPAIRER TO ROYAL AUTOMOBILE CLUB.

MOTOR CARS—OPEN OR CLOSED—ON HIRE.

STOCKIST FOR MICHELIN, PALMER, DUNLOP, AND CONTINENTAL TYRES.

Telegrams—"OWEN, STIRLING."   Telephone—120.

THOMAS MENZIES & CO.

Carpet, House-Furnishing and

General Drapery Warehousemen,

HIGH-CLASS DRESSMAKERS, MANTLEMAKERS, MILLINERS, SILK MERCERS, FURRIERS, HOSIERS, GLOVERS, &c.

Specialities.

CLAN TARTANS OF EVERY DESCRIPTION.
REAL SHETLAND HAND-KNIT GOODS.
SCOTCH HOME-SPUNS, HARRIS, AND DONEGAL
COSTUME TWEEDS.

PATTERNS FREE ON APPLICATION.

Marriage Trousseaux. **Family Mournings.**

LETTER ORDERS HAVE PERSONAL ATTENTION.

36-38 KING ST., STIRLING.

Telephone 3Y2.

See page 149.

INTRODUCTION.

TIRLING, situated on the banks of the river Forth, is one of the oldest Royal Burghs in Scotland. Long a residence of royalty, favoured by reason of the strength and beautiful situation of the Castle, it may well be claimed that the most historic area of Scotland is in and around Stirling. The ancient buildings in the town are among the finest in Scotland, these including the Castle, the Palace, Parliament House, East and West Churches, Mar's Work, Argyll Ludging, and the Guild Hall; while in the neighbourhood are the famous Old Bridge of Stirling and the ruins of Cambuskenneth Abbey. Being a market centre, a royal and parliamentary burgh, and the county town of Stirlingshire, and situated on the borders of West Perthshire and Clackmannanshire, embracing an extensive district largely devoted to agriculture, the merchants and manufacturers of Stirling are in an excellent position to supply the needs of the inhabitants of the surrounding districts. Visitors are agreeably surprised at seeing the spacious and up-to-date business premises to be found in the burgh, and many have expressed the opinion that these are amongst the finest in Scotland, being equal to the best in the cities and much superior to those of towns of a similar size. In addition to a large and permanent population, Stirling and district is much frequented throughout the year by visitors from all over the world, while during the summer large excursion parties from various quarters visit the town.

The town may be said to owe its origin to its nearness to what must have always been the principal ford across the Forth, and hence Stirling is known as "The Key to the Highlands." The ancient fortress and royal residence also accounts for the growth of the burgh, as from the earliest recorded times Stirling Castle has held a prominent position in Scottish history.   From its picturesque situation and beautiful surroundings, the Castle has been compared with the Acropolis of Athens, while it also has a resemblance to Edinburgh.   The higher parts of the town, and more particularly the Castle, command very beautiful and extensive views.   The foregrounds on every side are rich, highly cultivated plains, while to the

Stirling Castle (Autumn).

north rise the woods above Bridge of Allan and Dunblane, capped by the stretch of the historic Sheriffmuir; the picturesque cliffs of Abbey Craig, surmounted by the handsome monument to the memory of Sir William Wallace, occupy the middle distance, with the pastoral slopes of the Ochil Hills as a magnificent background; to the east are the fertile carses of Stirling and Falkirk, with the Forth winding its silvery course to the sea, and beyond are seen the distant hills of Fife and the Lothians; to the north-west lie the flat but nicely wooded valleys of the upper Forth and the Teith and the Braes of Doune; in the middle distance towards the west and south are the Campsie Fells and Menteith Hills, while sweeping round from west to north is the great semi-circular range of mountains, several of which are among the monarchs of the Grampians, conspicuous peaks being Ben Lomond (3192 feet), Ben Venue (2393), Ben A'an (1851), Ben Ledi (2875), Ben Voirlich (3224), and Uam Var (2179).

LINKS OF FORTH, FROM STIRLING CASTLE

Stirling is a railway centre of considerable importance, being on the main line between the north and south of Scotland, and the Callander and Oban Railway to the Western Highlands, while it is also the terminus for trains of the North British Company from Edinburgh by the Forth Bridge, and for branches to Fife and along the valley of the Forth to Balloch. Owing to the windings of the river Forth there is not much shipping trade at

Stirling, though a connection with North Sea and Baltic ports, which has existed for centuries, is still maintained.

In recent years Stirling has become one of the most favoured towns in Scotland as a centre for the sale of live stock, largely attended sales being held weekly, with frequent special sales; and there is also a weekly grain market of long standing.

The coalfields now opened up in the neighbourhood of the town have added considerably to the earning and spending power of the district, whilst

Stirling from Polmaise.

situated sufficiently far away to prevent the residential amenity of the burgh being affected adversely.

As an indication of the importance of Stirling as a business centre, it may be stated that on an average 1,137,130 letters, &c., were handled monthly at the Post Office, while 28,280 parcels monthly were also dealt with. The staff at the head office numbers 82, with every prospect of increasing, as during the last few years the additional work has been very noticeable. With a thoroughly capable staff, the business at Stirling head office has all

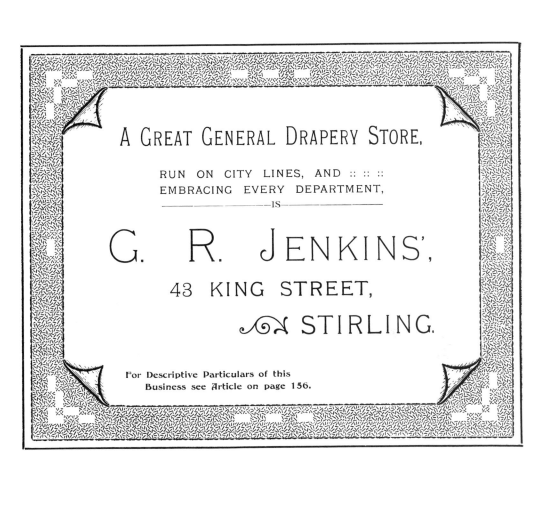

A GREAT GENERAL DRAPERY STORE,

RUN ON CITY LINES, AND :: :: ::
EMBRACING EVERY DEPARTMENT,
————————IS————————

G. R. JENKINS',

43 KING STREET,

℘ STIRLING.

For Descriptive Particulars of this
Business see Article on page 156.

along, but particularily of late years, been carried through in such a manner as to call for favourable comment. The counter service is of a praiseworthy description, and the efficiency of the telegraphic staff has earned the enconiums of pressmen—than whom there are no better judges—on many occasions when a large amount of matter has had to be wired to newspapers throughout the United Kingdom.

Argyll Ludging, Stirling.

From statements supplied by Mr. Goudie, burgh surveyor, and by Mr. Papworth, burgh electrical engineer, regarding the water and electrical supplies of the burgh, the reader cannot fail to be impressed with the fact that these two very necessary adjuncts to modern businesses are in an excellent position, both departments being quite capable of responding to a larger consumption than the present demands made upon them. In addition, the circumstances that the Stirling Corporation is in the position of granting sites for works, &c., on very favourable terms—and heartily invite applications for the same—together with the admirable railway facilities of the town and the coalfields in the neighbourhood, is an inducement to manufacturers and others to establish industries in the burgh.

It may be observed here that the business of the Stirling Gas-Light Company, Ltd., is marked by continuous progress, the output for the current

STIRLING OLD BRIDGE

year having increased to 136,000,000 cubic feet. The works, as will be noted from our review, are of the most complete and up-to-date character.

Regarding the climate, it may be claimed that the burgh of Stirling is fairly dry, the total rainfall for last year (1908) being 36.04 inches. The winter mildness of Stirling, compared with many other towns in the midlands of Scotland, is also noticeable, the fact that very little snow falls, and that the frosts are less severe, being often commented on.

A casual glance over the pages of this volume will readily indicate the size and character of some of the businesses carried on in Stirling. While these are representative of the whole, we would particularly draw attention to the fact that some old-established and prosperous enterprises are not included. In compiling the list, an endeavour was made to secure the history of the earliest commenced local commercial undertaking, and only one in each trade, but in some instances it was not found possible to carry this out, and we can only request our readers to take note of the advertisement pages in this book, where will be found notices of other important businesses which, for the reason stated, are not included in our review.

Mar's Work, Stirling.

East and West Churches, Stirling.

BURGH AND COUNTY INFORMATION.

POPULATION OF PARLIAMENTARY BURGH.

	Census 1901.	1891.	1881.
Males, ...	8,592	7,819	———
Females, ...	9,811	8,957	———
	18,403	16,776	16,013

Estimated Population, 1909—21,000.

MUNICIPAL CONSTITUENCY.

	Males.	Supplementary.	Totals.
Ward No. 1, King Street,	453	189	642
,, 2, Port Street,	800	271	1071
,, 3, Baker Street,	554	140	694
,, 4, Cowane Street,	994	257	1251
,, 5, St. Ninians,	452	134	586
	3253	991	4244

Area, 1377 Acres.
Mileage of Streets, 19 Miles.

VALUATION OF BURGH, 1908-1909.

Lands, Houses, &c., ...	£109,643 16 2
Railways, Tramways, and Gas, ...	7,700 0 0
	£117,343 16 2

1896-97,	...	£87,765 7 4
1897-98,	...	89,440 1 9
1898-99,	...	92,765 4 1
1899-1900,	...	95,351 17 0
1900-1901,	...	96,726 14 4
1901-1902,	...	98,664 8 5
1902-1903,	...	101,903 15 6
1903-1904,	...	104,587 7 1
1904-1905,	...	107,162 15 3
1905-1906,	...	109,874 14 0
1906-1907,	...	112,881 8 8
1907-1908,	...	115,799 5 1

RATES AND ASSESSMENTS,
1908-1909.

	Owners.	Occupiers.
Burgh General, ...	—	1/1¼ per £
Burgh Improvement,	½d. per £	½d. ,,
Sewers, ...	½d. ,,	—
Roads and Bridges, ...	3¼d. ,,	3½d. ,,
Old Road Debt, ...	¼d. ,,	—
Public Health--namely, Public Health, 4⅜d. per £, and Special Sewer, ⅛d. per £, ...	2¼d. ,,	2¼d. ,,
Public Libraries, ...	—	1d. ,,
Registration of Voters,	¼d. ,,	¼d. ,,
Lunacy, ...	½d. ,,	½d. ,,
Domestic Water Rate for Dwelling-houses,&c.,	—	8d ,,
Public Water Rate, ...	1d. ,,	—
Domestic Water Rate for Shops, 4d. per £ on Occupiers, ...	—	—
Poor and School, subject to deductions, ...	1/ ,,	1/0½ ,,
Occupiers of Agricultural Lands, 3½d. per £, ...		
	1/8½ per £	3/5½ per £

Combined total, ...	5/2	
Income Tax (on unearned income), ...	1/- per £	
Do. (on earned income), ...	9d. ,,	
Subject to Statutory deductions.		

PARLIAMENTARY REPRESENTATIVES.

STIRLING COUNTY.

Donald MacKenzie Smeaton, C.S.I., 12 Chester Square, London, S.W., and Downsland, Basingstoke, Hants.

Agent—Henry D. M'Lellan, solicitor, 48 Barnton Street.

Parliamentary Constituency, 19,796.

PARLIAMENTARY REPRESENTATIVES.

STIRLING DISTRICT OF BURGHS.

(Stirling, Dunfermline, Queensferry, Inverkeithing, and Culross.)

Arthur Augustus William Harry Ponsonby, Shulebrede Priory, Lynchmere, Sussex.

Agent—Robert Taylor, solicitor, 46 Barnton Street.

Parliamentary Constituency, 3253.

TOWN COUNCIL, 1908-09.

Ward No. I. — King Street Ward.

George Plenderleith, blacksmith, ...	... Bailie
William Montgomery Reyburn, banker, ...	Hon. Treasurer
Robert M'Culloch, draper, ...	Councillor
Daniel Stewart, jeweller, ...	,,

Ward No. II.—Port Street Ward.

John Steel (Police Judge), plumber,	Dean of Guild
Hugh Gavin, draper, ...	Councillor
William Gourlay (Police Judge), builder,	,,
James Fletcher Macintosh, bootmaker,	,,
John Raffan, chemist, ...	,,

Ward No. III.—Baker Street Ward.

Oliver Petrie Derrick, auctioneer, ...	Councillor
John Duff, plumber, ...	,,
Robert Menzies, grocer, ...	,,
Henry Pender Watt, cabinetmaker,	,,

Ward No. IV.—Cowane Street Ward.

James Thomson, coachbuilder, ...	... Provost
David Bayne, grocer, ...	... Bailie
Parlan Macfarlan, seed and manure merchant, ...	... ,,
Ridley Sandeman, laundryman, ...	Councillor
Daniel Wylie (Police Judge), printer,	,,

Ward No. V.—St. Ninians Ward.

Andrew Buchanan, grocer, ...	... Bailie
James Hay, joiner, ...	Councillor
Archibald Thomson, law cashier, ...	,,

WATERWORKS COMMISSIONERS.

The PROVOST OF STIRLING, Chairman *ex officio.*

From Town Council.

Bailie Parlan Macfarlan.
Treasurer William Montgomery Reyburn.
Councillors Oliver Petrie Derrick.
John Duff.
Daniel Stewart.
Archibald Thomson.

From Ratepayers.

Messrs. George Christie, draper.
John T. Dale, hairdresser.
Thomas Ferguson, joiner.
John A. Gordon, chemist.
John F. Oswald, bookseller.
John S. Ralston, confectioner.

Clerk—David B. Morris, Town Clerk.

COMMISSIONERS OF THE FORTH NAVIGATION.

Royal Burgh of Stirling.

The Provost, Magistrates, and Councillors.

Perthshire.

Col. Home Drummond of Blair Drummond, Stirling.
William Watson Murray, Catter House, Drymen.

Stirlingshire.

Andrew Mackay, Fairfield, Grangemouth.
Alex. Young, Craigview, Causewayhead, Stirling.

Clackmannanshire.

George Cousin, The Walk, Alloa.
T. S. Knox, The Cottages, Cambus.
Clerk—David B. Morris, Town Clerk, Stirling.

RIVER FORTH DISTRICT SALMON FISHERY BOARD.

Upper Proprietors.

The Earl of Moray, Doune Lodge, Doune.
Colonel Home Drummond of Blair Drummond, Stirling.
Captain Stirling of Keir, Dunblane.

Lower Proprietors.

The Provost of Stirling.
John M. Morries of Blackgrange, Gogar, Stirling.
Major Alastair Murray of Polmaise, Stirling.
Chairman—Holmes Ivory, W.S., Crown Receiver, New Register House, Edinburgh.
Clerk—Henry Robb, solicitor, Stirling.

Old Town Mansions.

STIRLING EDUCATIONAL TRUST.

ELECTING BODIES—

Magistrates and Town Council of Stirling.

(*a*) Town Councillors.

Provost James Thomson.
Bailies David Bayne.
      Andrew Buchanan.
      Parlan Macfarlan.
Dean of Guild Judge John Steel.
Councillors John Raffan.
      Henry Pender Watt.
      Hugh Ferguson, bootmaker.

(*b*) Minister from other than Established Church.
    Rev. Thomas Wright, M.A., U.F.C., Stirling.

School Board of Stirling.

Daniel Barker, stair-railer.
Rev. Colin Mackenzie, U.F.C., St. Ninians.
James C. Muirhead, solicitor.

University Court of Glasgow.

Charles M. King of Antermony, Milton of Campsie.

University Court of Edinburgh.

Rev. J. M. Robertson, D.D., E.C., St. Ninians.

Presbytery of Stirling.

Rev. James Paisley Lang, Stirling.
Chairman—Hugh Ferguson, Stirling.
Clerk—David B. Morris, Town Clerk.
Treasurer and Factor—Thomas J. Y. Brown, solicitor.

OLD AGE PENSIONS SUB-COMMITTEES.

Ward No. I.—King Street Ward.—Treasurer Reyburn, chairman ; Bailie Plenderleith ; Councillors M'Culloch and Stewart ; Messrs. George Begbie, law clerk ; William Hynd, tailor ; John M'Gregor, blacksmith ; William Simpson, pawnbroker.

OLD AGE PENSIONS SUB-COMMITTEES.

Ward No. II.—Port Street Ward.—Dean of Guild Judge Steel, chairman ; Judge Gourlay ; Councillors Gavin, Macintosh, and Raffan ; Messrs. John Blyth, hall-keeper ; Robert Gilchrist, carpet weaver ; William Somers, joiner ; William Low Thomson, solicitor.

Ward No. III.—Baker Street Ward.—Councillor Watt, chairman ; Councillors Derrick, Duff, and Menzies ; Messrs. John William Heron, teacher ; James Minty, clothier ; James Tainsh, coach painter ; John B. Taylor, gardener.

Ward No. IV.—Cowane Street Ward.—Provost Thomson, chairman ; Bailies Bayne and Macfarlan, Judge Wylie, Councillor Sandeman ; Messrs. Adam Elder, railway agent ; William Law, grocer ; John Merrilees, plumber : Hugh M'Master, foreman carter.

Ward No. V.—St. Ninians Ward.—Bailie Buchanan, chairman ; Councillors Hay and Thomson ; Messrs. Peter Aitken, builder ; Archd. B. Laidlaw, surgeon ; Bernard Reynolds, builder.

STIRLING PUBLIC LIBRARY COMMITTEE.

Rev. David Duncan Ormond, Chairman.

Council Representatives.

Bailies Andrew Buchanan.
      George Plenderleith.
Dean of Guild Judge John Steel.
Councillors Oliver P. Derrick.
      John Raffan.
      Archibald Thomson.
      Henry P. Watt.

Householder Representatives.

James W. Drummond, seedsman.
Daniel Ferguson, banker.
Michael J. Hare, insurance agent.
Robert Kidston, LL.D., residenter.
Hugh M'Master, foreman carter.
Rev. David Duncan Ormond, minister.
Robert Whyte, solicitor.
Librarian—William G. Waugh.

WALLACE MONUMENT CUSTODIERS.

The Provost, Magistrates, and Councillors.
First Minister of Stirling.
Master of Cowane's Hospital.
The Lords Lieutenant of the Counties of Stirling, Clackmannan, and Perth.
The Sheriff Deputes of said Counties.
The Dean of the Guildry of Stirling.

(Provost Thomson, *Convener*.)

Committee—

Provost Thomson, Dean of Guild Steel, Judge Wylie, and Mr. John Crawford—Dean of Guild Steel, *Convener.*

National Wallace Monument, Stirling.

WILLIAM AITKEN,

Family Bread & Biscuit Baker,

Established 1858.

Wedding,
Christening,
and
Birthday
Cakes.

TRADE MARK.
THE STEEPLE, ST. NINIANS, NEAR STIRLING.

Shortbread
and
Currant
Loaves.

ST. NINIANS BAKERY,

St. Ninians.

SPECIAL.—Our Famous **ABERNETHY BISCUITS.**

VANS deliver Bread to any Address in Town or Country.

Telegraphic Address : " Cowbrough."
Telephone No. 44.

ESTABLISHED 1839.

COWBROUGH & MERCER,

FAMILY GROCERS,

. . .

Wine and Scotch Whisky Merchants,

Port Street,

STIRLING.

Branches : WALLACE STREET, FORTH CRESCENT, and MILLAR PLACE, STIRLING.

COUNTY OFFICIALS.

Lord Lieutenant of the County of Stirling—
His Grace the Duke of Montrose, K.T., Buchanan Castle, Drymen.

Sheriff of the Counties of Stirling, Dumbarton, and Clackmannan—
John M. Lees, Esq., LL.B., K.C., 4 Darnaway Street, Edinburgh.

Sheriff Substitute at Stirling—
And. Mitchell, M.A., advocate, Springwood, Stirling.

Honorary Sheriffs Substitute—
James R. Buntine, Robert MacLuckie, Provost Thomson, Stirling ; John B. Young, advocate, Edinburgh.

*Sheriff Clerk—*John Gilchrist Curror.

Depute, and Auditor of Sheriff Court—
Donald Cowan.

*Chief Constable—*Charles Middleton.

County Clerk and Clerk to Police Committee—
James Learmonth.

*Procurator Fiscal—*James Rennie Archibald.
*Depute—*Robert Waugh.

*Clerk of the Peace—*Andrew C. Buchanan.

Depute Clerks—
George Begbie and James Macpherson.

*Procurator-Fiscal to Justices—*Charles Middleton.

County Council—Central District.

*Clerks—*Thomas Lupton and James M. MacLuckie.
*Sanitary Inspector—*John Barr.
*Road Surveyor—*Donald Cox.
*Inspector of Weights and Measures—*James Fraser.

BURGH OFFICIALS.

*Town Clerk—*David B. Morris.
*Town Clerk Depute—*David G. White.
*Chamberlain—*John A. Clark.
*Master of Works—*Andrew H. Goudie.
*Electrical Engineer—*John W. Papworth.
*Chief Constable—*Thomas Ferguson, Burgh Police Office.

BURGH OFFICIALS.

*Factor, Cowane's Hospital—*John Crawford, 3 Port Street.
*Factor, Spittal's Hospital—*William M. Brown, 10 Princes Street.
*Collector of Rates—*Eben. Gentleman, 2 Wolf Craig.
*Medical Officer of Health—*Dr. Andrew F. Wilson, 1 Viewfield Place.
*Auditor—*J. Maxtone Graham, C.A., 34 Charlotte Square, Edinburgh.
*Veterinary Surgeon—*John M. Stewart, 72 Murray Place.
*Inspector under Diseases of Animals Act—*Thomas Ferguson, Burgh Police Office.
*Sanitary Inspector—*John Fyfe, 15 Spittal Street.
*Health Visitor—*Miss Mary Molloy, 15 Spittal St.
*Burgh Assessor—*Thomas Currie, 16 King Street.
*Firemaster—*Robert Oswald, 82 Spittal Street.
*Burgh Analyst—*Andrew Wilson, F.I.C., Hayford House, Cambusbarron.
*Inspector of Weights and Measures—*James Fraser, County Buildings.
*Overseer, Cemeteries—*Peter Lees, Mount Pleasant Place.
*Bellman—*Matthew Kidd, 25 Broad Street.
*Burgh Officer—*John Burns, 3 Middle Craigs.

Guildry of Stirling.

*Dean—*Judge John Steel.
Joint Clerks and Treasurers—
Thomas Lupton and James M. MacLuckie.
*Officer—*William M'Naughton.

Seven Incorporated Trades.

(Bakers, Fleshers, Hammermen, Shoemakers, Skinners, Weavers, Tailors.)

*Convener—*Judge Daniel Wylie.
*Clerk—*David Chrystal, solicitor.
*Officer—*John Syme.

Omnium Gatherum.

*Deacon—*James J. Miller, brewer.
*Clerk—*Hugh M'Master, foreman carter.

STIRLING PARISH COUNCIL,
1907-1910.

William Somerville, J.P., tobacconist, Chairman.

Ward No. I.—King Street Ward.

John Gray, seedsman.
James Minty, clothier.
James Kemp Smith, engineer.

Ward No. II.—Port Street Ward.

John Brown, grocer.
Thomas J. Y. Brown, solicitor.
William Somerville, tobacconist.
William Somerville, ironmonger.

Ward No. III.—Baker Street Ward.

John Blyth, insurance agent.
John W. Heron, teacher.
William Simpson, pawnbroker.

Ward No. IV.—Cowane Street Ward.

Peter M'Neill, draper.
James Oliphant, confectioner.
Daniel Sinclair, joiner.
David W. Soutar, clothier.

Ward No. V.—St. Ninians Ward.

John Corser, grocer.
Archibald Duncan, printer.

Landward Part of the Parish.

John H. Pride, insurance agent.
Inspector of Poor, Clerk to Council—John Paterson.
Medical Officers—Dr. James H. Murray and
Dr. Alex. Chalmers.

Cambuskenneth Abbey and Tomb of James III.

Stirling Combination Poorhouse.

Governor—Donald M'Millan.
Matron—Mrs. M'Millan.
Clerk to Combination—Henry Robb, solicitor.
Medical Officer—Dr. James Ernest Moorhouse.

18

CHURCHES AND CLERGY.

Established.

East, St. John Street—James P. Lang.
West, St. John Street—Archibald J. Miller, M.A.
North, Murray Place—David P. M'Lees.
Marykirk, St. Mary's Wynd—Thomas Skeoch.

United Free.

Peter Memorial, Park Terrace—John Chalmers, M.A.
South, Murray Place—John Arnott, M.A.
West, Cowane Street—
Erskine, St. John Street—Robert Primrose.
Viewfield, Viewfield Place—Thomas Wright, M.A.
Allan Park, Dumbarton Road—John Tait Gowan-
 lock, M.A ; colleague, James W. Purves, M.A.

Episcopal, Holy Trinity, Albert Place—R. Percival
 Brown, M.A.
Congregational, Murray Place—James C. M'Lachlan,
 M.A.
Baptist, Murray Place—George Yuille.
Wesleyan, Queen Street—John Keddie.
Roman Catholic, St. Mary's, Upper Bridge Street—
 The Very Rev. Monseigneur Smith, V.G.

St. Ninians.

Established—John M. Robertson, D.D.
North United Free—Colin Mackenzie.
South United Free—Robert Frew, D.D. ; colleague,
 David Smith, M.A.

Registrar of Births, Marriages, and Deaths—
 Ebenezer Gentleman, 2 Wolf Craig.

Session Clerk for Stirling Parish—
John Brown, solicitor, 10 Barnton Street.

Session Clerk for Marykirk Parish—
William J. Nicol, clerk, 59 Wallace Street.

Session Clerk for St. Ninians Parish—
Thomas J. Y. Brown, solicitor, 53 Port Street.

MEDICAL PRACTITIONERS.

Alexander Chalmers.
John Drew, M D.
Surgeon-Lieut.-Colonel F. J. Greig.
Robert C. Highet, M.B., C.M.
W. L. Johnston, M.B., Ch.B.
Archibald B. Laidlaw.
Peter M'Fadyen, M.D.
P. F. M'Farlan.
William A. Mackintosh, M.B., C.M.
James E. Moorhouse, M.A., B.Sc., M.D.
James H. Murray, M.D.
Grahame H. Skinner, M.B., Ch.B.
A. Whytt, M.B., C.M.
Andrew F. Wilson, L.F.P.S.G.

BANKS AND AGENTS.

Bank of Scotland—James W. Campbell.
British Linen—John R. Park.
Clydesdale—William M. Reyburn.
Commercial—Hugh S. Robson.
National—Daniel Ferguson.
North of Scotland and Town and County—Hill &
 Whyte.
Royal—Thomas L. Reid.
Union—Thomas Lupton and Robert Cairns.

SOCIETY OF SOLICITORS AND PROCURATORS.

Dean—David B. Morris.
Sub-Dean—James Dobbie.
Secretary and Treasurer—James C. Muirhead.
Dean's Council—Robert Whyte, E. W. Simpson,
 J. S. Henderson, and J. M. MacLuckie.
Procurators for the Poor—Alexander Jenkins and
 H. D. M'Lellan.
Curator of Library—
Fiscal—David W. Logie.
Board of Examiners—A. C. Buchanan, Robert
 Whyte, and James C. Muirhead, *ex officio.*

Adams, Alexander E.,	1908
Brown, Thomas J. Y., and N.P.,	1897
Buchanan, Andrew C.,	1880
Chrystal, David, and N.P.,	1888

SOCIETY OF SOLICITORS AND PROCURATORS.

Curror, John G.,	1877
Darling, Thomas C.,	1903
Dobbie, James, B.L., and N.P.,	1890
Donaldson, William, and N.P.,	1885
Douglas, Peter,	1905
Fleming, James S., and N.P.,	1872
Gentleman, Ebenezer,	1868
Gibson, James A.,	1895
Henderson, James S.,	1905
Hendry, Alexander,	1902
Hill, Robert Alex., S.S.C., and N.P.,	1885
Jenkins, Alexander,	1865
Jenkins, John,	1896
Lennox, William M.,	1904
Logie, David W.,	1873
Lupton, Thomas,	1893
M'Lellan, Henry D.,	1906
MacLuckie, James M.,	1896
Morris, David B.,	1891
Morrison, Alex., jun.,	1905
Muirhead, James C.,	1900
Muirhead, Thomas,	1898
Paterson, Alexander,	1901
Robb, Henry, B.L.,	1889
Simpson, Ewen W.,	1906
Taylor, Robert,	1897
Wardlaw, Andrew M.,	1893
Whyte, Robert, and N.P.,	1881

Keeper of Library and Officer—A. Johnston.

NEWSPAPERS.

Stirling Observer—Wednesday—1836.
Stirling Saturday Observer—Friday—1873.
Bridge of Allan Gazette—Friday—1884.
Callander Advertiser—Friday—1884.

John Jamieson.

Stirling Journal and Advertiser—Friday—1820.
Stirling and Bridge of Allan Reporter—Saturday—1859.

James Hogg & Co.

Stirling Sentinel—Tuesday—1888.
The Visitor—Wednesday—1892.

Cook & Wylie.

Town House, Stirling.

20

D. & J. MacEwen & Co.

STIRLING

(Branch Establishments—Callander, Crieff, Dunblane, Bridge of Allan,
Killin, Fort William, Aberfoyle ;
also at Inverness, under the name of MacDonald & Mackintosh),

For over a Century

THE LEADING GROCERS

In Central Scotland.

Every article sold is the best of its kind procurable, and our
prices will compare favourably with those charged by the best
City Houses or Stores.

We hold a very rare selection of Old Vintage Ports, Clarets, and
Sherries, and are also the Proprietors of

The Famous " Sterlini " Whisky,

which is guaranteed Pure Malt, and Ten Years' Old.

Telegrams—" MacEwen."   Telephone No. 15.

Telephones :
GLASGOW—National 154, Charing X.
Do.   Post Office 4299.
STIRLING—National 244.

Established
1867.

ARGYLE JOINERY WORKS,
1070 ARGYLE STREET,
GLASGOW.
CANAL STREET. CLYDEBANK.

Robert Anderson & Sons

Wrights & Building Contractors,

21 BARNTON STREET,

Stirling,

DOORS, WINDOWS, MANTELPIECES,
&c., made to any Design, at
Special Terms to the Trade.

Estimates Given
for all kinds of Joiner and
Architectural Cabinet
Works.

Estimates Given
for all kinds of Mason,
Brick, and
Granolithic Works.

ROYAL INFIRMARY AND DISPENSARY.

President—

Henry David Erskine, C.V.O., of Cardross.

Vice-Presidents—

Major Alastair Bruce Murray of Polmaise.
Sir Alan Henry Seton Steuart, Bart., of Touch.
Provost Thomson, Stirling.

Trustees—

H. D. Erskine, Esq., of Cardross,
    President of the Institution, and his successors in office.
Sir Alan H. Seton Steuart, Bart., of Touch,
    Chairman of the Central District Committee of the
    Stirling County Council, and his successors in office.
Provost Thomson, Stirling,
    and his successors in office.
Sir James B. Smith, of Clifford Park.

Directors—

H. D. Erskine, *Chairman.*
James Thomson, *Vice-Chairman.*
Edwin Bolton of Carbrook.
Robert Christie, Caledonian Railway Station.
David Chrystal, 15 Victoria Square.
W. G. Crum, Auchenbowie.
Captain Dundas, Ochtertyre.
John Jenkins, 11 Clifford Road.
Alex. M'Grigor of Cairnock.
Sheriff-Substitute Mitchell, Springwood.
David B. Morris, Town Clerk.
Hugh Murnin, 24 Princes Street.
Major Murray of Polmaise.
William Renwick, Langgarth.

Consulting Physician and Surgeon
(With a Seat at the Board)—
William Haldane, M.D., F.R.C.P.E.

Visiting Medical Officers—

J. H. Murray, M.D.
J. E. Moorhouse, M.A., B.Sc., M.D.
F. J. Greig, Lieut.-Col., R.A.M.C. (Retired).
Grahame H. Skinner, M.B., Ch.B.

*Radiographer—*Grahame H. Skinner, M.B., Ch.B.

Consulting Dental Surgeon—
Leon J. Platt, L.D.S.R.C.S.E.

ROYAL INFIRMARY AND DISPENSARY.

*House Surgeon—*W. M. L. Johnston, M.B., Ch.B.
*Matron—*Miss Peebles.
*Secretary—*James Dobbie, solicitor, 3 Port Street.
*Treasurer—*Robert Cairns, Union Bank.

Auditors—

Andrew C. Buchanan, solicitor.
Henry Robb, solicitor.

SCHOOL BOARD, 1909-1912.

Rev. Colin Mackenzie, minister, *Chairman.*
Mrs. Williamina Macfie Graham Drummond.
Daniel Barker, stair-railer.
William Berrie, traveller.
William Brown, outfitter.
Thomas William Reid Johnston, editor.
Alexander Paterson, solicitor.
William Simpson, pawnbroker.

*Clerk—*James Calder Muirhead, solicitor.

Stirling High School.

George Lowson, LL.D., *Rector.*

*Lady Superintendent—*Mrs. K. L. Hagemann.

*Classics—*James Sheridan, M.A. (Glas.); Marshall
    P. Constable, M.A. (St. And.); Miss Mary
    S. Mackenzie, M.A. (Glas.).
*Mathematics and Arithmetic—*The Rector; Alex.
    Goldie, M.A. (Glas.); John Rushton, M.A.
    (St. And.); Alexander Adam.
*English—*John Inch Low, M.A. (Edin.); Arch.
    Menzies, M.A. (St. And.); Archibald Cunning-
    ham, M.A. (Edin.).
*Modern Languages—*Julius F. Schilling, Univ. of
    Gottingen, F.E.I.S.; Miss Eliz. Scott, M.A.
    (Glas.); Miss Janey Keddie, M.A. (Glas.).
*Writing, Book-keeping, and Shorthand—*Robert
    Dawson, Univ. of Glas.
*Art—*Edmund Baker, art master; John K. Baker,
    art teacher; James Ferguson.
*Science—*Alexander S. Third, M.A., B.Sc. (Abdn.);
    James Chisholm, M.A. (Glas.); Alexander
    Adam, M.A., B.Sc. (Abdn.).
*Music—*George Forbes Forsyth.
*Sewing—*The Lady Superintendent; Miss Eliza
    Fraser.

SCHOOL BOARD, 1909-1912.

Boys' Gymnastics—Sergeant Griffiths.
Girls' Gymnastics—Miss Mary Mackerchar.
Cookery and Laundry Work—Miss May C. Thorburn.
Dancing and Calisthenics—George Low.
Manual Work—Alexander D. Sangster, John Brisbane.
Playground Master and Janitor—Alexander Scott.

Primary High School.

Head Master—Alexander Moyes, F.E.I.S.
Infant Mistress—Miss J. Coutts, F.E.I.S.

ELEMENTARY BOARD SCHOOLS.

Allan's—Master, Charles Johnston. Infant Mistress, Miss Margaret C. M'Callum.
Craigs—Master, William Yule.
Territorial—Master, John Jamieson.
St. Ninians—Master, John M. Taylor.
Cambuskenneth—Mistress, Miss Hannah H. Reid.
Episcopal—Master, John W. Heron.
Roman Catholic—Master, Samuel Murphy.

Doorway, High School, Stirling.

CLUBS AND CLUB SECRETARIES.

Agricultural Association—A. C. Buchanan, solicitor, 26 Port Street.
Amateur Boating and Swimming Club—John H. Pride, 12 Union Street.
Arcade Hall—G. Begbie, 26 Port Street.
Back o' Hill Angling Club—John Campbell, jun., 53 Lower Bridge Street.
Bowling Club—John Fyfe, 1 Princes Street.
Burns Club—R. Sandeman, Forth Crescent.
Chess Club—D. Lindsay, *Observer* Office.
Choral Society—E. W. Simpson, Port Street. Conductor—Arthur W. Marchant, Mus. Doc., Oxon., 10 Glebe Crescent.
Chrysanthemum Society—R. C. Dickson, Raploch.
County Bowling Association—T. W. R. Johnston, *Journal* Office.
County Cricket Club—W. Wilson, 10 Drummond Place.
Fine Art Association—E. Baker, High School.
Fishing Club—J. M. MacLuckie, solicitor.
Girls' Club—Mrs. J. W. Drummond, Westerlands.
Golf Club—Andrew Swan, 7 Clarendon Place.
High School Cricket Club—J. E. Adam, 9 Douglas Terrace.
High School F.P. Association Football Club— P. Dun, 37 Barnton Street.
High School F.P. Rugby Club—Alex. W. Wilson, 10 Drummond Place.
Horticultural Association—Alexander M'Lellan, Laurelhill Lodge.
Horticultural Society—James M'Arthur, 13 Murray Place.
King's Park Football Club—A. Dun, 37 Murray Place.
Ladies' Chess Club—Miss Ure and Miss Fisher, 37 Snowdon Place.
Ladies' Golf Club—
Ladies' Hockey Club—Miss Morris, 2 Laurelhill Place.
Livilands Tennis Club—Alex. E. Adams, Manse, St. Ninians.
Natural History and Archæological Society— R. Kidston, LL.D., 24 Victoria Place, and D. B. Morris, 15 Gladstone Place.
Ochilview Tennis Club—John Clark, Alexandra Place.
Operatic Society—D. T. James, 5 Coburg Avenue.
Spittalmyre Bowling Club—John Campbell, jun., 53 Lower Bridge Street.
St. Ninians Rifle Club—R. Muir, Williamfield Cottage.
Tennis Club—Dr. Whytt, 20 Clarendon Place.
U.Y.M.C.A.—R. Goldie, 64 Murray Place.
Victoria Golf Club—J. Kenny, 10 Nelson Place.
Victoria Square Lawn Tennis Club—R. Yellowlees, 6 Victoria Square.

Filter Beds.

STIRLING CORPORATION WATER SUPPLY.

TIRLING is amply provided with a good and sufficient water supply. The works are situated on the Touch Hills, about four miles from the town. The average rainfall, taken over 30 years, amounts to 44.62 inches, and the average for the three driest years in that time was 34.77 inches. The drainage area is over 1300 acres, and the water from the streams and springs is collected into three reservoirs, of a total holding capacity of about 200,000,000 gallons. The reservoirs are so constructed that they decant into one another. They are also provided with bye-passes, so that they can be drawn upon independently.

The water from the reservoirs discharges into a small pond holding about two days' supply, which acts as a settling and break pressure pond. It then passes through a system of sand filters, and discharges into two clear water tanks, which hold fully one day's supply.

All water, before leaving the works, is measured by three self-registering Deacon Meters, and a very careful record is kept of the consumpt, so that any sudden increase is instantly detected, this being absolutely necessary owing to the very heavy pressure at which the water is supplied to large sections of the water district.

The town is supplied through three different mains, which lessens the danger of the supply being wholly cut off, and facilitates the making of repairs to the different systems.

The mains are connected together inside the burgh, but the town is also divided into districts, on which Deacon Meters are placed, so that any rise in the consumpt can be located in any particular district or part of a district, thus facilitating the checking of waste. The pressure is also reduced in various districts to minimise the waste as far as possible.

The population supplied is estimated at 26,490, and the average daily consumpt is about 1,520,000 gallons, thus making 57.38 gallons per head over all, of which 42.84 gallons per head are for domestic use, and the remainder for trade purposes.

ANALYSIS.—Clorine, 38; Nitrogen, in Free or Saline Ammonia, .0033; Nitrogen, in Albuminoid Ammonia, .0041; Nitrogen, in Nitrates, 0; Nitrogen, in Nitrites, 0; Total Solid Residue, 3.76; Hardness, in Clark Degrees, 3.5.

The Burgh Analyst characterises the water as exceptionally wholesome and desirable for potable and general purposes.

AND. H. GOUDIE,
Water Engineer.

THE QUESTION OF THE HOUR

SUPPORT HOME INDUSTRY !

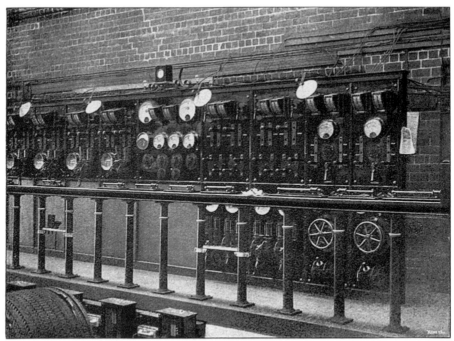

 Switch Board.

STIRLING CORPORATION ELECTRICITY WORKS.

HE Corporation, in providing the town with an electric undertaking, have placed the latest and most up-to-date method of lighting and power within the reach of all classes. Every ratepayer is a shareholder in the undertaking, and it is to them the Corporation look for support in making the works a success financially. Each new consumer of electricity not only benefits himself thereby, but the public at large.

Judge Wylie has been Convener of the Lighting Committee since the commencement, and to his care and foresight the present position of the undertaking is largely due.

Opened in 1900 by Provost Forrest, the electricity works are now entering on their tenth year of working.

The Buildings, which are substantially built of red brick, consist of engine room, boiler house, battery room, engineers' and general offices, etc.

The Engine Room, 52 feet 6 inches by 55 feet wide, contains four sets of engines, two by Bellis & Morcomb, of aprox. 100 horse power (H.P.), each direct coupled to two Mather & Platt generators, and two by Messrs. Allan, of aprox. 300 H.P. each, coupled to Siemens generators. There are also two engines by Bellis & Morcomb, of 32 H.P. each, coupled direct to (two each) generators of Messrs. Mather & Platt's make, for balancing purposes. A battery booster, for charging and discharging the battery to its maximum, is installed in front of the switch board.

Engine Room—Lighter Section.

The total horse power of the steam plant is well over 800 H.P., and the plant is capable of an overload of 25 per cent. for short periods.

The Switch Board, by Messrs. Kelvin & White, is placed on the west side of the engine room, and raised about 4 feet above floor level. It is 21 feet long by 7 feet 6 inches high, and consists of 11 panels of enamelled slate fixed into an iron frame. On the panels are mounted the switches and instruments controlling the generators, battery and booster, and also the feeder cables supplying the various districts of the town. Automatic switches, fuses, and a meter are provided for each generator. Instruments for recording the pressure in the various districts are fixed behind the board, and a continuous record over the 24 hours is kept.

The Battery Room, 26 feet by 21 feet, contains 250 cells of The Tudor Co.'s make, and is in constant use.

The Boiler House, 47 feet wide by 58 feet deep, is built parallel with the engine room, and directly behind the engines, thus shortening the length of steam pipes to a minimum. It contains four Lancashire boilers, 28 feet by 8 feet, working at 160 lbs. pressure per square inch. Three of these are now required for use, leaving one for reserve. Each boiler is provided with two safety valves as a safeguard against accidents.

The main flue, placed directly behind the boilers, is 7 feet 6 inches high by

Engine Room—Heavy Section.

4 feet 6 inches wide, and connects through a Green's economiser to the chimney shaft. The shaft, 7 feet 6 inches internal diameter by 120 feet high, provides a good draught for the boilers. A reserve flue for use during the cleaning of the economiser is also provided.

The Pump Room, on the north end of boiler house, contains two Worthington pumps and an exhaust steam heater. The water is obtained from the town mains, and supplied through a Kennedy water meter to a storage tank of ample dimensions. From there it is drawn by the pumps through the heater, which raises the temperature to aprox. 120 degrees F., passed through the economiser, which still further raises the temperature to aprox. 212 degrees F., before it enters the boilers. Automatic feed valves are provided on the boilers for controlling the water.

A railway siding affords facility for the delivery of coal, etc., and there is considerable ground for extension in the future.

The output of the plant which, for the year 1902, was aprox. 120,000 units, has risen steadily to aprox. 400,000 units in 1909.

The supply has been maintained throughout continuously, practically without hitch of any kind. The results for the year have been satisfactory, and it is confidently expected that this will continue.

The manufacturers in the district are appreciating the fact that foreign competition cannot be met unless the latest up-to-date methods be employed in their businesses, as a consequence, quite a respectable motor load is being obtained. The convenience, ease of starting, cleanliness and economy of the electric motor is highly appreciated by all classes of consumers.

Electric lighting is steadily increasing, and is now being used by all classes. The metallic fillament lamps on the market have enabled the consumers to obtain three times the light without increase of consumption, or, as has occurred in many cases, decreasing the consumption to one third. Many other combinations have also been made. The cleanliness and saving in cost of decorations more than compensates for the cost of installation.

J. W. PAPWORTH,
A.M.I.E.E., A.M.I.Mch.E.,
Burgh Electrical Engineer.

THE NEW METHOD OF HEATING!

BY

WRIGHT'S
"ST. ANDREW" RADIATORS

FOR

CHURCHES, PUBLIC HALLS, SCHOOLS,
THEATRES, OFFICES, WAREHOUSES, &c.,

IS

Rapidly superseding the older forms of heating everywhere. The reason for their wide popularity is simple—they require neither steam-piping, flue, nor attendance, they only need a Gas Connection.

GAS CONSUMPTION AUTOMATICALLY CONTROLLED.

Absolutely the SIMPLEST and CHEAPEST Heating Method in the World.

FULL PARTICULARS FROM GAS OFFICE.

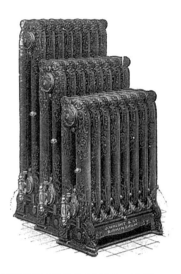

Wright's "EUREKA" Gas Cooker.

NO SYSTEM SO CHEAP!
NO SYSTEM SO SIMPLE!
NO SYSTEM SO CLEAN!

AS

COOKING WITH A "EUREKA!"

FIRST IN 1866.
FIRST IN 1909.

The "EUREKA" is a first-class Bread and Tea Cake Baker.
The "EUREKA" improves the quality of the Food Cooked.
The "EUREKA" ensures a delightfully cool Kitchen.
The "EUREKA" is installed in more than **1,000,000** households.

FULL PARTICULARS FROM GAS OFFICE, THISTLE STREET.

THE STIRLING GAS-LIGHT COMPANY.

POLMAISE AND BANDEATH COLLIERIES.

Much has been written about Stirling, historic-ally and otherwise, and it is not an easy task, with the field already so well harvested, to find anything novel, and at the same time interesting, on which the pen might be employed. But that there is something yet left for the diligent gleaner we feel convinced, and that is the reason why we in this issue commence a series of articles on the local and district industries of Stirling. At first sight this may appear a waste of time, space, and energy, as the name and fame of the "City of the Rock" is usually not connected with industrial affairs, the historic past being mainly her portion. But that Stirling has like-wise a present and a future in the arts of peace, now that the warlike past is dimmed, it will be our object to show in this series of articles The town itself may not be the centre of any industry of great extent, but there are numerous concerns of lesser size, and not a few of these are of an age, in the way of continuous, unbroken existence, that renders their history all the more interesting. To deal weekly with these and other industries, manufacturing and otherwise, is the object we have in view, and we have to thank the many cordial responses and promises of co-operation we have received from those we circularised as to our intention. It is possible, however, that someone has been forgotten, and if that is the case, we trust he will not think this is a slight, but will regard it as an un-intentional overlook—wnich it is—and communi-cate with us in that spirit.

Coal mining is an old industry in Stirlingshire, and particularly in the eastern district, where it has been carried on for at least two hundred years in one form or another. The "black diamond" is known to exist all over the county, but until within a very recent period the nearest spot to the town of Stirling at which the coal was worked was Bannockburn. Round about that village of historic name there are yet to be seen old pit shafts. denoting the locality of mines, which have long since been abandoned, but this fact does not necessarily imply that the minerals have been wrought out. Far from it. There is yet plenty of coal in the district, and whilst new shafts have been sunk, old coal fields have been re-opened, modern scientific appliances and machinery having made it possible to sink pits and work the minerals at a depth and under conditions which were beyond the reach of achievement half-a-century ago, and even less No further back than 1843—only 65 years ago—contemporary history tells us that there were then no winding engines and cages in use in the collieries of Scotland, and women and also chil-dren of tender years were employed at under-ground work, carrying the coal from the "face" on their backs up steep slippery ladders to the pithead, or acting as "drawers," being yoked at the latter occupation in a kind of harness, after the manner of the ponies which are now utilised for that purpose, and which are also much better treated than the human beasts of burden were at the time we refer to.

About a dozen years ago the development com-menced of the coalfield in the Plean and Cowie district, and it has extended north and west-wards, till we find it at the very door of Stirling, so to speak, whilst the miner, who had no place in local life half-a-dozen years ago, is now in his black face and working garb a familiar figure in the streets, as he passes between his place of abode in the burgh and his employment at the pits.

The agency responsible for this transformation is the enterprise of the well-known firm of coal-masters, Messrs Archibald Russell, Ltd.. who have opened the Polmaise and Bandeath collieries in the Carse, a little to the south-east of Stirling, and as this is easily the largest industrial under-taking in the immediate vicinity of Stirling, we regard it as being the most suitable for opening the present series of articles on the subject. Polmaise Colliery is situated at Millhall, near Kersemill, about a mile and a quarter from the county town, and Bandeath is at Fallin, three miles away. Both collieries are in the parish of St Ninians, and on the estate of Major Alastair Murray, of Touchadam and Polmaise. The mineral fields comprise the following leaseholds—Polmaise, 2100 acres; Townlands, 600; Black-grange and Westgrange, 400; Stewarthall, 270; Broadleys, 125; and Clayslaps, 30—a total area of 3525. Numerous bores put down at former times on Townlands and Stewarthall, along with seven diamond bores sunk by the present mineral tenants on Polmaise, Blackgrange, and West-grange, go to prove the existence of the seams of coal under practically the whole of the field. Blackgrange and Westgrange, it may be noted, are on the opposite side of the river Forth from the present coalfield being worked at Bandeath, but indeed there is coal all round Stirling—east, west, north, and south—and those versed in the matter inform us that in the near future the county town will be the centre of a much larger coal-mining community than we have at present, indeed Stirlingshire, and particularly the Stirling part of it, is, in their opinion, destined to become one of the biggest coal-producing counties in the country. How this prospect will be relished by some people we have a shrewd notion, but within the last half-dozen years a great many persons in Stirling have learnt sense regarding mining and miners, and though hostile to their advent, would now be among the first to deplore their departure. Other communities have had to lament the working out of the coalfield in their vicinity, and the consequent loss of trade and employment caused by the closing of pits, and Stirling would in the same circumstances prove no exception to the rule. The first appearance of the miner is the worst of him, and like other people whose outward aspect may not be exceedingly attractive, he may, and does in the majority of cases improve on closer acquaintance. Despite his great affection—mistaken affection, if you will—for the Co-Operative Store, in which he deposits most of his earnings, the miner has always something left to spend elsewhere, and it will be admitted that he is no niggard in this respect. And free-handedness in this way makes up for other traits of character which are not so desirable.

But to return to the pioneers of the coal-mining development in our immediate neighbourhood, Messrs Archibald Russell, Ltd. This is an old firm, and it is interesting to learn that the founder of it was born within sight of the walls of Stirling Castle. The first Archibald Russell saw the light at Clackmannan, but moved westwards in early life, and became connected with the mining industry in Lanarkshire, in which county the interests of the firm are still largely concentrated. He began business in 1843—65 years ago—as a coalmaster at Cambuslang, and gradually extended it till he was the owner of half-a-dozen collieries. His son, Archibald Russell, got control of affairs in due time, and very largely developed them, being the owner of 21 pits—17 in Lanarkshire and 4 in Stirlingshire —at the time of his death. There was a third Archibald Russell, but he died, and in 1894 the business was, for family reasons, turned into a limited liability company, the leading members

of it being four grandsons of the founder of the firm.

The sinking of Nos. 1 and 2 pits, Polmaise Colliery, was commenced in December, 1902, and finished in June, 1904. Mr Tom Salmond, eldest son of the genial general manager of the Company, Mr Thomas Salmond, cut the first sod when sinking was started. This was a tedious and also costly operation, and it would stagger most people unacquainted with mining matters to learn the amount of money expended in this work. The sinking was rendered very difficult owing to the surface strata, which was soft and troublesome, being composed in the following order of soil—yellow clay, very soft blue silt, peat, fine sand with water course sand and shells, red clay and stones, very soft red clay, sand, gravel, and boulders, and broken rock, the last being come upon 101 feet 6 inches from the surface. The pits were sunk through by means of a steel crib 24¼ feet long, 9½ feet wide, and 7 feet deep. The water got during the sinking was saltish, and was observed to be most abundant in quantity at the time of high tide in the river Forth, which is about 1 mile distant, indicating that the river really drained to some extent into the pit, which of course was at a lower level. The sinking of Nos. 3 and 4 pits at Bandeath was begun in August, 1904, and finished in April, 1906. The surface was of the same soft nature, although not so deep as that at Nos. 1 and 2 pits, being in this case 60 feet thick. The same method of sinking was adopted, a crib of like dimensions being used. The depth at which the coal is worked at Polmaise Colliery is 85 fathoms—510 feet—and at 210 fathoms—1260 feet —at Bandeath.

At Polmaise Colliery twelve seams of coal were passed through in the shafts, amounting in thickness to 23 feet 3 inches. The thicknesses of the seams which are at present being worked, and the depths at No. 1 pit, are as follows:— The Hartley seam, 2 feet at 291 feet deep; the Greenyard seam, 3 feet 3 inches at 372 feet; the Main seam, 3 feet 1 inch at 447 feet; and the Knott seam, 3 feet at 486 feet. At Bandeath the seams at present being worked, and the depths are as follows:—The Hirst seam, 2 feet 2 inches at 102 feet; the Hartley seam, 2 feet 4 inches at 1,008 feet; and the Knott seam, 2 feet 6 inches at 1,242 feet. The index limestone, 33 inches thick, was got at 786 feet. In the sinking of the Bandeath pits the shafts passed

Polmaise Colliery.

Bandeath Colliery.

through twenty seams of coal, over 1 foot in thickness, the total amounting to 32 feet 6 inches. In the pits at both collieries household coal, steam coal, and anthracite are found. The latter is a rare coal in Scotland, and the Polmaise and Bandeath variety is very good. It is a very hard, smokeless coal, and burns best with forced draught, such as is to be got in stoves, etc. Most of the anthracite is shipped to the Continent, and some also goes to America. The Hartley seam is a household coal, and there is a good home market for it, whilst the steam coal is largely used in industrial centres, and is also sent abroad. Needless to say, when referring to a firm of the high reputation of Messrs Archibald Russell, Ltd., everything in connection with the working of the collieries—both above and below ground—is of the most up-to-date description. It would serve no purpose to dwell at length on this phase of the enterprise, because the general reader would not understand the technical references that would have to be used, and it is sufficient to say that the machinery employed is of the finest pattern, and that every provision is made for the safety and comfort of the employees. Safety-lamps are in use throughout the pits. They are magnetically locked and electrically ignited: the underground appliance for relighting them being so constructed that it cannot be operated nor can a spark be produced unless the lamp is in position underneath an airtight closed-down lid. Two machines are fitted in the lamp-cabin: one for charging the accumulators, and the other for cleaning 100 lamps per hour. The pumping and ventilating apparatus are elaborate and most effective, and electricity is very largely used for motive, lighting, and other purposes. Preparing the coal by screening, washing, etc., are interesting processes that require to be seen to be understood, as have many

other matters about a coal pit, where, alike in regard to human and mechanical equipment, some of the finest types of industrial development are to be seen.

Most collieries have in their near neighbourhood a range or two of what are termed "colliers' rows," for the household accommodation of the miners, but there is nothing of that sort at Millhall. The proximity of Polmaise Colliery to Stirling, St Ninians, and Bannockburn, where houses can be got, has rendered it unnecessary for the Colliery Company to provide these, and the entrance to Polmaise Colliery is marked by thirty neat brick cottages, erected principally for the use of officials. At Bandeath, however, which is further away from Stirling and other residential centres, housing accommodation for a large number of the employees has been provided. There are twenty cottages for officials erected at the entrance to the colliery; eighty workmen's houses of the room-and-kitchen type, with all conveniences, have been built near it; and a hundred more are in course of erection. Water for domestic purposes is led in pipes for a distance of 2 miles from the town mains; and, owing to the supply being scarce, storage tanks have been erected. The pit-water, pumped into tanks, is conveyed to the houses for flushing purposes.

Between both collieries, when at full working strength, over 1200 hands are employed, and the wage bill is a large one. Just now there is an easing off, owing to the slackness in the coal trade, but with the return of brisk time the Polmaise and Bandeath collieries will undergo further development, giving more employment, and leading to the circulating of more money, and it will be the wish of everyone that the valuable enterprise introduced into the district by Messrs Archibald Russell, Ltd., should have a prosperous future before it.

ROCKVALE SPINNING MILL.

As may be assumed, looking to the important part the humble sheep has always played in the feeding and clothing of mankind, wool-spinning is an ancient industry all over the world, and it is certainly one of the oldest, if not the oldest, in Stirling, though in extent it is now but a shadow of what was once the case, and that down to very recent times. Wool-spinning is also the only survivor of several local trades that were in operation two or three centuries ago. Among these time-honoured occupations were dyeing, soap-making, cotton-spinning, and ropemaking; all of which have now ceased to exist so far as Stirling is concerned, though middle-aged people can remember of the whole quartette being carried on. In the Statistical Account of Scotland, published in 1793, we are informed that woollen manufactures were carried on in Stirling a hundred years at least before 1796, and in the 17th century a fabric called shalloon was made and exported to the Low Countries—Belgium and Holland. It is also stated that latterly the manufacturers "debased their goods and lost the trade, and the town became miserably poor," which shows that even in these far-off days the standard of commercial morality, so far as adulteration was concerned, was not what it should have been, any more than it is now. The trade, however, never entirely dropped away, and in 1793 220,000 yards of shalloon were manufactured in the town. What shalloon actually was we have not been able to find out, as the name is not known amongst people engaged in the wool-spinning trade at the present time. But we know it is a Yorkshire term for some woollen fabric, said to have been made at Chalons, in France.

"In blue shalloon shall Hannibal be clad,
And Scipio trail an Irish purple plaid."—Swift.

The Oxford Dialect Dictionary vaguely defines it as a "worsted material," and quotes from p. 330 of W. Cudworth's "Bradford" (1876)—"They were about the first to start the worsted business, . . . the principal make being shalloons and wildbores." However, so far as wool-spinning is concerned, we read that in 1793 100 hands were employed at the work of "teasing, scouring, and combing the wool to make it ready for the wheel." At that time, as now, women labour appears to have been largely used, but the wages paid were a good deal lower. What would a female wool-spinner think of a "pay" of threepence a day,

which was all that women spinners got in 1793? The wage men employees received at that period we have not been able to find out, but it could not have been much more than what would be regarded as a pittance nowadays, seeing that in 1793 the earnings of masons were only 1s 8d per day, joiners 1s 6d, tailors 1s, and labourers 1s to 1s 2d. On this matter of wool-spinners' wages in 1793, it is no surprise to find the chronicler in the Statistical Account remarking:—

Such small encouragement destroys industry, and the female having so little prospect of advantage from her labour, is at no pains to be expert at it. When necessity urges they are incapable of proficiency, and must either starve or beg, but many of them would rather be idle altogether, than turn a wheel. There are perhaps fewer places in Scotland where the quantum of female labour is less than in Stirling, because it is so unproductive. Manufacturers should consider themselves as obliged to increase the price of female labour.

The next we read about wool-spinning in Stirling is in the New Statistical Account of Scotland, published in 1840, and there we are informed that "since 1832 the woollen manufacture has more than doubled." About this time machinery was beginning to supplant hand labour, and in 1840 there were three spinning mills in the operation in the town, employing 140 workers. The locality of these establishments is not stated, but probably they were the Bridge Mill, near the Old Bridge, the premises in the "'Oo Mill Entry," which is now known as Douglas Street, and the old mill near the Abbey Ferry. The Old Bridge mill and the Abbey Ferry one are still standing, but it is many years since wool-spinning was carried on in them, and as for the establishment in the "'Oo Mill Entry" no trace of it remains. In 1840 the hours of labour in the wool mills were eleven hours a day for five days a week, and nine on Saturday, and we are informed by the chronicler of that period that

The occupation of wool-spinning has an excellent effect on health, the regular employment and the attention paid by the masters appearing to have a good effect on the morals of those employed.

Following upon the Crimean War woollen manufacturing entered on a period of prosperity, and about this time the Cambusbarron Mills were established by the Messrs Smith, whose father had the small business in the "'Oo Mill Entry" already referred to. At Cambusbarron both spinning and weaving were carried on, and a similar state of affairs prevailed at Bannockburn, where the Messrs Wilson's mills had even then been long in existence. In 1868 Cambusbarron Mills employed 950 hands, but now there are none, the establishment having been closed sixteen years ago. In the same year there were between five and six hundred workers in the Bannockburn Mills, which, two years ago, shared the fate of the Cambusbarron ones, and as in their case silence now reigns where once industry hummed briskly. In the early sixties, a new wool-spinning mill was erected at Forthvale, Cornton Road, Stirling, by Mr John Todd, and in 1868 65 hands were employed in it, whilst the value of the annual production was £30,000. After Mr Todd's death the business was acquired by the brothers Messrs Andrew and David B. Robertson, but they ceased operations about a dozen years ago, and the establishment is now used as a factory by the Rubber Coy. of Scotland.

Now the only place in the district where wool-spinning is carried on is at Rockvale Mill, Stirling, and it is the youngest of all the establishments erected for this purpose in the town or neighbourhood. Built on what was the site of a farm less than half-a-century ago, the mill stands at the foot of the Craigs where the old Burghmuir begins. Erected in 1870 by Messrs Jas. Lyle & Co., the business was retained by them but a few years, and in 1873 was purchased by the late Mr John Aitken, salt merchant, The Shore, Stirling. He was connected with the Lyle firm from the start, and shortly after getting sole control of the business, transferred it to his son, Mr John Aitken, jun., the latter carrying it on till his death in 1902, and his trustees for two years later. In the beginning of 1905, the undertaking was acquired by Messrs Jas. Templeton & Co., Glasgow, the well-known firm of carpet manufacturers, who are the present owners. Mr Aitken used to supply them with part of their yarns, and their purpose in taking over the mill into their own hands after his demise was to utilise it as an auxiliary to their carpet manufacturing business. Under their regime the Rockvale Mills are more prosperous than ever they were, and it is to be hoped, for the sake of Stirling, if for no other reason, that this state of affairs will long continue. The town

has few industries that employ so many hands, and it was a great relief to those interested in the welfare of the burgh, and who were apprehensive that Mr Aitken's death might be followed by the closing of the establishment—as has happened in similar circumstances in Stirling more than once—to learn that the enterprise was to be taken over by a firm of the strength and reputation of Messrs Jas. Templeton & Co., whose local manager is Mr R. B. Neil, Craigs House. There are bigger wool spinning manufactories in Scotland than Rockvale Mills, but there are few, if any, better equipped alike in regard to facilities for carrying on the business or with respect to the conditions under which the employees work. There are 150 hands—80 per cent. of whom are female workers—and with respect to lighting, ventilation, and what may be termed housing accommodation generally, their circumstances leave little or nothing to be desired. Since the Messrs Templeton acquired the establishment the buildings have been enlarged to some extent by the erection of extra storage, etc.

A visit to the mill is a very instructive experience to those who are interested in the conversion of the fleece of the sheep into yarns, which is the first process in the manufacture of cloth and carpets of various kinds from wool or worsted. In reality both mean the same thing, but to the uninitiated it may be explained that worsted is a finer spun kind of yarn than the ordinary woollen variety, though each is produced by the same process to a large extent. When Mr Aitken had the business, more worsted spinning was done at Rockvale than is the case now, but on the other hand the woollen yarns branch has doubled since the Messrs Templeton acquired possession, and the machinery is there for the production of more worsted whenever the trade requires it. The wool used is largely of the home variety, but the raw material is also imported from Australia, South America, New Zealand, and the East Indies. In its raw condition there are two kinds of wool. That shorn from the sheep is known as fleece wool, whilst skin wool is that which is pulled off the carcase of slaughtered animals. The initial process in the conversion of the wool into yarns is known as batching or blending. The latter is a term usually more intimately associated in the public mind with the marketing of whisky, but a somewhat similar mixing method is utilised to obtain equality in the yarn. A better illustration

Rockvale Mill, Stirling.

Carding Machines.

Spinning Department.

however, is afforded by the means gardeners employ to obtain the kind of soil they desire for the cultivation of some classes of plants. The gardener produces the earth he requires by heaping one variety of soil upon another, in this way building a strata into which the plant is put, and the blending of the wool is carried out in a similar fashion. Several qualities of the material are placed on top of each other, the same as a hay-stack is built, and then when the wool is required for spinning purposes, it is pulled out of the face of the strata or stack that has been formed, which makes certain that an equal proportion of all the varieties will be obtained towards the preparation of the yarn. The next process is to convey the wool to the washing machine, from which it is transferred to the teasing apparatus, being also oiled in connection with this operation in order to assist the carding. The teaser, it may be explained, opens up the material for the carder, which in turn improves upon this process for the comb, by removing all foreign substances and laying the fibres of the wool in one direction, whilst the comb completes the process by separating the short fibres from the longer ones. Following the combing, the wool, which is always attaining a whiter, thinner, and more ostrich feather sort of consistency as it passes through the various machines, goes under another series of processes, which may be summed up in the term "finishing," and which brings it into the "roving" stage, from which it is passed on to the spinning frames. So far as woollen yarns are concerned, there is no intermediate process, the wool passing direct from the carding machines to the spinning mules. After the yarns are spun in both cases, only the auxiliary processes of twisting, reeling, and bundling remain, which mean putting the yarn into a commercial form for the market, in the way of bobbins or reels and "hanks." Worsted yarns, it may be stated, being of a closer texture, are used in the manufacture of the finer classes of carpets, ladies and gentlemen's dress goods, furniture covering materials, etc., whilst woollen yarns go to the making of coarser articles, such as blankets, horse and travelling rugs, and the heavier kinds of carpets and dress goods.

But whilst we have shown our readers what modern machines, with human beings attending and controlling them, can accomplish in the way of saving manual labour in preparing the fleece of the sheep for its manufacture into cloth, it must not be thought that the old primitive processes utilised in the attainment of this end have been swept into oblivion. Far from it. Certainly the old wife and her distaff and spinning-wheel are now a rarity, and are generally only to be seen in pictures in industrial centres, but the ancient process of hand manufacture is still the common one in the Highlands of Scotland and Ireland. Instead of teasing, carding, and spinning machines, the time crusted, laborious operations of pre-scientific times are to be witnessed at the present day in the before-mentioned parts of the United Kingdom. To the people in the remote Highlands the sheep which they rear is still the animal that both feeds and clothes them. The old wife yet prepares the wool for spinning by placing it between two flat boards, which she rubs one against the other, and thereby draws out the fibres in a parallel fashion. These she hangs on her distaff, which is a piece of wood placed in the stool of her spinning-wheel, and using her foot on the treadle, turns the wheel, at the same time twisting the fibre into a thread, and thereby carrying out the spinning process. In this connection it is interesting to learn that the Messrs Templeton have been co-operating for sometime with the Duke of Portland and the Duchess of Sutherland in developing home industries at Lybster in Caithness, and Helmsdale in Sutherland, in the way of preparing woollen carpets by hand method. This provides remunerative winter occupation for the girls who find their summer employment at the herring curing. This home industry has been established in Ireland for some time, and has been a success there, and the same thing may be confidently expected in the Highlands of Scotland.

And finally a word or two regarding the firm of Messrs Jas. Templeton & Co. The business, we understand, was started in the year 1839 by the father of the heads of the present firm, and it has gradually grown until it is now the largest carpet manufacturing concern in Scotland The founder of the business was Mr James Templeton, a native of Campbeltown, who, after being some years on the Continent as a merchant, returned to Scotland and settled in Paisley as a manufacturer of Chenille shawls. Whilst engaged in the manipulation of that fabric, he was struck with the possibility of adapting the principle employed in the making of these shawls to the manufacture of carpets, and after any difficulties, he invented the Patent

Axminster carpet. The Axminster fabric is of very fine quality, and is named after a small town in Devonshire, where carpet manufacturing was introduced into Britain in the 16th century by Huguenots, who had to flee from France on account of religious persecution. Besides being a fine carpet, the Axminster was also a very costly one, but Mr Templeton's invention enabled it to be manufactured much more cheaply, whilst retaining and combining the eminent characteristics both in appearance and quality of the original Axminster. But not only did Mr Templeton invent the Patent Axminster ; he was also one of the pioneers, if indeed not the pioneer, of artistic manufacture in carpets—a reputation which is worthily maintained by his successors. Mr Templeton removed in 1839 from Paisley to Glasgow, where he began to perfect and weave the Patent "Victorian" Axminster, but he had a long and costly fight in the law courts in maintaining his patent, and it was not until 1847 that his right was fully established. By patiently improving his process and employing the highest skill in design—an example which the present firm still follows—he gradually established the well-known "house" of James Templeton & Co., which, besides being the leading carpet manufacturing business in Scotland, has nothing to learn from the best firms in England or anywhere else in the matter of artistic production. The finest Axminster, Brussels, and Wilton carpets are made, and also rugs and mats, but not only that, the goods manufactured are in a great many qualities, to suit the desires of the most luxurious, as well as the popular demand. "Templeton's carpets" are to be found practically in every part of the civilised world, and an idea of the widespread ramifications of the firm's business may be gathered from the fact that it has warehouses in London, Manchester, Newcastle, Melbourne, and Montreal, and representatives on the Continent,

and also in South America and South Africa. Last, but not least, as giving an indication of the extent of the enterprise of the firm, it may be stated that it has four factories in Glasgow and the Rockvale Mill auxiliary in Stirling, and employs 2500 hands.

In conclusion, a word or two may be said concerning the human and social side of this great industrial hive. There is a tradition in "Templeton's" that their workers are human beings, and not merely so many "hands," and this tradition takes various practical shapes. One of these is a Savings Bank which the firm manages for its workpeople—and which, by the bye, the employees in Rockvale Mills, Stirling, get the advantage of if they chose to accept it. The method of the Bank is simplicity itself. If the worker wishes to deposit, he merely marks on a ticket supplied by the firm the amount of his wages which he requires, the balance being placed to his credit in the Bank, and 5 per cent. per annum paid on the deposit. In connection with the Glasgow manufactory there is also a Recreation Club, which is supported by a capital sum given to the workers by the two senior partners of the firm, Mr J. Stewart Templeton and Mr James Templeton, whilst a large sum has also been provided for benevolent purposes. These social arrangements, whilst they have been initiated by the Messrs Templeton and provided with funds, are managed by a committee of both sexes from among the workers. In the club, meals are provided at a moderate rate, and in the evenings the rooms are available for art, music, and other classes, as well as games and reading, whilst lectures on various subjects and concerts are given during the winter months. "Templeton's, Glasgow," is a firm of which Scotland may be proud, and Stirling feel honoured in having association with.

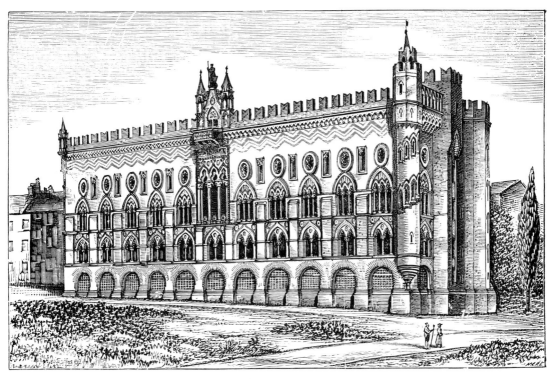

Greenhead Carpet Factory, Glasgow.

James Thomson.

GEORGE THOMSON, CARRIAGE AND MOTOR BUILDER.

The art of Carriage or Coach Building is a very old one, and, if space permitted, an interesting history of its beginning, its steady evolution, and its fuller development might here be written, and prints of ancient vehicles as well as more modern carriages might be shown. This ancient craft, whose crest in heraldry is Phœbus driving the chariot of the Sun, was, until the Reform Bill, peculiarly exclusive, and kept strictly secret the various arts and industries which combined to uphold this important manufacture. It was not merely one industrial art, the knowledge of which was sufficient to make a coachbuilder, for a carriage is a complex thing, and one man cannot complete one carriage from start to finish. For instance, the wheels of a carriage are made by the wheelwright, the axles, springs, drag, and all iron parts are forged by the coachsmith ; the carriage-maker again fits and finishes the locking wheel and under-carriage, the shafts and pole, and adjusts and fits up the various parts ; the bodymaker builds the frame-work and fits in the panels, in fact makes the body of the carriage ; the coachpainter, with time and skill, puts on a beautiful finish in colour and bright varnish ; while the coachtrimmer upholsters the inside with leather, satin, or cloth, and makes the carriage comfortable and luxurious for the owner. Each journeyman in the coachbuilding trade learns his own branch only, and it is by a combination of the skilled workmen in all the various branches of the craft that the master coachbuilder, who supervises and guides the various workmen, is able ultimately to present the perfectly finished carriage.

The town of Stirling has long been one of the principal centres of this industry, and its carriages have been widely known and appreciated, not only in Great Britain and Ireland, but in our colonies and dependencies. In addition to this, Stirling has been an important school in carriage building, for many hundreds of apprentices in its different branches have been trained here, and have carried the knowledge of their craft to our great cities, and many have gone to India, Australia, South Africa, and Canada, where not infrequently they have risen to the highest positions in this industry.

The firm of George Thomson, Coach Builder, Stirling, is a very old established one, as it is more than one hundred years since the business was founded. While last century was only a few years old, the grandfather of the present proprietor of the business came to Stirling. Like most enterprises that have attained considerable proportions, this well-known coachbuilding firm had a small beginning. At first the business was conducted in the Craigs, and from the earliest day-books it would seem that for a year or two smith-work for saddlers, for gigs and coaches, and also for general smith-work for the Town Council of Stirling, formed the principal business. After a very few years there is a distinct increase of business, and several neighbouring proprietors' names appear as clients, such as those of Airth, Kennet, Polmaise. Lanrick, and Leckie.

The Mr Thomson of these early days, in addition to being master of his own business, was elected Deacon of the Hammermen, and afterwards Convener of the Seven Incorporated Trades and a member of the Town Council of Stirling. About 1832 George Thomson, his second son, took sole charge of the business, and under his management there took place a marked development. In 1833 a partnership was entered into between George Thomson and John Buchanan, the founder of J. Buchanan & Co., coachbuilders, Glasgow. For some years this union of the Stirling and Glasgow firms lasted, the style of the Stirling firm being altered to Thomson & Buchanan. The partnership, however, came to an end, and George Thomson decided to carry on the Stirling business, while John Buchanan took over the Glasgow branch. An era of prosperity was in store for both partners. The premises in the Craigs soon became too small, and new coachworks were erected in Orchard Place. Mr George Thomson, alert to interpret the wants of users of carriages, and ready to adopt the best methods of production, soon became known as a manufacturer of dogcarts and wagonettes, and many other styles of carriages which were popular throughout the country. The London Exhibitions of 1851 and 1862 afforded Mr Thomson the opportunity of exhibiting in competition with the best coachbuilders in Britain, and his business-like enterprise again and again brought him numerous additional customers, not only in Great Britain and Ireland, but throughout the Colonies. The export business was for a time no small part of his successful labours. In 1860 large additions were made to the coachworks, mainly large showrooms, which were well lighted and capable of containing about

Front View of Works.

Part of a Carriage Showroom.

A "Victoria" of the Latest and Most Fashionable Design.

A Motor Landaulette.

one hundred carriages. In 1865 the Dublin Exhibition was held, and there, as in London, Mr Thomson exhibited and obtained high awards and many orders for his manufactures.

Until the middle of the last century the old stagecoaches were the principal means of communication throughout England and Scotland. Their slow but picturesque progress is still fascinating to think of, the heavy lumbering coach, with its inside and outside passengers, its prancing team of four horses, its portly coachman, who handled the reins so deftly, and the conductor, who made the echoes ring again in passing through many a sleepy village with his sounding horn. For many a township, and town even, the coming and going of the mail coach formed the principal event of the day. Many are the tales, full of humour, pathos, and even tragedy, connected with the old coaching days, tales of accidents and stoppages in snow or storm, of runaway matches by loving couples, of terrible experiences at the hands of blood-thirsty highwaymen. Stirling was on the main route through Scotland, and the coaches came in by the Port and passed out of the royal burgh by the old Stirling Bridge. Some few are still left who can recall vividly the old coaching days, with their delights and drawbacks. But in the Fifties a new era dawned, and with it came the railway train, with its easy, rapid, and regular communication. The days of the old stagecoach were then numbered, but it did not die without a final struggle. Notably in Stirling district Mr Ramsay of Barnton kept his fast coach, the Defiance, on the road in the vain belief that he could ruin the railways and render their companies bankrupt. His was a fine example of the good old, dour, determined Scottish spirit, but the more powerful enterprise easily won, and in Stirling, as elsewhere, the mail coach gave up the unequal struggle, and was seen no more.

The railways were to do away entirely with the need of horses and carriages, but these were turned to good account by Mr George Thomson. Fortunate in securing orders for the construction of railway carriages, for some years he devoted much energy to this new department of work, and both in the old factory in the Craigs as well as in the new coachworks in Orchard Place, many of the first carriages supplied to the pioneer railway companies in Scotland were built and finished under his careful superintendence. The railways, which were to

wipe out coachbuilding, brought prosperity to such an extent to everyone that, instead of fewer carriages being required, far more were in demand : because of greater wealth more people were able to keep their horse and carriage. The carriages were also of a more elaborate design, of a more luxurious finish, and of a greatly increased price.

One outstanding feature of the coachbuilding trade is its great variety of design. When one considers that the coachbuilder was expected to be able to supply the farmer with his gig, the merchant with his delivery wagon, the sportsman with his dogcart and game wagon, the St Andrew's Ambulance Society with their special ambulance wagons, the medical man with his mail phaeton and brougham, and the more extensive class of those who keep their carriage, with their victoria, wagonette, brougham, landau, or omnibus, it will be seen that here is a business in which a great opportunity is given to the individual workman, to the designer, to the inventor, and to the man of good taste and practical sense. Many minds have been applied to the perfection of the carriage, and at no previous time has there been such light, graceful, luxurious, or more highly finished carriages built.

Since 1873 the business of George Thomson has been carried on by his son, Mr James Thomson, now Provost of Stirling. During his management the high reputation of the firm has been well maintained. In the great Industrial Exhibitions of Edinburgh and Glasgow, the firm of George Thomson was represented by exhibits which did credit to their well-known manufactures.

During the last few years a great advance has taken place in the means of locomotion. Motor cars have come into regular use, and have in many instances displaced the horse and carriage. George Thomson has recognised the new departure and the new demand, and is now manufacturing not only the high class carriage, but the most modern motor car. He is building motor car bodies of every description, finished with all the latest improvements, and these can be fitted wih any well-known type of engine and chassis. With a well appointed staff of workmen, with commodious premises, and with a long experience gained in carriage building, it may be anticipated that this new departure and extension of their old established business will, in the interest both of employer and employees, be abundantly successful.

STIRLING FOUNDRY.

JAMES DAVIE & SONS, IRONFOUNDERS AND ENGINEERS.

The previous three articles we have dealt with have had reference to industries in the town and district, and are hoary with age, as it were, all having been practised in one form or another for upwards of a century and a half. This week we deal with a trade which is comparatively modern, and though fairly old as years go, is yet in its infancy, contrasted with coal mining, woollen spinning, and coachbuilding. This is the iron age, and it is not more than sixty years since the first foundry was established in our midst. Of course there were workers in iron many years before that, but it was almost entirely confined to smith work, and there was none of the heavy castings of beams, columns, etc., that are so familiar nowadays. Falkirk has been a seat of the iron industry for over a century, and it is not easy to tell why it did not also take root in Stirling, seeing there is plenty of coal in this district, but the fact remains that whereas Falkirk has been identified with the iron trade ever since Scotland entered into the manufacturing arena, Stirling, up to very recent times, ranked more as a country town, dependent a good deal on the surrounding agricultural population for its trade, and the advantages it enjoyed as the headquarters of the legal and public administration of the county, along with its status as a military station, and the residential element attracted to the burgh as a result of its central situation and scenic beauty. The first iron foundry in the immediate district was located in "The Hollow" of St Ninians, and was carried on by a Mr Thos. Smith, whose biggest undertaking was the casting of the railing that goes round the King's Park, Stirling. The St Ninians establishment was a small one, and was confined mostly to making fire-bars and articles for the hand nail-making industry, which was then carried on on a big scale in St Ninians and Whins of Milton. About the same time the late Mr John Christie, ironmonger, King Street (opposite the head of Friars Street), had a small foundry in the Shore Road, where the Stirling Cooperage now is, and here the work turned out consisted mainly of farm threshing-mill wheels, railings, and other light castings. There was also a small foundry at the Burnside, opposite where Macdonald, Fraser & Co.'s auction mart now is, but in course of time the three establishments referred to were closed for various reasons, the chief one being that the trade was undergoing a change in its character, and larger concerns were superseding the smaller businesses.

The Foundry, situated in Orchard Place, was built by Mr John Christie, ironmonger, Stirling, who had removed from his Shore Road premises, and had it only about two years when it was sold to Messrs Wylie, Smith & Davie, in 1857. Mr, afterwards Bailie, Davie (father of the present head) being of the firm. Mr Davie was a blacksmith ; Mr Wylie, a millwright ; and Mr Smith, a moulder, the latter gentleman being the former owner of St Ninians foundry. After a few years Mr Smith retired, followed in another year or so by Mr Wylie, leaving Bailie Davie, who was joined by Bailie Brown and Mr Wm. Young, farmer, Taylorton, both of whom still reside here. After working together for a few years, Messrs Brown and Young likewise retired in 1873, when Bailie Davie was joined by his two sons, John, and the present principal of the firm, James. The latter was born at Tillicoultry in the year 1850, and attended Mr Paton's School there, where, with a year or so at the Stirling High School, he received his early education. He commenced his apprenticeship when he was fourteen years old, under the firm of Wylie & Davie. After his apprenticeship was out he worked for two years with Moses, Cairns & Co., Hayfield Foundry, Glasgow, and two years with Boyd, North Street Foundry, Glasgow, going then to Hull, and working with Rose & Douns. From Hull he went to the Patent Moulding Machine Works at Manchester, but returned to Stirling in 1873, and joined with his father and brother, on the retiral of Brown and Young from the firm. On the death of his father in 1885 Mr James Davie succeeded to the whole business, and carried it on for seventeen years, till he took his two sons into partnership in 1902. Mr James Davie, senior, has seen in Stirling Foundry five generations of Davies, viz., grandfather, father, himself son, and grandson.

Whilst various descriptions of iron founding work are carried on at Stirling Foundry, the principal trade is the casting of columns and beams, so largely used nowadays in the construction of all classes of buildings. At one time, and that not so long ago, iron entered very

James Davie.

little into the erection of any structure, except large sheds and warehouses, but now we find it extensively utilised in the putting up of houses. more particularly where there are shops on the ground floor with dwellings above. In this country we have not yet attained to the distinction of the sky-scraper which is so familiar a sight in large American cities, but probably that monstrosity in iron and steel will in time become a feature of our great towns, where building sites are both scarce and dear. That is by the way, however, and meantime our reference may be confined to the Stirling Foundry, which was amongst the earliest, if not the very earliest, in this district, where the casting of iron beams and columns was undertaken on an extensive scale, and indeed almost made a speciality. The reputation the Davie firm gained for good, solid work in the early days has always been maintained, and the Stirling Foundry has a wide business connection. So far as the process of "casting" is concerned, it is a very interesting operation, but is much more easily understood when seen performed than explained on paper. Briefly, however, it may be stated that after a drawing or sketch of the article wanted is presented at the office, the patternmaker first takes the job in hand. A patternmaker is an expert worker in wood, and he makes an exact model in that material of the article that is to be cast in iron. The pattern is next taken to the moulder, who places it in what may be termed a bed of specially prepared sand, which, it may be mentioned, comes from London and Belfast districts, and has a clayey consistency, that makes it stick together when damped with water. The material is mixed with coal dust and also sprinkled with ordinary local sand; and both these elements are necessary if a good cast is to be made, as will be explained a little further on. But to return to the wooden pattern or model that has been placed in its sandy bed. After remaining there for some time to give a due impression in the sand, the pattern is carefully lifted away, the sprinkling of the ordinary dry sand helping in the separation of the pattern from the mould—and the casting follows. This is done by molten metal—which has previously been produced by the smelting by great heat of pig and scrap iron in a blast furnace—being conveyed in iron ladles coated inside with a composition that prevents the metal burning them, and poured into the sandy mould where the impress

of the article required to be manufactured has been left by the wooden pattern or model already referred to. The metal is then left to cool, what may be styled air holes being bored in the mould at regular distances from one another to allow the steam and gases to escape. If this were not done they would soon escape of their own accord by blowing the whole thing up. This is one of the reasons why a "cast" is such a ticklish process, very little may spoil it, and the greatest care and skill has to be exercised. Whilst the molten metal poured into the mould is cooling down and hardening into a beam, a wheel, or a column, as the case may be, the coal dust mixed with the sand comes into play. It burns away by the heat of the metal, and helps to set up a draught which makes the heated air blow off gradually. After the "cast" has sufficiently cooled it is taken out of the mould, and this is easily done, as the sand has, by the action of the heat, been dried, and has become hard and gritty, so that it falls away of its own accord from the iron. The "cast" is now complete, and the next thing is to convey it in turn to the dressing, fitting, and engineering departments as required. where it is planed, polished, cut, etc., until turned out the finished article. For these operations machinery is used, and in the moulding shop there are no fewer than five cranes, which are so fitted up that heavy articles—and almost everything about an iron foundry is more or less heavy—can be swung from one to another without requiring to touch the ground. Beams and columns can be made to any required length or thickness, and not only that, but they can be cut through, a powerful machine fitted with strong knives soon making short work of halving an iron or steel beam into two. The largest joist or beam this machine takes in is 12 inches by 6 inches. Three men can cut a 12 inches by 6 inches joist in three minutes actual cutting, but of course there is the putting in and taking out to be considered. The cutting machine is the latest addition to the firm's stock of tools, and they consider it is the most successful they have introduced for some years. When one looks back to the time that the joists were cut with the hand, one wonders how people had the patience to do the cutting. In this connection it may be interesting to mention that whilst no steel beams are made at Stirling Foundry, there are plenty of them to be seen there. Steel is a metal which "gives," whilst cast iron is brittle.

Part of Moulding Shop.

Section of Girder Yard.

and would break much readier under certain forms of pressure, and accordingly steel is mostly used for cross beams, whilst iron is the material of which pillars or columns are composed. The Messrs Davie get the steel casting supplied, and cut them into the required lengths. Finally, it may also be stated that whilst there are Belgium iron beams on the market at a cheaper rate than Scottish ones, architects fight shy of the foreign article where a substantial job is required, and the Messrs Davie have the confidence of all local architects who make a point of scheduling the home "product" in the specifications they issue.

Amongst the principal contracts which Mr Davie has carried out are weaving sheds at Glasgow Green for Messrs Templeton, carpet manufacturers, and when their new buildings were erected he received the contract from Sir Wm. Arroll. All the castings for the Singers Sewing Machine Works at Clydebank were made at Stirling. These were the largest works ever built in Scotland at one time. In 1900 the castings of 350 tons for Messrs Aird & Coghill, printers, buildings erected in Cadogan Street, Glasgow, were made in Stirling. This building was eight storeys high, and the bottom columns weighed about 2 tons 10 cwts. each, the architect being Mr H. E. Clifford, Glasgow. In 1902, 200 tons of castings were sent to West George Street, Glasgow, for the building for the West George Street Property Company, and the Stirling Foundry also supplied the castings for the handsome building in St Andrew's Square for Messrs Stephen Mitchell & Son, tobacco manufacturers, and also the steel roof, beam, columns, and stable mounting for Mr Stephen Mitchell's new steading at Boquhan; R. W. Forsyth, drapers, Renfield Street; Messrs Blacklock & M'Arthur, paint merchants, Dale Street. The steel columns at Carlisle Race Course were machined and sent from Stirling, likewise the steel columns in Greenock Theatre, done to the order of Messrs Bladen & Co., whom the Stirling Foundry has also supplied with a large quantity of castings. Mr Davie had the contracts for the columns,

joists, tanks, coolers, piping, etc., for Messrs R. & D. Sharp, Ltd., brewers, Blackford; also for the ironwork of Messrs Thomson, brewers, Blackford, and Bo'ness Distillery, the latter job consisting of tanks, columns, joists. The Bo'ness contract was only completed about a month when the place was burned to the ground, Mr Davie thereupon got this contract again, this keeping him busy for over two years.

Of local undertakings, it may be mentioned that Mr Davie cast all the columns and beams for the Arcade and the Arcade Hall, and provided the ironwork for the block of property in Port Street erected by Mr Gillespie, grocer, the architect being the late Mr John M'Lean, Stirling. Other local contracts were the columns for the Albert Hall, steel roof for the Volunteer Drill Hall, Princes Street; the iron work for new stores for Mr Walls, Kerse Mill; the iron work at the Stirling Electric Light Station; building in King Street for Messrs M'Aree Bros., drapers; premises in Murray Place for Messrs W. Drummond & Sons, seedsmen; tenements and shops in Barnton Street for ex-Bailie Brown and Mr Young, Taylorton: tenements and shops in Barnton Street for Messrs J. & A. Young, bakers; Allan Park buildings for Bailie Gourlay; Baker Street buildings for Lawsons Limited; tenements and shops in Port Street for Messrs Cullens, butchers; tenements and shops in Port Street for Mr R. Adam, china merchant; iron work of the new buildings for the "Stirling Observer;" likewise all the Stirling Co-Operative Society's new buildings and alterations.

The firm does all classes of castings up to five tons, and structural, mechanical, and agricultural engineering. Last year the firm made a new waterwheel for His Grace the Duke of Montrose, and erected the same at Buchanan.

At the time of the "Singers'" job the number of hands employed were about 100. At the present time, owing to the depression in trade, there are the smallest number employed that has ever been on the firm's books.

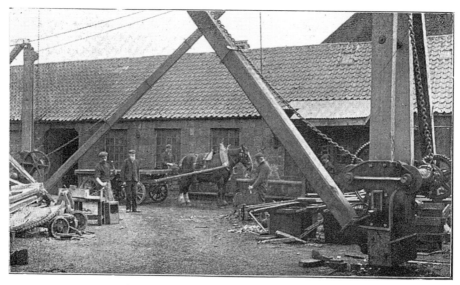

Part of Yard for Dressing Heavy Castings.

Part of Machine Shop.

STIRLING CARRIAGE WORKS, WILLIAM KINROSS & SONS.

As was pointed out in a previous article, coach-building or carriage-making is in one form or another a very ancient industry, probably about the oldest in existence. From the earliest times —Biblical ones—we read of chariots, and we see them represented on Assyrian and Egyptian bas reliefs. These vehicles appeared to have been used more as fighting machines than as regular conveyances, but still they embodied to a considerable extent the principles of the coach and other horse-drawn conveyances on wheels, and coming down to a later period in the world's history there is no doubt about carriages—both open and covered—being used in Rome when she was the Mistress of the World. After the fall of the Roman Empire, coaches went out of use again—as did a good many other things—and during the feudal ages the custom was to ride on horseback, the use of carriages being considered effeminate. They do not appear to have become common till the 15th century, and even then were regarded exclusively as vehicles for women and children. Later on they became, especially in Germany, part of the appendages of royalty. They seem to have been introduced into Stirling about the middle of the 16th century, but were for long confined to the aristocracy and the wealthy classes. Hackney carriages were first used in London in 1625. Stage coaches came into use about the same time, and 1784 saw the establishment of mail coaches, which continued to be the means of travelling both in Scotland and on the other side of the Tweed until their place was taken by the railways, about sixty years ago. There is little doubt that coach-building has existed in Stirling for a century and a half, but the trade was a small one until the establishment of the mail coaches. Being on the high road between Edinburgh and Perth, Stirling was extremely well situated for the purpose of getting any repairs executed to the coaches, and looking to the state of the highways in these days it may be assumed that the vehicles would require a good deal of overhauling.

The firm which is the subject of our article this week—Messrs William Kinross & Sons, Stirling Carriage Works—appears to be the oldest established business in the town. It was begun in 1802—106 years ago—by Mr William Croall, "formerly of Airthrey," and Mr Henry Kinross, who also belonged to the district, and had served an apprenticeship to Mr Croall. His indenture of apprenticeship, drawn by a Stirling lawyer, is still preserved. Their place of business was most likely the old premises at the head of the Shore Road, as the present firm have a copy of a new lease which was entered into in 1817, and which refers to their former tenancy of workshops "at the head of the shore causeway." There was no Barnton Street in those days, the great north road leading down Maxwell Street, and turning at the head of the Shore Road up Viewfield Street. The business was carried on here for sixty-three years, until the late Mr Wm. Kinross decided to remove to the premises now occupied in Port Street. These premises had previously been used as a brewery, and as a woollen mill, but were converted by him into the present spacious workshops, and have now been used for the last forty-three years as a carriage manufactory. These two periods make up the hundred odd years during which the business has been carried on by the founder, then by his nephew, and in these later years by his two grandnephews —ex-Provost George Kinross and his brother, Mr James Kinross. It should be mentioned here that the sons of Mr Croall, after learning the trade, were not satisfied with Stirling, and removed early in the century to Edinburgh, where they founded a very successful business. We can say little as to the personality of Mr Henry Kinross, the young man of 1802, but we know one or two things about his skill. A valued customer (the late Mr Robert Moubray, of Cambus) stated that his father had given the firm one of its first orders, if not the very first, which was to make an improved two-seated gig, with the result that it turned out the first gig made in Scotland. At that time there were very few coachmakers in Scotland. There was no instruction to be had, no work to copy, no choice of materials from makers of special parts, as there is now ; every part had to be designed and made, and the details of construction had to be evolved from the brain. Another interesting fact shows that the firm must have made a name for itself during the stormy years at the beginning of the century, for another of the orders with which it was entrusted was to build a family carriage for Sir David Baird, on his return from the great Indian and Peninsular wars, in which, next to the Duke of Wellington, he had been a brave and skilful leader. To show the

substantial character of the work, this carriage, built in 1816, was finally broken up in the firm's yard in Port Street so late as 1896, the body timbers being still fresh and good, after being in use for 80 years.

There is little to indicate the progress of the business for many years, but there was no want of ability and enterprise, for during the Thirties Mr Henry Kinross had advanced so far that he introduced into his premises the first steam engine used in Stirling, and one of those who took a deep interest in this was one Charles Randolph, then an apprentice in the smith shop. Any one who knows the size and capability of the Fairfield Shipbuilding Yard in Glasgow, should also know that this same Charles Randolph was the founder of it. By 1837 Mr Henry Kinross had been recognised as the leading coach-maker in Scotland, for shortly after the accession of the late Queen Victoria, he was appointed coachmaker to Her Majesty, being the only trades-man in this branch of business in Scotland so honoured. The present firm preserve the Royal Warrant of 1838, and the letter of the late Lord Dalmeny forwarding it, as valuable documents. From the local papers of that year, it would appear that Mr Henry Kinross and his workmen took a notable part in the reception of the late Queen and Prince Consort, on their visit to Stirling in 1842. It is also worthy of note, from the original minute book of the Stirling School of Arts and Mechanics' Institute, that he had been one of the founders of this useful institution in 1825, and was present at the preliminary meeting. Having no sons, he had been training his nephews to his business, and on his death in 1845, it was carried on by them. There was no falling off in the skill and ability with which it had been conducted. The Scottish Central Rail-way Company, after opening its line through Stirling, entrusted the firm with considerable orders for railway carriages, and one of ex-Provost Kinross's boyish recollections is of climbing the steps on to the outside seat provided for the guard of those days.

A disastrous fire in 1850 destroyed the whole workshops, stock and tools in a few hours, and the firm had to make a new beginning. But it proved equal to the emergency, and was able to send the first genuinely improved street omnibus to the great exhibition of 1851 in the Crystal Palace in London. This exhibit attracted much attention, gaining a silver medal, and being adopted as the design best suited for the purpose, brought many orders. A recent writer in the "Glasgow Herald" on the history of street locomotion in that city omitted to notice the part that Stirling took in supplying it with its best omnibuses. From the departure of the last of his brothers for Melbourne in 1852, the late Mr William Kinross, father of the present partners, carried on the business alone, and during the Fifties, when Scotland was not so well-known as now to the dwellers in England and Ireland, he had orders from the Duchess of Bedford, the Earl of Derby, the Marquis of Londonderry, Viscount Shannon and others, including Scottish settlers abroad, all showing that the character of the work was fully maintained. It may sur-prise many to learn that the first Perth dogcart was made by Mr William Kinross in Stirling, and a good many more like it. In 1857, a Scottish gentleman, Mr John Ross of Shandwick, Inver-ness, engaged in business in India, had a phaeton built by Mr Wm. Kinross's father to take back with him to Bombay. This carriage must have been a very attractive one, for it was the begin-ning of a very extensive business with India. More orders came than it was possible to execute, and the workshops never looked so gay as when five or six of these carriages were being finished for shipment, in their bright, lively colours, fawn or drab linings, and silver mountings, a great contrast to the dull colours in use now. For three or four years in succession, nine-tenths of the work done went to India. Down to this time the business had grown with the demand. There was no such thing as keeping a finished carriage in stock, every one being made to order. Others throughout the country had been noticing the opportunity, and carriages were beginning to be kept for sale. From the change of premises in 1865 down to his death in 1874, Mr William Kinross was making changes to meet this. Since then the firm have had to recognise the desire to buy a finished carriage on the part of a large section of customers much more fully, and in 1890 they added their present large and com-modious showroom, which will hold its own with anything of the same kind, even in the great city of London. Ex-Provost and Mr James Kinross took up the business in 1874, and have carried it on till now.

It takes a long time to make a coachbuilder. To get a skilful knowledge of these branches no period of years spent at one of them suffices.

Section of Carriage Showroom.

Section of Carriage Showroom.

View of Part of Paintrooms.

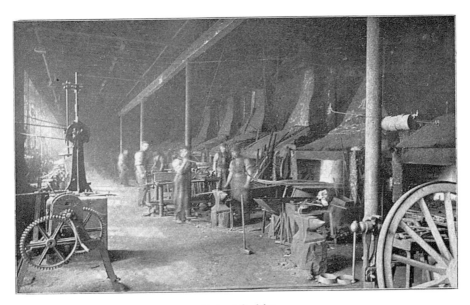

Part of Smithy.

For a well made, well hung, and highly finished carriage is entitled to rank as a work of art, for which very high prices are paid. There are nearly 200 different parts in a carriage (not reckoning bolts or screws), and ten different trades are combined. Yet several successful coachbuilders in this country and the colonies have been trained in Stirling, and as to American competitors, some of these have gone from Scotland. One contributor to a local paper, writing some few years ago from a city in the Far West, stated that he was a native of Stirling, and was trained in the college of Henry Kinross.

The rivalry of the motor car has interfered considerably with the making of new carriages, and the output of these is not so great as it was, but there is a fairly good amount of work going on, and the firm continues to maintain its high standard of reputation, whilst it has a band of loyal workmen, several of whom have been in its employment for very many years. In this connection it is interesting to mention that whilst some other industries find a difficulty in getting apprentices, Messrs Wm. Kinross & Sons have never had any trouble on that score. They can always get lads when wanted, and not only that, but their best apprentices come from the country villages round about Stirling. Boys brought up in town are, as a rule, not so steady in their habits nor so anxious to perfect themselves in their trade.

The buildings in which this industry, or rather combination of industries, is carried on, were not erected specially for it, except the more recent showroom entering from Port Street. Going down the carriage entrance at the side of it one of the buildings is the old guard-house, part of the Town Wall, now occupied by a long steam boiler. Attached to this building is a modern engine-house with a high-class Corliss engine. On a lower level, and close by, is the machine shop, with circular and band saws, turning lathes, and machines for wheel timber. Parallel with it is a large airy smith shop, with ten forges, having patent fanner blast. Here the forging, filing, and fitting of springs and all the other details of coach iron work goes on entirely by hand labour, the only machines being the verticals for boring. Opening from it is the large bodyshop, with benches all round, where the making of carriage and motor bodies is going on. The other branches of under-carriage and wheel-making are also going on here, and when tested for weight, balance, etc., the carriages are sent up to the higher level to be painted and finished. Two flats above this are occupied as carriage stores, the upper one carrying also finished wheels and mahogany panels.

Entering through the middle flat, to the right is a long, spacious, and well lighted painting room, and to the left another, with part of it used for the trimming and upholstery work. Coming outside again, there are large timber sheds, in which a variety of woods are stored, some taking years to season properly. One shed under the paint loft holds mostly four-in-hand and other coaches used through the summer season. There is also a fire-proof store where all the smaller furnishings, varnishes, etc., are kept, and a special room for the sewing done by the only female employee. Last of all, the long saloon, extending up to Port Street, where new and second-hand carriages for sale are shown.

One outstanding feature is that the making of carriage springs and the different parts of iron work has always been, and is still, carried on here. Coachmakers elsewhere have given up making these, and supply themselves from wholesale makers and dealers in Birmingham. The firm has a high reputation for first-class work, and as evidence of this can refer to carriages turned out recently to such distant places as Thurso, the Hebrides, places both in England and Ireland, and Gibraltar, while in previous years many carriages have gone to South Africa, India, Jamaica, Trinidad, and one to Victoria, Vancouver Island. Long may this old and worthy firm continue to flourish and to uphold the good name of the "City of the Rock" in the branch of industry in which its reputation has been gained.

Front View of Premises.

Part of Washing-House.

BRAEHEAD LAUNDRY, ALVA.—T. W. HENDERSON.

Liebig has been credited with the remark that the quantity of soap consumed by a nation would be no inaccurate measure whereby to estimate its wealth and civilisation, and if the word soap may be interpreted as synonymous with laundries, then the Stirling district must be highly favoured in this respect, as it includes a large number of these institutions among its industries. It is said the earliest mention of the term soap, as applied to the substance now known by that name, occurs in the writings of Pliny, and in the excavations of Pompeii a complete soap-boiling establishment was discovered containing soap, still perfect, though it must have been prepared many centuries ago. It is therefore surely not claiming too much if we assume that, even though the rich in the Middle Ages are reputed to have concealed a want of cleanliness in their clothes and persons under a profusion of costly scents and essences, the launderer's trade (although perhaps not as we know it) is a very ancient one. The good Queen Bess appears to have been a fashion leader in her time, and is reported to have engaged and brought from Holland an expert laundress experienced in the starching and getting up of the lace ruffles and frills worn at that period.

The washing of clothes, however, as an industry by itself seems of comparatively recent date. The power laundry only came into existence in the latter half of last century, laundrying, prior to that time, being conducted more or less as a branch of domestic work; consequently records of former customs are somewhat vague. In Eastern countries, however, customs change more slowly than among the more advanced Western nations, and the Indian "dhobie," carrying his basket of clothes to the side of a stream, there to perform the operation of washing in the running water, aided by pounding the clothes on a flat stone, is probably, after making due allowance for necessary differences arising from climatic and other causes, a very good example of the primitive methods in vogue generations, or possibly centuries, ago. Even at the present time in some parts of Southern Europe it is still customary for washerwomen to carry baskets of clothes to the side of a spring or stream for washing purposes, elsewhere the operation is carried on in sheds erected for the purpose in suitable situations, which are evidently a forerunner of the public wash-houses erected by the local authorities in many of our own cities and towns. Writers describing Glasgow as it existed a century ago mention that Glasgow Green was a favourite haunt of the washerwomen of that time, who conducted operations in the open-air, much to the surprise of English visitors, who witnessed with astonishment the process of scouring blankets, by treading them with the feet, being conducted in a public place. Gradually, partly as a result of more modern town life restricting the facilities for doing washings in the home, probably also because of the increase of wages generally tending to encourage the use of labour-saving appliances, and also because of the ingenuity of engineers and inventors stimulating this growing demand, the tendency, for many years past, has been more and more in the direction of families giving out their washings instead of doing them at home, first to the ordinary washerwoman, then to the cottage or hand laundry, and finally to the power laundry. The prejudice which existed a few years ago against power laundries is rapidly dying out, and as the public taste becomes better educated its appreciation of high-class laundry work increases, until it cannot be satisfied except by the more perfect appliances in the power laundry, or from the similar appliances in those whose only right to the use of the term "hand" arises from the fact of their machines being driven by hand instead of power. Among the industries of its kind in our own neighbourhood, Braehead Laundry, Alva, the subject of our present article, occupies a prominent position, both as to extent of trade and quality of output.

This establishment, which was started by Mr T. W. Henderson, the present proprietor, fully a dozen years ago, is now not the least important of the works in the town of Alva, situated in the Hillfoots district, about seven miles eastwards of Stirling. While selecting a location for his work, Mr Henderson held very pronounced opinions as to the disadvantages a limited water supply and smoky atmosphere entailed on laundries by proximity to towns of even comparatively small size, and in going further afield and selecting his present site, he has been singularly happy in securing an altogether ideal situation for a business such as his. The laundry, standing as it does on the rising ground to the north of the town, at the entrance to Alva Glen, possesses splendid facilities for open-air bleaching and drying, which are, after all, generally recognised as the best methods of dealing with a large number of articles. The water supply is drawn from the Alva Burn, and is so abundant as not only to provide copiously for washing requirements, but also to supply a considerable proportion of the motive power required, and as, on analysis, it has been found to be exceptionally soft, and peculiarly free from impurities, it undoubtedly contributes very largely to the success of the operations conducted in the laundry. Of course, sufficient support could not be obtained in the immediate vicinity of Alva for a trade of the kind, and it is therefore necessary to maintain an efficient and somewhat expensive van service, for collecting and delivering purposes, working the country eastwards as far as Dunfermline, and westwards as far as Callander and Aberfoyle. To maintain this service it is necessary that a number of horses should be kept, and the stables form a very important part of the laundry premises.

When the vans return from their collecting rounds, the parcels they contain are handed into the receiving room, where they are taken charge of by a squad of sorters, who, after carefully counting the articles they contain, and comparing particulars with the quantities advised in the washing lists that accompany the parcels, make the necessary entries in the "goods received" book, and after putting on each article a distinguishing mark (either with coloured thread or marking ink) to permit of identification at a later stage, separate the goods into the different grades necessary for their proper treatment in the washing-house, which adjoins the receiving room. Of course the washing machines are the leading feature in this department, and consist of two cylinders, the one inside the other, a rotary motion being imparted to the former by means of gearing placed outside the outer cylinder. After running in a sufficient quantity of water, the clothes are placed inside the inner cylinder, the lid shut, and the machine started. A strong solution of soap dissolved in water is then poured into the machine. This, with the water already in the machine, forms the washing liquor, which, through holes in its circumference, is allowed to circulate freely through the clothes inside the revolving cylinder. This cylinder has, on its inner surface, spars with smoothly-rounded edges, running in the direction of its length, and these gently rub and beat the clothes

as the cylinder revolves. In addition to the pipes for inlet and outlet of water, a steam pipe is connected with the washer, and by its means the liquor can very speedily be raised to boiling point, and the washing carried through from start to finish without any intermediate removal of the clothes from the machine for treatment in a separate boiler. After completion of the washing process, the clothes are transferred to the hydro extractors, or centrifugal wringer, which consist of a swiftly-revolving perforated basket (in which the clothes are placed) inside a case. This basket is perfectly smooth inside, and there is absolutely nothing in the machine which can possibly injure the goods, the wringing effect being entirely due to the well-known tendency of centrifugal force to cause water to fly outwards from the centre of any quickly twirled body containing it. A very few minutes suffice to wring a load in one of these extractors, and while the work is much more efficiently performed, there is less wear and tear on the goods than is the case with the common domestic roller wringer, or even the still older fashioned method of twisting between the hands. There are, of course, a few articles which, as they require special treatment, it would be injudicious to put into the washing machines, and these are provided for by the row of hand washing-tubs running along one side of the house.

On leaving the washing-house, a door to the right gives entrance to the boiler-house, which stands in a convenient central position, and contains two steam boilers of the Cornish type. The older of these was put in nine years ago, to replace the original boiler, which, by that time, had become too small to meet the requirements of a rapidly increasing trade, but as it has now in its turn been found unable to fully cope with the demands made on it, especially by the expanding trade in the carpet-beating department, another boiler, capable of being worked at a much higher pressure, has this year been added to the plant. The boilers not only supply steam to the engine, which, in conjunction with a turbine wheel, supply power for driving the various machines, but also supply steam for heating purposes. With the exception of a stove in a small detached office there are no fires in the laundry except in the boiler-house, all boiling and heating being done either by steam or gas. The exhaust or waste steam from the engine is utilised for heating the dry houses, in which clothes are

Part of Ironing Room.

dried, also for providing a supply of hot water for use in the washing-house, as well as for feeding the boilers.

After leaving the washing-house, many articles, for which the open-air treatment is deemed desirable, are taken outside to the drying grounds, and the extent to which this system is practised, when circumstances permit, is evidenced every fine day by the lengths of well-covered ropes stretching across the grass plots. It is impossible to do more than a portion of the drying in the open-air, and ample provision for inside drying is therefore a necessary adjunct to a laundry of this kind. The dry houses are in convenient proximity to the washing-house, and after the wet clothes have been hung in them, a fan is set in motion, causing a strong current of air, warmed to a high temperature by passing through a coil of steam-heated pipes, to circulate rapidly through the houses, quickly removing all moisture from the clothes, and preparing them for the next operation. Such a system as this insures thorough ventilation of the goods, and altogether very nearly secures the benefits of open-air drying.

Starching, so far as it concerns the articles to which starch is applied, takes a most important place in the programme of laundry operations, as on the thoroughness with which this operation is performed, the success of succeeding processes depends to a very great extent. So that nothing may be left to chance, it is customary not only to carefully weigh the starch and measure the water used for each mixing, but before using, and to ensure perfect regularity of density, to test with a hydrometer. Shirts and collars are the articles to which these latter remarks chiefly apply, and which are probably responsible for the greater part of the starch consumption in a laundry. At Braehead this part of the work is done by mechanical means, the shirts by a machine of ingenious, but extremely simple construction. In this process there is nothing which can be injurious, and indeed the cloth must suffer less than by ordinary hand starching, as results are produced, not by rubbing or squeezing, but simply by a steady flow of liquor passing gently through the cloth. Collars are starched by an equally simple machine, which, as visitors often remark, strongly resembles an ordinary barrel churn, and, indeed, it is nothing else than a small barrel hung inside a frame by suitable bearings, and which, on power being

applied, is set in motion, revolving end over end. The collars, with a sufficient quantity of starch liquor, are put inside, and after the lid has been securely fastened the machine is started, and kept going for a few minutes, then it is stopped, emptied, and the collars wrung, wiped, and taken to the ironing room. In this machine also the treatment is extremely gentle, as the barrel is perfectly smooth inside. The effect is obtained entirely by the tumbling about of the collars among the liquor.

In the ironing rooms both machine and hand ironers are employed, the latter, probably, to a greater extent than is generally supposed by many who are not conversant with power laundry routine. There are many articles which cannot be done except with the hand iron, and many others that require to be partly done by it. In the power laundry, however, it is possible to use a type which is more economical in time and fuel than that in common domestic use. Among ironing machines, the largest, and perhaps the most important, are the calenders or steam mangles for flat work. There are various makes of these machines, but those in Braehead Laundry are of the Decoudun type. They are composed of a steam heated cylinder covered by a jacketing of felt and cotton, and revolving slowly in a concave highly-polished bedplate formed by the upper side of a steam-heated chest. The pressure betwixt cylinder and bedplate is adjusted to a nicety by means of the springs on which the cylinder rests. The articles are slightly damp when brought to these machines, which are generally operated by four workers. The two in front feed in the damp clothes, the two behind receive them as they pass through, and when sufficiently dry, fold and lay them aside ready for removal to the packing room. These machines deal with a most varied assortment of articles, comprising tablecloths, serviettes, sheets, bedcovers, towels, pillowslips, etc., and when at work an almost continuous snow-white stream of varying width is seen passing through them. Articles up to nine feet in width may be ironed without a crease or fold of any kind. The collar machines, though small in size, are not the least important in this department, and Braehead has a full equipment of these, both of the reciprocating and rotary types. These machines are, like the hand irons, heated by a mixture of gas and air, which burns inside a highly polished metal roller, immediately beneath which, but at some little distance apart,

Carpet Beating Machine.

to permit of a jacketed board or table passing between, there is an ordinary metal roller. These rollers are geared by toothed pinions which run them at slightly varying speeds, and the power is transmitted to the machine from the main shaft by belts and pulleys, the former being controlled by guides, acted on by a pedal worked by the operator's foot, by means of which the run of the machine may be instantly reversed. The board having been prepared by covering with some thicknesses of felt and cotton, has collars carefully spread on it, and is then inserted into the machine betwixt the rollers, the motions of which, governed by the foot of the operator, run it rapidly to and fro, until, after several passes, the collars, having meanwhile been turned once or twice, are considered sufficiently dry to be removed from the board and laid aside for glossing and finishing. The shirt machines, at all events those which do the breasts and cuffs of shirts, are practically the same in construction as the collar machines, the principal difference being that the rollers are placed further apart to suit the different make of board. The less important machines in the ironing room include body and skirt ironers, the former being used for the bodies of shirts and other articles for which it may be suitable, and the latter for the skirts of dresses, etc. The first of these two machines consists of two parallel rollers, about 36 inches in length and 6 inches in diameter, extending outside a frame, the upper of the two being heated with the gas and air flame, and the lower jacketed with felt and cloths. The body of the shirt or other article is drawn over the lower roller, then, by the application of the operator's foot to a pedal, the two rollers are brought into contact, and the article allowed to pass slowly through between them. When sufficiently ironed the raising of the foot allows the rollers to open and the garment to be removed. The second machine is somewhat similar in construction, but the heating is done by steam, an inverted steam chest taking the place of the upper roller, while the jacketed roller is of much larger diameter, and the articles done through it consist of the skirts of dresses, etc., which are done in the same way as the shirts on the body ironer.

In the upper flat of the Laundry is situated the curtain frame house, where lace and other curtains, after being cleaned and starched, are stretched and dried. This is a most important branch of the trade at Braehead Laundry, and its extent indicates very strongly the appreciation with which its output is received by customers. The house, which is a small steam-heated dry house of suitable construction, contains a number of frames, each having a movable side and end to permit of its size being adjusted to the size of curtain about to be stretched. Along the sides and ends of the frames are rows of short metal teeth, and on these the edges of the curtains are fixed, and then the frame, which slides on little rails, is pushed inside the house and shut in for the curtains to be dried while stretched.

On the same flat there are also several cold and hot water storage tanks. Owing to the water supply being drawn from a stream, it was found advisable to run it first into settling tanks, from which it is pumped to tanks in the top flat of the main building, and from these distributed over the Laundry. The tanks on the top floor and the pumps on the ground floor are connected by an ingenious contrivance, which, by the falling or rising of the water in the tanks, causes the pumps to start or stop automatically. In this way, and with practically no attention, a constant supply of water is retained in the tanks. The water in the hot water tanks is heated by the exhaust or waste steam from the engine, and provides, at very little expense, a constant supply of hot water for various purposes.

The packing room is, in ordinary succession, the last department of the Laundry proper, and is conveniently placed for receiving the finished goods from the ironing room, and after they have been properly parcelled, passing them over to one or other of the well-known green painted vans, by which they are conveyed to their respective destinations. This room is suitably furnished with tables and sorting bins, and the finished goods, when received from the ironing room, are sorted into their respective lots, and gradually, as these lots are one after another completely gathered together, parcelled for delivery.

A small but very important branch of the trade at Braehead Laundry is the chemical cleaning process (French or dry cleaning it is more generally termed) which, owing to the highly inflammable nature of the materials used, is carried on in an outlying portion of the premises set apart for it alone. This department is complete within itself, and contains steam engine, washing machine, hydro extractor, still, etc. The process consists in washing the goods in benzine in a machine very similar in appearance and working to those in the ordinary washing-house. This benzine cleaning process may be successfully applied to practically all articles liable to suffer shrinkage or loss of colour when washed with water and soap, and is especially valuable in the case of bright coloured articles. But however valuable benzine may be as a cleaning medium, it should never be forgotten that its cleansing power is not equal to that of water and soap, and consequently it is even more necessary that goods intended for the chemical cleaning process should not be kept in use too long, as the marks of excessive soiling cannot always be completely eradicated, and in many cases this result can only be attained by touching up and sponging with water, either alone or with chemicals dissolved in it, a treatment which, to some extent, detracts from the advantages of the benzine process.

Carpet-beating is another side line, and also forms a separate department, the machine being placed by itself in a large apartment on the ground floor of the main building. The old fashioned hand system is very closely followed by the machine, the beating, however, being done by balata or leather straps instead of canes. The carpets are fed in by a slit in the side casing of the machine, and rest on a bed of leather bands stretched on a frame supported by springs, which yield slightly beneath the rapidly descending shower of blows delivered by the beaters. These beaters are merely straps attached to a swiftly revolving shaft, and by their means the dust is speedily and effectually removed from the carpets, which, after being passed into the machine, are drawn back, passed in again several times in succession, and at last leave the machine thoroughly freed from the dust which has been sucked away by a fan and blown into a pit, so that none is allowed to escape out of the machine into the house. The process is extremely simple, and risks of injury are reduced to a minimum.

The public, however, should fully realise that exemption from risk depends to a very great extent on the owners of carpets themselves, being careful to see that before having them beaten they are thoroughly protected along the edges by hemming or binding with tape, as it is only a very natural consequence of beating that unprotected edges or torn places will slightly tease out by the action of the process, and nothing else need be expected. The strongest evidence of the carefulness with which carpets are handled, and the harmless character of the treatment, is to be found in the fact that during the eight and a half years which have elapsed since the machine was put into Braehead Laundry, there have been only three occasions on which it has been found necessary to make compensation for alleged injury, that the subject of one of these had admittedly passed fifteen years on active service, and had been beaten at the Laundry on many previous occasions, while the costs of making repairs in the whole three cases only reached a total of six or seven shillings. Notwithstanding the advent a few years ago of the vacuum cleaning machine, which at one time threatened to be a serious opponent of the carpet-beater, the trade of this department has always shown an expanding tendency, and the present year again gives promise of outstripping its predecessor. A feature of the carpet-beating trade is the limited time allowed for collecting, beating, and delivering carpets, but this demand has been successfully complied with by furnishing an extended van service during the months of March, April, and May of each year, and except in the more distant parts of the district, deliveries are made the day following that on which carpets are received.

SCOTTISH CENTRAL WORKS, STIRLING.

KEMP & NICHOLSON.

This week our article deals with a firm which, though not old as age goes, is supplying the most of the requisites needed for the carrying on of the oldest industry that man has engaged in, and which it may also be safely assumed will be the last that this world will see. We refer to agriculture, or the cultivation of the soil for the purpose of bringing forth the fruits that are the staff of life. In the presence of agriculture, all other pursuits and industries are but things of yesterday. The tilling of the soil is practically coeval with the beginning of the world, for in the Garden of Eden, or at least soon after they were ejected from it, Adam delved while Eve span. The chief operations of agriculture are the same to-day as they were when first practised. Ploughing, sowing, harrowing, reaping, and threshing are all mentioned in the Old Testament, and they are still as necessary in the twentieth century as they were in the first. More than that, the implements of husbandry are, with slight modifications, taking into account the thousands of years that have elapsed, very similar to what they were when the world was in its youth. Reaping machines are certainly modern inventions, but not nearly so modern as might be imagined. Most people are in the belief that mechanical reapers are creations of the last half century or so, and whilst this is true to a large extent, it is none the less interesting to learn that reaping by machinery is no modern invention so far as the idea is concerned, but is simply the re-discovery of an art which was known to the ancients. Pliny the elder, a famous Roman writer who was born in the first century of the Christian era, found a reaping machine in Gaul (France) which was in the form of a modern two-wheeled barrow, with boards on three sides. The front of this barrow was armed with a row of projecting teeth, and this machine was pushed against the standing corn by an ox, with the result that as the barrow moved forward the ears of the grain were cut off, and fell into it. Ploughing and harrowing are still carried on as they were in early times, though by more improved methods. In these operations, human beings, oxen, and horses have furnished the motive power according to the stage of civilisation the people of various countries have attained, but machinery has found little or no place. Certainly steam ploughs have been

invented, and put into use, but for various reasons the experiments have never been a success, and the old methods continue to be used. The threshing or separation of the grain from the straw has, however, undergone a change akin to that of reaping. In early times the Egyptians and Israelites used oxen to tramp over the sheaves and thus press out the grain, but this damaged the corn, and afterwards wooden, and then iron rollers were employed. For many centuries this was the method in use, until in 1787 when Andrew Meikle, a Scotsman, invented the stationary threshing mill, which is part of the equipment of most farms at the present day. Though the threshing mill has been improved since Meikle's time, and travelling threshers drawn by a traction engine have come into vogue, the principle of the machine is essentially the same as that employed by the original inventor. Farm threshing mills used to be driven by horses walking round in a circle, but nowadays in most cases the motive power is an oil engine. An old-fashioned way of threshing the grain, which is still practised in remote districts in Britain, is carried out by means of the flail. This implement is in the form of a short, thick club attached to a slender pole about three feet long, but hanging loose from it for an inch or two. The operator grasps the pole with both hands, swings it round his head, and brings the club down with a smack upon the sheaf which is lying on the floor. At first sight this would not appear a very difficult operation, and so it isn't—if one is an expert at it. In the hands of an inexperienced operator, however, the flail is a dangerous weapon—to the man who uses it. If he does not give the proper swing which keeps the club well away from his body, the chances are that he will find out how easy it is for a man to commit an assault upon his own person. When he picks himself up from the ground and tenderly rubs the back of his head where the club has struck him, the unskilled wielder of the flail will probably recollect Shakespeare's saying that "there are more things in heaven and earth than are dreamt of in our philosophy."

As we have previously remarked, the plough, the harrow, and the sickle are all implements of agriculture which have in one form or another been in use beyond the dawn of history. All are referred to in the earlier books of the Old Testa-

View of Works.

ment, and the old writers in their beautiful imagery make frequent use of the terms by way of illustration of matters outside the cultivation of the soil. We have all read of the time when swords will be beaten into ploughshares, when the foes of the Israelites will be punished even as the land is broken up under the teeth of the harrows, and when man shall be cut down in the flower of his youth, as the corn falls before the sickle. Scythes are not mentioned in the Scriptures, probably because they are of comparatively modern invention. They are, however, an obvious development of the sickle, and in modern harvesting operations filled in the gap between the reaping hook of the ancients and the self-binder of the nineteenth century. The latter has wrought the greatest revolution that has been witnessed in the practice of agriculture, and it is difficult, when one looks upon a field of grain being harvested by a machine drawn by a couple of horses, and guided by a single man who enjoys a comfortable seat on the reaper, to realise how farmers got their crops cut and housed in the olden days, when the scythe or the sickle was the only implement in use. The seasons were then as uncertain and changeable as they are yet, but for all that the grain was cut and secured quite as expeditiously. The explanation is found in the condition of the people half a century ago. This was before the great industrial boom had set in, and all the country villages were the centres of considerable populations—mostly handloom weavers. To them the "hairst" was the chief event of the local year, and when it came round the looms were stopped, and the population, young and old, flocked to the harvest fields. Bands of Irish "shearers" also perambulated the country, and the farmer had no lack of willing hands to assist him, labour being cheap and plentiful, whilst high prices were obtained for grain, this being previous to the days of American and Canadian wheat imports. Bands of weavers and Irishmen took on contracts for the cutting and "stooking" of the grain, the fee being at the rate of from eight to fifteen shillings per acre. Sometimes board and lodging—of a kind—was given by the farmer, and an old chronicler records in the case of the Irish harvesters that the quantity of porridge, which was the staple meal, consumed by these men was astonishing. One man, it is stated, ate no less than 5 lbs. of porridge, and consumed $1\frac{1}{2}$ lbs. of milk at one meal. Many of the finest idylls in Scottish song and story derive their inspiration from the

incidents of the "hairst," but the picturesqueness has long departed from the harvest field, the introduction of the self-binder and the whirr of its machinery having given the death-blow to this interesting phase of Scottish rural life.

The firm of Kemp & Nicholson, which is a familiar name of good repute in agricultural circles both at home and abroad, was founded 60 years ago by Mr John Kemp, who in the Seventies and Eighties was a well-known and highly respected public man in Stirling, he having held office in the Town Council, School Board, and Water Commission. Though not a Son of the Rock, Mr Kemp was a native of the adjoining county of Perth. Born in 1823, at Loanside, a small hamlet in the parish of Fowlis Wester, near Crieff, he learned the trade of a joiner and cartwright at Methven in the same district, and afterwards worked for some years as a journeyman in Perth. Coming to Stirling in 1848, he entered the employment of the late Mr Thomas Reid, joiner and cabinetmaker, Craigs. In a few months, however, Mr Kemp changed his position, and ceasing to be an employee, became a master. In November, 1848, he commenced business as a joiner and cartwright on his own account, his first workshop being in Murray Place, in "Waugh's Pend," opposite the Baptist Church. Mr Kemp had a severe struggle for a year or two, but by sterling integrity he gradually built up a good business, and in 1851 assumed as partner the late Bailie Murray, who was a joiner. Two years later, a third partner joined the firm in the person of the late Mr Peter Nicholson, who was of the same trade as Bailie Murray. The Bailie and Mr Nicholson attended to the joinery department, while Mr Kemp took charge of the agricultural section. For several years the firm did a big joinery business, many important contracts being executed by it, not only in Stirling, but all over the country. It is also an interesting fact that several gentlemen who afterwards established joinery businesses in Stirling and elsewhere received their training in the service of the firm of Kemp, Murray, & Nicholson. During this time, however, the agricultural section of the firm's business was rapidly developing, and the joinery part was gradually dropped, and closer attention given to the department of trade on which the name and fame of the Scottish Central Works has been built up.

About fifty years ago, the reaping machine began to supersede the scythe in harvesting operations, and Mr Kemp, who was of an inventive and also

Kemp & Nicholson's First Reaper, 1856.

The Modern Self-Binder.

practical turn of mind, adapted and improved upon the pattern of reaper then in use, with the result that his machine became the leading favourite in the market. An honoured local firm was the first to give him an order for a reaper, the "Good Samaritan" being Messrs Wm. Drummond & Sons, seedsmen, who at that period were also agents for agricultural implements. For a considerable number of years the reaper turned out by Messrs Kemp, Murray, & Nicholson held the field at home, and besides being also largely used in England and Ireland, found a market on the Continent of Europe, and even in Syria, Australia, and New Zealand. The machine gained the prize medal at several international exhibitions, notably London in 1862, Hamburg 1863, Dublin 1865, Stettin 1865, and Cologne 1865, whilst premier honours were secured at the Highland Society's Shows and numerous agricultural exhibitions all over Scotland down to 1875, and during the "boom" in reapers, the firm turned out as many as 400 in one year.

In 1876 Bailie Murray retired from business and Messrs Kemp & Nicholson carried on the firm until 1887, when the latter also left, Mr Kemp remaining as sole partner. Previous to that, however, the firm had again removed to larger premises, and this time they built for themselves, instead of renting workshops. In 1884, a feu was taken off in the Cow Park, at what is now known as Forth Street, which had the advantage of being adjacent to the railway, and here in 1884, the extensive Scottish Central Works were erected. Though the frontage to the street is to-day much as it was then, the establishment has been added to since, and the manufactory is a very complete and well-equipped one indeed for the business carried on. The frontage to Forth Street is 140 ft., and the premises comprise a suite of well-appointed general and private offices, with extensive workshops, stores, sheds, &c., whilst the working plant is of a thoroughly up-to-date character, lending itself to rapid and also economical production. The number of departments of one kind or another is somewhat astonishing, looking to the space the Works occupy, and can only be fully realised by a visit to the premises.

About the time Mr Nicholson retired from the firm, the ramifications of the business carried on were again undergoing a change, and continued to do so right up to the time of Mr Kemp's death in 1892. The old reaper was being ousted by the American and Canadian self-binder, and our Transatlantic cousins were also getting a hold of the British market with their ploughs, which implement had up to this time also been largely manufactured by Kemp & Nicholson. Owing to certain natural advantages, the Americans were able to supply lighter reaping machines and ploughs at a cost for production which the home makers could not compete against, and realising this fact, Kemp & Nicholson turned their attention to the manufacture of not only other agricultural implements in which they could hold their own, but likewise to some new forms of industry altogether. The beginning of this change was almost coincident with the taking over of the control of the business by the present head of the firm, Mr James Kemp Smith, who as a young man succeeded his grandfather, Mr Kemp, in 1892, but had been closely associated with him ever since he left school, which was some years before that. Entering as an apprentice in 1884, Mr J. Kemp Smith spent five years gaining a knowledge of the work of the various departments, and following this employed two or three years more in familiarising himself with the commercial side, having in this connection attended the annual shows of the Highland and Agricultural Society since he was a boy. But though, as we have already stated, Kemp & Nicholson found it impossible to manufacture self-binders at the American price, they did not give up connection with reaping machines. What they did was to develop the trade in another way, by taking up the agency for central Scotland of one of the most famous Canadian makes of reaper and binder, the Massey-Harris. This agency was negotiated for shortly before Mr Kemp's death in 1892, and it has remained with the firm ever since. Kemp & Nicholson started with a sale of three self-binders the first year, but since then the machines have been disposed of at the rate of well on to three figures per annum, and the sale still continues steady. One might think that in the course of years farmers would all get supplied, and the sale would be bound to fall off, but a reaping machine is like a bicycle in one respect—it is always developing. Change of lightness of build and of draught are always going on, and the self-binder can now be used as easily on hilly and irregular surfaces, such as the Braes o' Doune, as in the flat Carse of Stirling. Moreover, a farmer is very like a cyclist in his feelings regarding his machine. After he has had a reaper for five or six seasons, he likes to go in for a more modern pattern with the latest improvements, and he accordingly returns to the agent with the

Section of Blacksmiths' Shop.

Part of Fitting and Turning Shop.

request that the old machine may be taken back, so that he may get a new one. This is easily arranged, as there is always a market for the older reapers among small farmers, who wish to make a start with a self-binder, but cannot give the price for a new one. Another thing that keeps up the demand for reapers is the fact of its life not being a long one. In this particular the self-binder is not so good as the old-fashioned reaper, but it has to be remembered that the former does the work of a large number of persons in the harvest field, and accordingly a lot is taken out of it. Machines no more than human beings can go on for ever at high pressure. The firm also has an extensive connection in the supplying of ploughs of American manufacture, for which it likewise holds an agency.

But if Kemp & Nicholson have ceased to manufacture reaping machines, and only make ploughs to order, they have an extensive trade in the production of every other requisite required for agricultural purposes. Under Mr Kemp Smith's management and business enterprise the output of the Works is much more varied in character than it was in his grandfather's time, even at the date of his death, sixteen years ago. This is an age of keen competition at low figures, and there must be big turnovers with quick returns if a profit is to be made, though it is the experience of all commercial men that the returns are not so quick as they might be by a long way. At the Scottish Central Works the number of articles manufactured is almost legion, and their multifarious nature gives one not intimately acquainted with agriculture an idea of the necessaries required for the carrying on of that industry. To select a few—and they are only a few—may be mentioned grubbers or earth pulverisers, harrows or field rakes, land rollers, turnip sowers, carts, chaff cutters, corn grinders, hay bailers, drill turnip cleaners, horse hoes, and cultivators, clod crushers, seed sowing machines, hay collectors, &c., &c. Since Mr Kemp Smith became head of the firm, he has enterprisingly struck out into several new lines of manufacture, which have been crowned with success. Amongst these may be mentioned the patent Morgan hay press, the making of South African ploughs and harrows, the construction of vans and lorries, and the preparation of steel axles for carts. This latter is an industry that has largely developed in recent years, and the trade is still going up. For a considerable number of years Messrs Kemp

& Nicholson made a considerable quantity of the wheels for the well-known Arrol-Johnstone Motor Car Company, Paisley. The vehicles supplied by this firm have a reputation for durability, and some cars fitted with solid tyred wheels manufactured at the Scottish Central Works are running in Scotland yet.

Though, as we have already stated, Messrs Kemp & Nicholson have ceased to manufacture ploughs for the home market, they have recently started doing so for South Africa, and have already completed two large contracts. The start of this department of the business was the outcome of an inquiry two years ago from a London firm, asking for a catalogue of the articles supplied by the Scottish Central Works. This was duly forwarded, and a few days later there was returned an illustration of a plough which was quite different from any implement the Stirling firm had made, and asking if they could undertake to do so, and at the same time to quote a price. This was done, and the outcome of further correspondence was that Mr J. Kemp Smith took a journey to London, saw the agent of a South African house there, and as a result an order was secured for the construction of three hundred ploughs for that colony. And not only that, but so satisfactory was the article supplied from the Scottish Central Works that "repeat" orders continued to come in until the firm had considerably over a thousand ploughs on its books for delivery before the end of the season. This was a big job to tackle, as the plant at the works was hardly capable of turning out the number of ploughs required in the specified time, but by working practically night and day, the contract was successfully carried through. On the 10th of December, 1907, Mr Kemp Smith was again invited to go to London to see the South African agent, and the outcome of that journey was the order for fifteen hundred more ploughs, to be delivered this season. Perhaps the most satisfactory feature of this new departure, however, on the part of Kemp & Nicholson was that the firm has taken the South African plough trade from the Germans, who had it previously, and also that out of fifty firms in Britain who got the chance of going into the business, Messrs Kemp & Nicholson were one of three who were accepted. It may also be mentioned in this connection that the firm some time ago executed an order for the British Government of 800 sets of harrows for South Africa, as part of the scheme of repatriating the Boers on their farms after the war.

But the ramifications of the industry carried on at the Scottish Central Works do not end with the matters to which we have called attention. The firm are not only agricultural implement makers, they are also agricultural engineers, and in this department of the business some important contracts have been executed. Amongst these may be stated—complete "installations" of agricultural machinery for two farms on the estate of Sir Charles Cayzer, Bart., of Gartmore; a similar undertaking for Mr J. Ernest Kerr of Harviestoun, Dollar; pumping plant, with oil engine, for Captain Stirling of Keir; and installations at the farms of Cornton, Alton of Bandeath, Home Farm of Auchterarder, Fintalich Farm, Muthill, etc. A good deal more could be written with reference to the operations of the firm, but sufficient has been said to give an idea of the position it holds in the agricultural world, and it need only be added in conclusion, that whilst Messrs Kemp & Nicholson, of Stirling, enjoy a worthy reputation all over the United Kingdom, they likewise have the confidence of customers in all European countries, and even further afield, goods being sent to Egypt, India, the Gold Coast, Australia, and New Zealand. Though there are older firms in our historic town, there are none more enterprising than the one that is identified with the Scottish Central Works, and it will be the desire of everyone interested in the prosperity of Stirling that Messrs Kemp & Nicholson will continue to flourish, and to maintain the good name which the founder of the firm bequeathed to it.

Part of Wood-Working Section.

ROBERT ANDERSON & SONS, BUILDING CONTRACTORS, STIRLING.

As we all know, the art of working in wood is almost as old as the world itself, and that the ancients were very skilled in this craft there is ample evidence to prove. The Bible contains many references to carpenters and wood workers, and that the craft was a highly skilled and honoured one, may be inferred from the fact that it would be old when the secret of working in metals was discovered. Going back to the time of Solomon, we read that in the erection of the Temple, and of his palace, he used wood very extensively as flooring, and also in lining walls and ceilings, etc., and right down through the different ages we can trace, both by manuscript and example, that the carpenter—or to use a good old Scottish term fast passing out of use, the wright or wricht—always filled a very prominent niche in the building world, alike in external and internal work involved in the erection of the lordly mansion or the humblest dwelling of mankind. But in this, as in other trades, there must either be progress or decay, there is no standing still, and the calling of the wright, like those of other crafts, has undergone very great changes within the last hundred years or thereby, both as to the class of work set before him to do, and the conditions under which it had to be done. These changes can be best understood when, on visiting, as most of us have done, some of these fine old castles or cathedrals built hundreds of years ago, we find such splendid examples of oak roofs and panelled walls and ceilings. As the wright of to-day looks upon such work with admiration, this feeling will be accompanied with surprise and respect for the old handicraftsmen as being tradesmen of no mean order, when the present day beholder thinks of the appliances at the disposal of the workmen of that period compared with those of the twentieth century. The hand saw, hand plane, chisels, hammer or mallet must have formed the principal instruments amongst the tools available for the wright of olden days in the execution of such fine work, which to-day is all manufactured by machinery, such as the power-driven circular saw, the morticing machine, and the planing and tennoring machine, and last, but not least, the irregular moulder or spindle machine, all as shown in illustration No. 1

Whilst the introduction of machinery nearly a hundred years ago began to gradually affect the methods of carrying on the joinery business, particularly in large industrial centres, the biggest change has undoubtedly been witnessed during the last half-century. During that time the transformation has almost been complete, both in regard to the timber used and the manufacture of the same into the finished article. Formerly logs were the only form in which wood was imported into Britain from the countries bordering the Baltic, and from America. Nowadays logs have largely given place to battens and deals, the trees being felled and cut up in Norway, Sweden, etc., into the standard sizes of planking, etc., required in this country, and this has resulted in doing away with the necessity of the master wright, on securing a job, having to go to the pond of the timber merchant, and there select the logs suitable for the different sizes of battens, deals, etc., required in his contract. When this had to be done, the logs selected were conveyed home to the master wright's place of business, where the sawyer was set to work with the hand saw to cut up the timber into the forms needed. This was called pit sawing, but it has for years been entirely supplanted. The master joiner can now order from the timber merchant the exact sizes, in most cases, of the deals, battens, etc., that he requires, as these are all made in standard sizes where the timber is felled, and then exported to this country, or if it should be necessary to cut up wood from the log—as is the case with certain classes of timber—the power-driven log or deal frame is requisitioned for the work. This machine, instead of cutting one board at a time, as in the old days of hand sawing, can produce a large number at one time. This is accomplished by the sawyer setting the required number of saws for the number of boards wanted out of the log or deal, and the machine does the rest, all at one operation. It will be seen from the foregoing that there is a great saving of time and labour compared with the old methods, and the same thing applies to the manufacture of internal finishings, such as doors, windows, etc.

Illustration No. 2 shows a large four cutter machine, principally used in the manufacture of mouldings, floorings, linings, etc., which has again supplanted the wright, producing at one

John Anderson.

Robert Anderson.

operation mouldings, etc., to the various shapes required at the rate of from 20 to 60 feet per minute. In bygone days the master joiner generally reserved this portion of his work if possible as a job for his men during the winter months, and there are still plenty of tradesmen with us to-day who can relate their trying experience of these earlier days when engaged on such employment, when hand labour was predominant, but under the old system of working it would be impossible to-day to supply the necessities of the trade—some of our mills turning out a million square yards per annum—in the way of floorings, linings, etc., if these had to be produced by hand. And there is this compensation under the new order of things—the materials required by the trade are now produced at a much less cost than formerly, which is all in the direction of expediting the work and cheapening the cost of building.

We give a view of a section of the joinery shop, in the corner of which will be seen the pulpit of Fallin Church. It is a fact, and a regrettable one, though it cannot be helped, that the wright or joiner of to-day is not the master of his craft that he was even twenty-five to thirty years ago, not to go further back, but the trade had to change with the needs of the times, machinery now does so much of what was formerly accomplished by hand, that the opportunity cannot be given the joiner to equip himself all round in a knowledge of his craft that his father was presented with. In fully equipped joinery establishments nowadays, machinery plays the all-important part, the operative wright's share being a small one, namely, putting the several pieces together after these leave the machines and subsequently finishing off—not like the old days, when he had to take the different parts out of the rough and work to their several shapes and sizes by the hand. However, for jobbing or repairing, as well as fitting work, there is always a field for the operative joiner, and of course that field is greater in rural places and new or undeveloped countries where machinery is not yet common. So much of the actual work of manufacture of the articles required for the trade is now done by machinery, that the joiner of this, the twentieth century, is little more than a fitter, he simply puts in their places the woodwork parts prepared by the machine.

We have now dealt with the different methods of manufacture, but it may prove interesting to add a few words on the timber itself, and on the marked changes that have taken place within the last half-century, both as regards the kind and the mode of importation, also the qualities at the disposal of the wright of to-day. American yellow pine at the earlier part of the above stated period was the principal timber in use, both for furnishings and rough timbering, and was of a very fine quality, but this timber is almost extinct, and is being supplanted by a very inferior quality, so much so that the first quality of to-day will not compare with the third quality of bygone times, even at double the price. The master wright of to-day has accordingly been compelled to turn his attention to other fields of supply, such as Russia, Norway, Sweden, etc., these countries supplying most of the timber for roofing, joistings, etc., while the doors and other internal furnishings are taken from wood supplied from Australia, New Zealand, America, Africa, etc.

Having said so much about the joinery or wright trade, we now come to deal with the firm which is the subject of this article, namely, that of Messrs Robert Anderson & Sons, wrights and building contractors, Barnton Street and Murray Place, Stirling, and the Argyle Joinery Works, 1070 Argyle Street, Glasgow. Though the firm is about the youngest of its kind, so far as establishment in Stirling is concerned, it is one of the most enterprising, and has done a large share of the local work during the brief term of its intimate connection with Stirling. The office of Robert Anderson & Sons was only opened in Murray Place four years ago, but in that time they have made themselves fairly prominent, having had, among other contracts, the Convalescent Home at Chartershall, the reconstruction of the old Royal Hotel for the Stirling Co-Operative Society, the joiner work of the new "Observer" Office, workmen's houses at Bandeath, Fallin Church; Governor's house, Simpson's Asylum, Plean; Mr John Gillespie's property in the Craigs, shops and tenement in Barnton Street for Mr Thomas J. Young, Tillicoultry; additions to Causewayhead School, and joinery work for tenements erected in St Ninians by Mr John Somerville, nail manufacturer. But Messrs Anderson & Sons claim a somewhat longer connection with this county and district, having executed the joinery contract of Duntreath Castle, Strathblane, as far back as 1890; the hard wood

Part of Machine Shop—No. 1.

Part of Machine Shop—No. 2.

finishings of Inglewood, Alloa, in 1897; and the joiner work of Logie Parish Church in 1901. Their last three contracts were worked from the firm's Glasgow Works, which were founded by the present partners' father as far back as 1867, and carried on successfully by him for upwards of thirty years, when he retired, and handed over the business to his sons.

Among the numerous important contracts carried out from the firm's Glasgow Works within recent years might be mentioned the Sports Ground, Glasgow International Exhibition, 1901, including cement cycle track, cinder track, timber terracing, grand stands and pavilion; the "Sunlight" Cottages, Glasgow International Exhibition; the Inebriates' Home, Girgenti, for the Glasgow Corporation. Other joiner work contracts have been—Rutherglen Road Baths, Glasgow Corporation; Baltic Street Baths, Glasgow Corporation; Truants School, Glasgow School Board; Radnor Park School, Old Kilpatrick Board; Boquhanran School, Dalmuir School, Primitive Methodist Church, Whiteinch; Pollokshields Congregational Church; Church of the Holy Redeemer, Clydebank; Renfrew and Clydebank Joint Hospital; workmen's dwellings, Clydebank.

The foregoing list of "jobs" will show the enterprising nature and up-to-date methods of the firm under review, and now that Messrs Robert Anderson & Sons have located themselves in Stirling, it will be the wish of all that they may flourish, and by doing so help to add to the prosperity and reputation of our old historic burgh.

Section of Joinery Shop.

View of Laundry.

ABBEY CRAIG LAUNDRY, CAUSEWAYHEAD.

Although the business of a launderer must of a necessity be an ancient one, the laundry trade, as we know it to-day, is a comparatively recent, but by no means unimportant, industry. From the last report of the Chief Inspector of Factories, we have in the United Kingdom 6940 laundries, giving employment to 100,000 persons, paying annually the sum of five and a quarter millions in wages, and employing probably upwards of £10,000,000 of capital. On the strength of the above statistics, we recently paid a visit to the Abbey Craig Laundry at Causewayhead, and an account of how the different departments are carried on, and the ingenious methods brought into operation, should prove of interest to most of our readers.

It is a matter of speculation and surprise to most people, when they consider their own weekly wash, how a large laundry can, with hundreds of such washings collected on a Monday, return all these clean as when new on Thursday, without one single error. The secret of the whole thing is method and up-to-date plant. When the collecting vans, so familiar in the town and district, return with their loads of soiled clothes in the beginning of the week, the goods are handed over to "checkers," who check them with their accompanying "lists," and see that every article that is marked on the list is included in parcel or hamper. These girls also mark the goods in coloured thread or indelible ink, with the customer's number. This is one of the most essential features of a laundry, as, without the mark or wrongly marked, the goods would get hopelessly mixed, and it would be nearly impossible to tell to whom they belonged. After being marked, they are sorted out according to the material of which they are made—silks, flannels, and fine goods are all treated by hand. Other goods are now re-sorted into their respective material classes, and sent to the washing machines. These are not quite of the domestic pattern, but are the most perfect of their class. They resemble large stationary barrels, with smaller perforated barrel revolving in both directions inside. Into the smaller barrel the clothes are put, with a quantity of soap, soda, and water.

"No; no chemicals, sir," was the answer to our query. "They are beneath the notice of a self-respecting laundry—for ordinary use, at all events. Sometimes we use them as a medicine.

to restore the complexion of a stained or spotted article, but only on request."

"Well, how about wear?" was our next query.

"Well, for getting to see through a thing, give me a good hefty washer-woman and a scrubbing brush—the machines haven't a chance against her," was the quiet answer—and we believe it.

After the clothes have had the dirt removed, they are taken to the hydro-extractors, and there wrung by centrifugal force. This obviates all damage to buttons, and is not nearly so hard on the clothes as the old-fashioned wringer.

Now for the drying. There are three methods —firstly, machine; second, hot air; and last, but not least, open air. There is little to comment on in the latter, but the drying machinery is worth a word. The machine consists of a large padded roller, steam-heated, revolving very slowly on a steam-heated metal bed. This takes in "flat work," such as sheets, etc., at one side, carries them through over the bed, and they come out not only dry but ironed at the other side, where they are picked up by girls and folded.

Next we come to the ironing and starching. This to a very great extent is done by hand. The irons are all heated by gas supplied through tubes attached to the irons. After starching, the shirts and similar articles are ironed by laundresses in the usual way. The fronts, cuffs, and collars are finished or polished in machines made for the purpose. These machines are supplied with double belts, by means of which the hob rollers can be made revolve in either direction, in imitation of the hand action. When each ironer finishes an article, it is taken to the forewoman, who examines it and folds neatly, preparatory to its being conveyed to the packing room, where the sorters who received them in the beginning of the week now become packers, and again sort out the goods according to their marks and districts, and pack them up ready for delivery by the various vans.

In conclusion, we were agreeably disappointed in not having to undergo the inconveniences of a Russian bath with our clothes on during the interview. The interior of the building is cheerful and clean, without a vestige of odour or steam. We understand Messrs Carruthers keep "open house" on Wednesday afternoons, and feel sure that it would be not only interesting, but satisfactory to know how and under what sanitary conditions laundering is done nowadays in an up-to-date establishment.

Robert Miller.

STIRLINGSHIRE POULTRY FARM, DENNY.

Hitherto the industries we have dealt with have had a historic past—merging in some cases into hundreds of years—but the one we bring under review this week is essentially of modern origin. Poultry have no doubt formed a portion of the live stock of farmers and cottars of the olden times, as is the case to-day, and in the New Testament there is at least one reference to the hen that gathereth her chickens under her wing, and in both Old and New Testaments there are many allusions to fowls, but these are the fowls of the air, not the domestic variety. But that in ancient times there must have been something in existence of the nature of present day poultry farming, would appear to be the case from the fact that both the Egyptians and Chinese used a variety of incubator in the hatching of chickens from the eggs So far as can be ascertained this hatching apparatus of the ancients was a kind of chamber heated by the burning of dried dung. This was very much different from the scientific methods in use to-day, when elaborately constructed incubators and "foster mothers," heated by hot air and water, are kept for weeks at the required temperature by means of automatic regulators, but modern experts admit that the Egyptians and Chinese of some thousands of years ago were likely enough to be successful with the primitive means they used, and in any event the fact that chickens were artifically hatched in past ages is but another proof of the truth of the saying that there is nothing new under the sun.

But poultry farming as a distinct branch of industry in its modern sense is not yet a quarter of a century old, and so far as Scotland is concerned is still practically in its infancy. There are at the present time not more than half-a-dozen undertakings of the kind in the country, and the leading one is the Stirlingshire Poultry Farm, situated at The Boards, about three miles from Denny, and five from Stirling, the proprietor being Mr Robert Miller, who is the pioneer of the poultry farming industry in Scotland. He has been at the business now for fourteen years, and from starting as a novice, with no more knowledge of the subject than that conferred by the fact of his coming of a race of agriculturalists, he has, by application and perseverance, gradually acquired a skill and knowledge which has placed him in the foremost rank of poultry farmers. Not only is he the leading exponent of

this branch of industry in Scotland, but his name is a household one all over the kingdom amongst people interested in poultry, and he holds as high a reputation abroad, having correspondents in the Colonies, on the Continent, and even in Constantinople. Though he is entirely self-taught, so to speak, Mr Miller has the advantage of being laird of his own ˙holding,'' which is a farm of 112 acres, with a nice house upon it. Had Mr Miller followed in the steps of his forbears, who had been in the district for generations, he would have continued to farm on the usual lines, but he early realised that this was a pursuit which gives little or no return for time, money, and labour, and fourteen years ago he entered upon the new departure with which we are dealing. No doubt many more agriculturalists would do the same thing were they in a similar position of freedom of action, but arbitrary landlords and lawyer factors curb their desires and ambitions. A Small Holdings Act such as the present Government has attempted to pass would widen the field for poultry farming, and until some legislation of that kind is got the foreigner will continue to obtain hundreds of thousands of pounds annually from the British public for eggs, which could, and would, be supplied at home more cheaply, and also in a more fresh condition. But at present landowners give no encouragement to poultry farming in the way of letting holdings to be utilised for that purpose, and until the land laws are altered the public must just grin and bear, and see large sums of money passing out of the country every year to people abroad for supplying what could easily be produced at home.

But to return to poultry farming itself, it may at once be stated that it is not a pursuit to be entered upon lightly if it is to be made a business conducted for profit. The modest domestic hen will do well for her owner if she is properly cared for, but not otherwise. Poultry which are kept as many cottagers and farmers do—allowed to pick up their own living to a large extent, and provided with more or less makeshift roosting places—will never yield a profitable return. Wnat must be done is to start with a pure breed or breeds, and provide them with proper food, a good open-air "run," and cleanliness, comfort, and ventilation in their housing. These requisites supplied, the hen will do her duty in the way of egg-laying in a fashion that will astonish the

Stirlingshire Poultry Farm—Landscape.

No. 1 Hatching House—21 Incubators, Containing 8000 Eggs.

uninitiated. The common barnyard or mongrel fowl costs quite as much to maintain as the pure bred strain, but when it comes to giving a return for her food and housing, there is a big difference. A pure bred hen will lay from 200 to 250 eggs a year easily, but the barnyard variety will not attain the half of that—60 to 90 being the average. From this the value of a breed of standard poultry will be realised, and at the Stirlingshire Poultry Farm none but the best varieties are to be found. The breeds of poultry are legion, but Mr Miller restricts his varieties to less than half-a-dozen of the best strains. This is the result of a long course of experimenting, and what the courteous proprietor of The Boards does not know about poultry and poultry farming is scarcely worth learning. Early and heavy layers are the first sine qua non, and Mr Miller has combined these two qualities to as near perfection as possible in a specialised breed produced by himself, and known as Exchequer Leghorns. Other breeds to be found at The Boards are White and Black Leghorns, Wyandottes, Crosses, etc., all fine, upstanding, robust varieties. The Game and Bantam, and other kinds which have little to commend them except their looks, are conspicuous by their absence at the Stirlingshire Poultry Farm.

A visit to the farm itself is a revelation, and it is not easy to credit the fact when one only sees in a field a number of what appear at a distance to be dog kennels, but are really breeding pens, and hens going about here and there scratching the earth and picking up grubs, etc., that there is a stock of 1300 fowls kept. Still more difficult is it to grasp the fact that in the few small buildings seen around there are over 3000 eggs hatching weekly, and that 1600 live chickens are despatched in a morning to various parts of the kingdom. Of course this would not be possible with "clocking" hens as the hatching mediums. "Clockers" are never made use of at The Boards. The first and foremost duty of the hens kept in stock is to lay eggs—the incubators and foster mothers or rearers do the rest. At the Stirlingshire Poultry Farm there are 34 incubators at work this season, and as they can accommodate from 360 to 390 eggs each, it will be seen that they have an immense capacity for producing chickens. From several points of view incubator hatching is much more preferable than trusting to the vagaries of a sitting hen. In her case there is no certainty as to when the

hatching will take place, but with the incubators this can be regulated to an hour. The hatching season usually begins at the end of February, and continues till August, and matters are so arranged at The Boards that there are two hatchings weekly, and the same number of despatches of live chickens. 3000 eggs are hatched every week, and it is calculated that 50,000 chickens will be produced this season. Most of these are sent off to their new homes within twenty-four hours of their "birth." And not only that, but they may be two or three days on the journey, and without food or water for that time. This would at first sight appear to be a somewhat cruel proceeding, but it isn't. Chickens of one day travel better than they would if they were a fortnight old, for this reason that they don't have the same need for food at that early age. Once they have been feeding for two or three days they could not want for any length of time. In the case of the older chickens there would also be great danger of the one crushing the other in the boxes. The birds are packed in cardboard boxes, each of which holds a dozen comfortably, and in these boxes several batches of chicks have been sent as far as the Island of Harris, to the Orkney and Shetland Islands, and to the south of England, and they have all reached their destination safely. It is very seldom indeed that a single bird comes by a mishap. All the preparation the "infants" get for their journey is the sojourn in a "foster mother" or rearer for a day, and at the end of that time they are quite strong. In this connection it may be mentioned that Mr Miller is himself the inventor of a special brooder or rearer bearing his name, and which is patented and commands a large sale at home and abroad. This brooder is warmed by hot air at any temperature, and can accommodate the chicks till they are four or five months old, when they are able to "fend" for themselves.

Mr Miller, in order to keep up his stock of layers to its proper number, rears annually about 1500 chicks. To rear this large number he does not enlist the services of one single broody hen, as he prefers to use his own patent brooders, which give only a fraction of the trouble. It may be wondered how it is possible to rear those tender chicks of one day old that have been sent out to purchasers in all parts of the kingdom. In the case of large buyers of chicks, brooders or foster mothers are generally made use of. These are put in order and held in readiness against the

Exchequer Leghorns—Mr Miller's Specialty.

After Reaching their New Home.

arrival of the chicks, whose despatch has been notified to the buyer a few days before. On their arrival the youngsters are placed in their new quarters, and in experienced hands everything goes on well. There are many, however, who adopt the natural, though the more troublesome, method of placing the chicks on arrival under a broody hen, and this method, too, is quite successful in every way, and a great improvement over setting the hen on eggs, as very often, after a hen has been sitting for three weeks on a lot of valuable eggs, a disappointing hatch is the result. A broody hen does not require to have been sitting three weeks in order to make her ready to receive an adopted family from the Stirlingshire Poultry Farm; half that time, or even a few days in the case of a quiet hen, is quite enough. Until the chicks arrive, the hen is allowed to sit on "dummy" eggs, and at the evening hour these are removed and the chicks are slipped gently under her. She tucks them comfortably under her wings, and next morning she struts proudly forth, taking full credit for the entire hatching arrangements. What the comments of the other hens are we cannot tell, but as poultry are in many of their habits very much alike to human beings, we may assume that the observations would not all be of a complimentary description. But in addition to the despatching of day old chickens a large trade is also done in providing fanciers with settings of eggs, the strain from The Boards being a favourite everywhere. At one time both eggs and chickens were imported from England by fanciers in Scotland, but the tide has turned. It is now recognised that the breeds which thrive in our severe northern clime are likely to do well in places where the conditions are not so severe, and as The Boards is not the most genial place even in Scotland in regard to climate, the chicks and settings from the Stirlingshire Poultry Farm are of a strain that is likely to thrive, and that vigorously. But in order that there should be no debilitating or weakening of his stocks, strong young birds are introduced into it every year. The breeding stock are never kept longer than two years, and are then sent to the market, where they are usually purchased by fanciers who desire a good strain. At the end of the season eggs, which are

now becoming scarce, are also forwarded to the market for table purposes, and good prices are obtained.

Much more could be written about poultry farming and the interesting nature of the industry, for there are a great many points of attraction about the modest little hen which, when looked after like prize cattle or horses, gives quite as much, if not more, in return. The farming of poultry can be carried on in conjunction with ordinary agriculture, at least so far as pasturage and the growing of hay is concerned. By penning off the fields and permitting poultry to run on certain portions for a time until all has been gone over, the land is thoroughly fertilised, and the result is a fine hay crop and plenty of grass on which cattle can be fed. So fully satisfied is Mr Miller with the past results of his venture that he has given up cropping his ground, and now devotes his entire time and attention to the development of the poultry business, and using his spare fields for grazing cattle.

With Scottish men and women, more especially if they be country-born and bred, old prejudices die hard, and to convince them of any improvements upon the practices that have prevailed in their families for generations past is no easy matter. To convince, then, the old-time farmer and cottager that the incubator-hatched and brooder-bred chickens may be, and are, as healthy and give as good results in the laying season as chickens that have had the care and attention of the clucking hen, is no easy matter. We feel sure, however, that those same folks would have their old-fashioned notions set aside were they to have the pleasure of a visit to Mr Miller's large and completely equipped farm at The Boards, and the ordinary layman would have his eyes opened in many ways to the possibilities contained in the humble but most interesting industry carried on there—and an industry, it may be remarked in conclusion, that gives employment to more "hands" than would be the case in ordinary farming. Visitors to The Boards are welcomed, and after they have had a look round they will leave with a greater respect for the capabilities of the modest domestic hen when treated kindly and encouraged to do her best for her owner.

J. C. Miller.

ST. NINIANS WELL BREWERY, STIRLING.

In noticing the St. Ninians Well Brewery, Stirling, we incidentally deal with one of the earliest industries or arts practised by mankind. History from its earliest stage shows that humanity has not been content with the water Nature provides for the quenching of thirst, but has devised ways and means of making artificial liquors of a more or less stimulating kind, and some of which are said to "raise a thirst" as well as quench it. The art of brewing or distilling—both are very similar processes—in one form or another seems to be an inborn accomplishment of all peoples, as it is, and has been, practised all over the world by the most lowly tribes of savages as well as the highly civilised nations. Barley has for many centuries been the favourite article in European countries from which beer and kindred liquors have been manufactured, although peas, beans, maize, wheat, etc., may be employed, and indeed are utilised in lands where grain is little grown. To go no further back, we read that barley was cultivated by the Romans and many other nations of antiquity, and the ancient inhabitants of Gaul (France) prepared a spirituous liquor, which was a kind of beer, from it. It is interesting as a mere "aside" to note that the superior qualities of barley are necessary for the brewing of beer, whilst the inferior qualities are utilised by the distillers who manufacture whisky. Beer, it may also further be mentioned, is a fermented liquid, which does not, like whisky, undergo the process of distillation. And whilst upon the subject of what is commonly—and erroneously—termed Scotland's national drink, it may be added that ale, which is a form of beer, was a favourite beverage of the poorer classes in Scotland centuries before whisky was heard of. Indeed up to less than a couple of centuries ago claret was the favourite liquor of the richer people, their humbler brethren having to refresh themselves with ale, which was home brewed. Many people, who are still on the sunny side of the half-century as regards years, can easily remember when they got ale to their porridge instead of milk. Anciently in Scotland the privilege of brewing was given by a license from the superior or laird to his vassals or tenants, but this right has been long done away with. At one time there were many ale houses in Stirling, and we find from the Burgh Records that regulations were made by tne Magistrates of these days as to the price at which the liquor was to be sold, under pain of fine for infringement. In the sixteenth century a proclamation was made at the Cross that "na broustar" was to sell ale dearer than 12d the gallon, under penalty, for repeated offences, of knocking the bottom out of the culprit's cask and dividing the liquor among the people. Then every brewer was required, as soon as his ale was ready, to send for the Bailie of that part of the town, who, along with two sworn "cunneis," or tasters, tasted the liquor, and put upon it the price at which it was to be sold, 40s of a fine being imposed if any selling was done before the tasting had taken place. In the fifteenth century Stirling was famous for distilled and fermented liquors, and when, by Act of the Scottish Parliament in 1437, various burghs were appointed to keep the standard weights and measures of the country, and issue duplicates to the other burghs as occasion necessitated, to the "City of the Rock" was given the custody of the pint measure, which is known as the Stirling Jug. This interesting relic of olden times is now domiciled in the Smith Institute.

But to return to beer and brewing as a local industry. Like most other trades, that of the manufacture of beer and kindred liquors has greatly altered during the last half-century. Though it still exists, and more so in England than Scotland, home brewing is very much a thing of the past, unless in remote and out-of-the-way districts. By the utilisation of machinery, and the application of chemical science in the brewery, the cost of production has been so greatly decreased, and the output so quickened, that it is cheaper for the public to buy than to brew. How the preparation of beer for the market is brought about will be described later on, but it may be stated here that it is a very delicate process, and if success is to be achieved, and waste and loss avoided, much watchfulness and ability is required. The brewer indeed has to be a skilful chemist, accurate in his reading of thermometers, an adept at flavouring, and an expert at mixing quantities, and doing a lot of other necessary things to secure a successful brew. Beer is usually regarded by most people as being one kind of liquor, with two or three varieties, but it is a much more comprehensive term than that. There are over a dozen classes of what is known as beer, and at the Brewers'

Exhibition in London last year no fewer than 350 samples were shown. This gives an idea of the numerous varieties of the liquor there are on the market. And all these varieties are found to be necessary by the manufacturers, for the simple reason that the public taste differs. For instance, the beer that is popular in Glasgow will not "take" in Fife, and the kind that is in demand on the Borders does not suit the Aberdeen palate —and so on all over the kingdom.

Of the materials used in brewing, it is almost needless to observe that an adequate supply of suitable water is the first necessary of every brewery, but there is no doubt that an undue importance and influence are popularly ascribed to the character of the water used in the manufacture of beer. So long as the water is clear and free from all traces of decomposing matter— animal and vegetable, as evidenced by the absence of any objectionable taste or smell—it will answer the purpose of the brewer, and throw no hindrance in the way of producing sound, palatable beer. It is absurd to suppose, as many do, that the peculiar flavour and other properties of certain ales are chiefly dependent on the composition of the local water. But whilst this is the case, the hardness of the "mashing" water has a sensible effect in aiding the spontaneous clarification of beer. Indeed, where water of the right degree of hardness, and having the proper saline ingredients in solution, is regularly employed, the use of finings is rarely required, and the beer is saved much probable injury in consequence. Although pure, soft water from any source will enable a brewer to obtain a good extract and prepare marketable beer without difficulty or disadvantage, except as regards the use of finings, it is certain that the water which contains a small amount of saline matter, especially sulphate and carbonate of lime, is the best adapted for brewing purposes. Such water produces quite as great an extract as the softer kinds, and has, in addition, the valuable property of causing the beer to clarify itself thoroughly in a short time after being cleansed. The reason of this action of hard water in brewing has not been satisfactorily accounted for, either by scientific or practical men, but long and varied experience in different localities makes the fact indisputable. Cleansing is greatly influenced by the quality or composition of the water employed in mashing. It was formerly believed that soft rain water, or tolerably pure river water, was the best for

brewers' use, as producing the greatest amount of fermentable extract from the malt. But it is now well known that well or spring water of a certain degree of hardness, arising from the presence of small quantities of lime salts, not only enhausts the goods as completely as the softer kinds, but through the reaction of the lime compounds on the mineral water contained in the malt, causes a precipitate, which, as it subsides, carries down with it the suspended mucilage and other impurities of the "wort," or extract of the malting, leaving the liquor above as fine as can be desired. Owing to the hardness of the well water at Burton it is rarely found requisite to adopt any artificial means for clarifying the ales brewed there, although it is done in nearly every case. It is commonly supposed that pale ale of the finest quality cannot be brewed elsewhere than at Burton-on-Trent ; but with proper management, minute attention to details, and the use of carefully-selected materials in the right proportions, it is within the power of any brewer, in whatever place his business may be carried on, to manufacture liquors of as good a quality in every respect as the renowned produce of Burton. The properties of the spring water obtained in Burton and the neighbourhood have no doubt, as previously observed in this article, some effect in promoting the natural clarification of the beer, and conferring upon it the keeping properties for which it is so justly celebrated. Apart, however, from the undoubted influence of the Burton water, or water of similar composition, there can be no question that the great secret of success in pale ale brewing lies in the use of selected pale malts and an abundance of finest hops. No portion of common dark sugar or quazza, or of other substitutes for malt or hops, is allowable in the manufacture of pale ale, as the least deviation from the proper materials or mode of brewing must infallibly injure the flavour and fineness of the beverage. Those who may not care to take the trouble of having the water of their locality tested by a competent person, and if it should be found wanting in the requisite saline ingredients, to have the defect remedied by impregnation with gypsum or other suitable salts, can nevertheless brew unexceptionable pale ale and bitter beer from the water they have at hand, provided such water is moderately hard, and free from all decaying organic matter. As it is generally required that bitter ale should be pale, or at least of a nice, sparkling golden colour, care must be taken to obtain a sound but pale malt, but many malts, although sufficiently pale, do not possess the thorough soundness, without which the ale will not keep ; indeed it will be preferable to use a somewhat darker coloured malt if there be the least doubt as to the soundness of a paler sample. As a general rule, spring or well water obtained from a considerable depth below the surface, and freshly pumped up, will be found the best in all respects for brewing purposes. But even in this case it is advisable that the water, however bright and sweet it may appear, should be carefully tested now and then to detect latent impurities which escape the eye and nose, and may yet exist to an extent most prejudicial to the quality of the beer, and also to determine whether the necessary degree of hardness is present. Mineral waters of any kind are of course quite inadmissible, particularly those which have the least trace of iron.

Malting is a process by which germination to a limited extent is artificially induced in barley or other grain, with the object of providing an eligible saccharine material for the use of brewers, distillers, etc. During this process a small quantity of a peculiar substance, termed diastase, is formed which changes a portion of the starch of the grain into dextrine or gum, and thence into sugar, and has also the property of saccharifying the whole of the remaining starch when the malt is subsequently infused in hot water, as in the "mashing" operation of the brewer. Wheat, rye, oats, beans, peas, and rice maize, or Indian corn, are each occasionally made into malt, but barley is found to be the most economical and the best suited to the purpose of the brewer. Both wheat and rye, being destitute of husk, do not afford that protection to the germ, or vital portion of the grain, which is found in barley and oats ; hence the grain is easily mutilated, and the grain in consequence soon becomes mouldy and undergoes decomposition. Oats, on account of their thick husk, small kernel, and slowness in germinating, are unprofitable, whilst the malt made from maize, beans, or peas, etc., has not hitherto been used with any great success in the brewing of beer, unless in suitable proportions. The barley chiefly malted in England, southern parts of Scotland, and Ireland, is the two-rowed variety, Hordeum Distichon. In the northern parts of Scotland and Ireland the six-rowed barley, Hordeum Henastichon, otherwise called bere or bigg, is also extensively used for malting.

In the manufacture of malt four principal operations are necessary, namely, steeping, couching, flooring, and kiln drying. In steeping the barley, after having been screened and cleansed, to free it both from small and useless corns, and from seeds of wild plants and other accidental impurities, is placed in a vessel called the steeping cistern, and is covered with water, and kept immersed under ordinary circumstances for a period of from 50 to 72, and sometimes 82 hours, according to the season, temperature, and condition of the barley. While in the steeping cistern the grain softens and increases in bulk over a fifth by the absorption of water, and nearly one-half in weight, and carbonic acid gas is also formed, which dissolves in the steep water along with a portion of colouring matter from the husk. Sometimes (especially in hot weather) a slight degree of fermentation arises from the vegetable matter in the steep water acting on decayed grains, and hence it becomes necessary or advisable to change the water during the period of steeping. The water is then drained off, and the grain removed into what is called the "couch," where it is kept in a mass of considerable depth for at least 24 hours, in order that heat may be developed and germination started or induced. Very little apparent change takes place in the grain for from 30 to 40 hours after removal from the cistern, but after that the temperature of the mass then begins to rise, and the rootlets, or, as the maltsters term it at this stage, the "chick" or "chit," shows itself as a small white bud, emerging from under the husk at the base or end of each corn—that is the end by which it was attached to the stem. In about two days afterwards the grain becomes moist on the surface, or sweats, and emits an agreeable odour compared to that of apples, and the white bud develops into several fibres or rootlets, which spread and shoot downwards. At about the same time the acrospire or stem, or that which would be the future stem of the plant, begins to grow. It takes its rise at the same end of the grain as the rootlets, but pursues its way under the husk along the back of the grain in an opposite direction to that of the roots, and may be readily perceived on removing part of the husk. To lower the temperature, and thereby moderate the germination or growing process, the grain is now spread rather thinly on the floor and frequently turned or stirred. By this means the corn is kept at an average temperature (which is decided by the maltster). Vegetation proceeds slowly and regularly, and the starchy matter of the grain becomes white, soft, and friable, and sweet-tasted, so far as the plumule or acrospire has advanced. In nine to twelve or thirteen days after the grain has been emptied from the steeping cistern, the frequent turnings and exposure to the air, together with the growth of the rootlets and acrospire, have dissipated or taken up the greater portion of the moisture absorbed in the steeping cistern, and the rootlets wither. The grain is then laid a little thicker on the floor to generate heat, liberate more moisture, and render it mellow, and by this time the acrospire ought to have grown to two-thirds or three-fourths the length of the corn. The grain is now properly malted, and is dried on the kiln to arrest germination, which if suffered to proceed beyond this point would exhaust the seeds of their soluble contents, the gum and sugar that had been previously formed rapidly disappearing to supply nourishment to the young plant. Drying has also the effect of enabling the malt to be kept in store without further change. Many maltsters work their floors on a plan somewhat different from the preceding. The floors are kept thick, and germination is forced, abundance of rootlets being formed. The heat generated in this process dissipates or takes up a part of the moisture absorbed by the grain while in steep long before the stem or acrospire has grown to a sufficient length. Hence it is requisite to sprinkle the corn with water in order to stimulate the germination. In a few of the malting districts, however, sprinkling is not resorted to as a practice, it being thought unnecessary and injurious. The drying operation is effected in a heated chamber termed a kiln, the floor of which is formed of perforated tiles or metal plates, wire gauze, etc. Heated air from a fire placed underneath passing through the malt stops the further progress of germination or vegetation in the grain, and rapidly carries off the moisture, which escapes through the windows or an opening in the roof. Other special modes of drying are occasionally resorted to, but some form of kiln is in general use. The process of kiln-drying varies according to the purpose for which the malt is required. There are three well marked varieties of kiln-dried malt, namely, pale, amber, and brown, the difference between these depending solely on the degree of heat to which each has been subjected and the manner in which

the heat has been applied. When the drying is completed, the rootlets are now termed "commings" or "culmins," and these are effectually separated from the malt by passing it over a screen which permits the "commings" or "culmins" to fall through. These are usually sold to farmers and dairymen to feed their cows.

In the process of malting, barley loses from eight to twelve per cent. in weight, and increases from three to ten per cent. in bulk. The grains of malt are generally free from wrinkles, although sometimes they have a slightly shrivelled appearance. The husk has a lighter colour than that of barley, and remains open at the end from which the rootlets protruded. Malt differs considerably in appearance from barley. The bright, yellowish hue or tint and shining aspect of the husk have disappeared, and instead of the tightly closed end, which characterises an unmalted barleycorn, an opening through which the rootlets have passed may now be observed at the base of each grain. As regards the internal changes, it is found that the toughness natural to barley is no longer present, and that the body of the grain has become mealy or friable, while underneath the husk the acrospire is seen to have grown nearly three-fourths of the length of the grain. It is, however, when ground or crushed and mixed with water, and kept for a suitable time at a certain temperature, that the alteration produced in barley by the process of malting is most strikingly exemplified. Under such circumstances the white and turbid solution of the remaining starch is observed to be converted into a sweet, transparent liquid—the starch, in fact, being almost wholly transformed into sugar.

Roasted malt, patent malt or black malt, as it is variously called, is used by brewers for the purpose of giving to porter or stout its rich dark brown colour and peculiar flavour. The process of roasting this kind of malt is very similar to that of roasting coffee. The malt is placed in a metal cylinder, which is made to revolve over a charcoal or coke fire, by this means the malt is slowly roasted at a temperature varying from 300 to 400 degrees Fahr. until it assumes a dark chocolate colour. If the heat exceeds 420 degrees Fahr. the malt becomes almost wholly decomposed, leaving nothing but a mass of porous charcoal. Carmel, which is now greatly used in porter or stout brewing, when pure is nearly tasteless. The substance met with in commerce under that name is prepared from cane sugar, and generally exists as a thick, syrupy, dark brown liquid, of bitter taste and intense colouring power. It is also used by rectifiers to impart a brown tint to compounded spirits.

Every malt liquor, properly so called, consists of extract of malt and hops fermented by means of yeast, the malt, as being the principal or characteristic ingredient, confers its name upon the compound. No materials besides these can be said to furnish a beverage entitled in strictness to the designation of a genuine malt liquor. In modern times, however, certain partial substitutes for malt, and occasionally also for hops, have been employed on an extensive scale without exposing the brewer to the charge of positive or intentional adulteration, and without altering the quality of the product, so far as to forbid its being classed under the head of malt liquors. Coming to the varieties of malt liquors—beer and ale—the word "beer" is nowadays most frequently used to indicate malt liquors in general, instead of being applied, as seems formerly to have been the case, to one particular kind only. Thus in a similar way wine stands as a comprehensive term for port, claret, Madeira, and all other descriptions of fermented grape juice. Spirits again collectively represent rum, brandy, whisky, and the like. In and around London that which is elsewhere styled porter is commonly spoken of as "black beer," and in some of the rural districts it is, or was, customary to distinguish the stronger or better classes of malt liquor by the title of beer. But with these slight exceptions the practice in the present day is as above stated—to regard beer as the type of malt liquors in general, and indeed of all other beverages prepared by a process of brewing, the several well-known varieties of ale, porter, and stout composing the principal members of the group. Whenever the term is used in a special or more restricted sense, it is with a descriptive prefix, as, for example, bitter beer, spruce beer, etc.

Before the introduction of hops into England, which is reputed to have taken place about the year 1524, during the reign of Henry VIII., ale seems to have been the popular name in this country for malt liquor. As the use of hops was derived from Germany, the German word "bier" (Saxon, bere, barley) was probably first adopted under the equivalent English form beer, to distinguish the hopped liquor from ale, the unhopped variety. There is strong reason for believing that the term ale is of Danish or Scandinavian extraction, since "ol" is still the designation of malt liquor in the Scandinavian tongue. On the invasion of Britain by the people of this race, it is not unlikely that "ol" or "ale" may have displaced the "beor" of the Anglo-Saxons, which that nation had in common with other Teutonic communities. Porter and stout are beverages of comparatively recent introduction. The supposed origin of the former term is described later. Ale of all kinds is brewed chiefly from pale malt, and is in most places of a nice golden colour, although occasionally a deeper tint is given, either by the use of a portion of high dried malt, or in some instances by the addition of a little roasted or black malt or sugar colouring to suit the taste of the locality; for in this, as in the case of many other beverages, such as coffee, tea, etc., depth of colour is with the great bulk of consumers regarded as an indication of strength or goodness. In the manufacture of what is called pale ale, only the finest and lightest dried malt is used, the flavour and odour of choice hops are caused to predominate slightly, and the whole, when skilfully prepared, is beyond doubt the most elegant, wholesome, and agreeable form of malt liquor that has ever been produced. It is in large request at the present day. Bitter beer has as a rule less body than pale ale, and is more highly hopped. It resembles, in fact, a medicinal tonic rather than a popular beverage, but it has many admirers. Mild ale differs from pale ale in being sweeter, somewhat stronger, and in having no marked predominance of the flavour or smell of hops. This is of the kind usually termed home brewed ale. Old ale has considerable strength, since a weak ale will not keep so as to remain sound and portable when it has attained to any age. In ordinary old ale there is a considerable development of acid, which leads to such ales being called also hard ales. Table beer or small beer has little body or spirituousness. It is, as the name imports, suitable chiefly for consumption at meals. Spruce beer (brown and white) is made from treacle or refined sugar, fermented with essence of spruce, an exudation from the Norway spruce trees instead of hops. This, however, should be classed as a wine rather than a beer. Of ginger beer and the various herb beers, it is unnecessary to treat them in the present article, as none of these, notwithstanding the names given to them, have any real similarity to a malt liquor.

The beverage known as porter differs from ale chiefly in respect of its being artificially coloured by the use of black or roasted malt, which also imparts a bitter flavour, if used to any extent. In point of strength, porter ordinarily stands about midway between light and strong ales although it is often brewed of a strength very slightly above that of table beer. Stout is simply a richer or stronger description of porter, and may be said to have nearly the same relation to the higher qualities of mild ale that porter holds with regard to pale ale or bitter beer. The origin of the term porter has been ascribed by most writers on brewing to the fact of the beverage having from its cheapness and refreshing properties being at first consumed principally by porters or other working men of that class; but the true explanation seems to be that the liquor was first manufactured by a brewer of the name of Porter, and that the invention came, as is often the case, to be called after the inventor.

After the malting of the barley, there are a number of other processes—and ticklish ones at that—to be gone through, such as mashing, boiling, cooling, fermenting, casking, and bottling, but these, though very interesting, have to be seen to be understood. The fermenting is the last stage of the preparation of the beer, and this process requires much skill to produce a good brew.

The St. Ninians Well Brewery, of which we give a view, is not the oldest establishment of the kind locally, nor is it the biggest in the country, but it is a compact, up-to-date manufactory, equipped with all appliances, and carried on with ability, vigour, and enterprise by the owner, Mr J. C. Miller. The name of his firm is J. & J. Miller, but some years ago a cousin, who was his partner, retired from the business, and since then it has been entirely under Mr Miller's control. The brewery, which is situated at Burghmuir, close to Nelson Place, was erected in 1865, and is in the form of a square, but in appearance does not differ materially from establishments of the same kind. The late Treasurer Andrew Colquhoun, who was a native of Tullibody, carried on the place for many years, but was perhaps too much occupied with municipal affairs, in which he played a leading part in Stirling for a considerable period, to develop the business as might have been done. In any case a great change has taken place since Mr J. C. Miller took it over. He came to the

business very well equipped for it by a lengthened and valued experience, though he is still a young man. A native of Clackmannanshire, he was seven years with M'Lay & Co., of Alloa; a similar period in the employment of Alex. Ferguson & Co., Glasgow; and a shorter time with J. & J. Stewart, Edinburgh. Altogether, Mr Miller had twenty years' experience before entering into business on his own account. After coming into possession of St Ninians Well Brewery he went in for a complete renovation of the establishment, and added a shed for loading lorries under cover. From the outside the premises give little indication of what is to be found inside the enclosing fences and walls, and it is rather surprising to come across so much in the space covered by the brewery. The establishment consists of aerated water department, syrup room, laboratory, private room and public office, storage cellars, brewhouse, beer and bottling cellars, coopers' workshop, malt barn, grain store, loading and storing sheds, etc., and last, but not least, an artesian well 200 feet deep. Everything, as we have already said, is on the most up-to-date principle, and it is a very interesting experience to visit the establishment and witness the various intricate processes employed in the conversion of barley into beer. The manufacture of aerated waters is a simple affair in comparison, and does not require to be minutely described. Under Mr Miller's vigorous superintendence—for besides acting as his own brewer, chemist, etc., he also keeps a grip of the commercial side of the undertaking—the business has practically quadrupled since he took it over. The plant he has fitted up is capable of turning out 2000 dozen bottles of aerated waters in a week, a thousand dozen of bottled beer, and 180 barrels of cask beer. This is a big capacity, but it is usually pretty fully employed, as Mr Miller's business connection is a wide one, his clientele of customers extending from Land's End to John o' Groats, though Scotland and the North of England are his chief markets. The extent to which his business has developed is ample proof of his ability in his profession, but if further evidence was wanted, it is provided in the fact that this year and last he is one of the judges at the Brewers' Exhibition in the Agricultural Hall, London, where there are 200 competitors. To be asked to act as a judge there is a high honour, and so far only two Scotsmen—Mr Miller being one—have had the distinction bestowed upon them.

St. Ninians Well Brewery, Stirling.

Peter Drummond.

THE STIRLING TRACT ENTERPRISE.

Than the Stirling Tract Enterprise—or to give it the designation, Drummond's Tract Depot, by which it is popularly known—no local agency has done more, or even half as much, to make the name of Stirling familiar all over the civilised world. In this respect indeed the Tract Depot may be said to vie with the old historic Castle, which is the crowning edifice of the "City of the Rock." The Stirling Tract Enterprise is not by any means the only organisation of the kind in the country, but there is none more widely known, or that has a more honoured past or respected present. Like most businesses or agencies which have attained to an eminent position, that of the Stirling Tract Enterprise, which is now housed in handsome buildings, and employs a staff of over 60, was the result of a very small beginning : indeed it may be said to have been —as will be shown later—the outcome of an impulse born of strong religious beliefs, than of any pre-conceived intention on the part of the founder to engage in the work. The originator of the Enterprise, Mr Peter Drummond, was a member of a family long and honourably associated with Stirling. Born at St Ninians on 26th February, 1799—over a century ago—he was the fourth of a remarkable family of eleven sons and four daughters. His father, William Drummond (who was twice married, Peter being the eldest son of the second family), was a man highly esteemed, of singular strength and purity of character. The business carried on by him was that of a land-surveyor and nurseryman. Success crowned his industry. Each succeeding year saw an enlargement of the business, which is now known under the name of William Drummond & Sons, Limited.

The early days of Peter were passed among the plants and flowers of the nursery lying near his home, as also in what is known as Stirling's magnificent recreation-ground, the King's Park, and if it be true that a man is affected by his environment, and imbibes the spirit which lingers round it, then we need not wonder that the Drummonds were all distinctly Scottish and patriotic—ardent lovers of their country, and devoted to the maintenance of its dearly-bought civil and religious liberties.

When comparatively young, Peter Drummond removed the seed department of the business from Coney Park, in Park Place, to the ground-floor of the Athenæum Buildings, now the Council Chambers, at the top of King Street, and evinced his enterprising spirit by forming an "Agricultural Museum," in which were exhibited the latest inventions in ploughing and harvesting implements, together with varieties of rare seeds, bulbs, and roots, and different models of farm steadings, etc. This was opened in 1831 ; and for many years it was visited by farmers and others interested in agricultural and horticultural science. To mark their appreciation of this effort, the Agricultural Society of Scotland awarded their gold medal for "originating and conducting" such an institution. It has long since been discontinued as unnecessary, owing to the multiplication of cattle shows, etc., and other facilities that have been provided for agriculturists and horticulturists gaining a knowledge of the outstanding elements of their respective industries.

Peter Drummond's father died in 1824 ; and at his grave, in the old churchyard of St Ninians, the sight of so many sorrowing sons, all distinguished for their fine physique, was exceedingly impressive. Sympathetic references were made to the event in the parish church on the following Sabbath.

Thus unexpectedly the two brothers, William and Peter, were left in charge of the business and of the upbringing of the younger members of the family, one of whom, David, was sent to Dublin to conduct a branch established there, and which is still carried on by the firm. Though now passed away full of years and honour, being a nonagenarian when he died, Mr David Drummond, by his energy and courtesy, by his Christian devotedness and large-hearted liberality, was a fountain of blessing, not only to the city of Dublin but to many parts of Ireland, where his name was long a household word. He was the last survivor of his family.

But it is with Peter Drummond that we are more immediately concerned at present, and, following his career, we find him in the "Fifties" of last century, as well established in business as a nurseryman and seedsman, and enjoying a large measure of prosperity. One result of this was his erection of the fine property of Viewforth House, adjoining Pitt Terrace, but standing in extensive and nicely laid out grounds of its own. Here, to show his love for the heroes of his country, he adorned his grounds with statues of Wallace, Bruce, Knox, Chalmers, and others, some of which are to be seen to-day in the Cemetery.

How Mr Drummond was led to engage in Christian work it is difficult exactly to say. No particular time is mentioned as forming the turning-point in his life. His early upbringing, and the influences that were brought to bear upon him in connection with the church; the great revival of 1839, under the fervent preaching of the Rev. William Burns, a modern John the Baptist; the stirring event known as the Disruption of the Church of Scotland, in 1843; these, and other public movements, no doubt, had a quickening and enlarging effect upon his mind. Besides, he had the privilege of sitting under the ministry of the Rev. Dr Beith, of the North Free Church, Stirling, who was one of the champions of evangelical religion, and whose earnest, eloquent, and faithful preaching could hardly fail to make a lasting impression upon a heart so sensitive and full of generous impulse.

Then, perhaps, it ought to be mentioned that his saintly sister, Helen, had a peculiar charm and power over the decisions of her brother. On the uprising of any doubt or difficulty it was to her he usually went, while her husband encouraged him to devote more of his time and extraordinary energy to various forms of Christian service. One day he was asked to address a Sabbath School at Causewayhead. With diffidence he agreed, but so well did he manage with his peculiar manner —being full of what is termed "life"—and anecdotes to arrest and keep the attention of the children, that he was induced to return again and again, so that in course of time Mr Drummond became locally famous as a speaker to children.

A booklet, "The Story of the Stirling Tract Enterprise," thus speaks:—

The Stirling Tract Enterprise was unconsciously commenced by Mr Peter Drummond in the year 1848, for when he issued his first tract, the idea of thereby starting an Enterprise, which should ere long have the whole world for its field, had never crossed his mind. For some years he had been grieved to learn the amount of Sabbath desecration in the neighbouring village of Cambuskenneth, to the fruit gardens and public-houses of which large numbers were in the habit of resorting, during summer and autumn, spending the Lord's Day in idleness and dissipation. For a time, along with several friends, he did what he could, by speaking to individuals among the pleasure-seekers, and occasionally by addressing as many as would gather round him in the open air, to persuade them of the evil of

their course. The thought one day occurred to him that it might be of use to issue a plain, pointed tract. That thought—a stray thought, as it may have seemed, was the beginning of the Stirling Tract Enterprise.

Immediately Mr Drummond set about the compilation of a tract (now No. 15, Sabbath Series, four pages), and in August, 1848, had 10,000 copies thrown off. These were distributed, Sabbath after Sabbath, in the village referred to, on the roads leading to it, and in the parishes around, the ministers of which took hearty interest in the work—knowing well the seriousness of the evil he and his friends were seeking to combat. There was nothing in the character or appearance of the tract itself to awaken unusual interest. It was printed on rather poor paper, and consisted almost exclusively of passages of Scripture, with brief extracts from M'Cheyne and Dr. Love, but it excited so much interest, that within a month the whole impression was exhausted, and applications for copies from all quarters were so numerous, that Mr Drummond resolved to issue another—this time of 100,000 copies. This accordingly he did, with the effect, however, not so much of supplying the demands as of further stimulating it; for within a few months a third edition had to be issued—also of 100,000 copies. The practical result, so far as concerned the direct object of the movement, was an immediate and most marked diminution in the amount of Sabbath desecration at Cambuskenneth. And while thus prospered in his attempt at good-doing at home, Mr Drummond was cheered by communications from friends at a distance, who had distributed the tract, and reported that, in not a few cases, the blessing of God had been manifestly vouchsafed in connection with it.

The success of his little effort took him by surprise. He felt as if a new, strange power had been put by God into his hand, to be used for His glory. He had no thought even then of founding a permanent Enterprise. But he felt constrained to go forward—again in a direction to which local circumstances seemed to point. The Stirling public had been accustomed to visits from strolling players, whose performances were accompanied by mischief to the morals of the community, and especially of the young. A company of these arriving in town just at this time, Mr Drummond had a tract prepared on theatre-going, and showered copies of it over the town and neighbourhood—having them distributed from house to house, in schools, in workshops, and on the streets,—and with special profusion among the crowds drawn to the doors of the theatre. The result was even more marked than in the first instance, the players in a day or two leaving the town, and not returning for years afterwards. Again successful, he again went forward. For a long time in Stirling "the Races" had been a source of dissipation and crime —the season of their annual recurrence being anticipated by many people with the deepest apprehension. It was resolved to bring the tract power to bear in this connection also. Tracts and large posting bills were prepared, and, although far from claiming for that agency the full credit of what soon followed, other circum- stances having aided in producing the result, yet in its own place it told powerfully ; and now horse-racing is unknown in Stirling, the last meeting of the kind being held in 1853 Nor was the good done in these connections confined to the locality—demands for copies of the tracts poured in from all quarters, and scores of thou- sands were sent in every direction, through Scotland, England, and Ireland. A number of simple, earnest, Gospel tracts were now added— including several on family religion, and several on intemperance. Altogether, the sphere of use- fulness widened so rapidly, that within three years Mr Drummond found to his amazement that no fewer than three millions of tracts had been put in circulation.

While he wondered whereunto this would grow, a further impetus of an extraordinary kind was given the work, and this from quite an unexpected quarter, by the institution of book-postage in 1859-60. The immediate result of this system, following as it did the penny post, was to con- stitute every letter-carrier in the kingdom a tract deliverer. While the penny post brought, the book-post within a few hours executed, the orders, conveying printed matter to the remotest hamlet or most solitary dwelling in the king- dom. So vast an impulse was thus given the work in which Mr Drummond was engaged, that he found himself face to face with a question he had been coming to see must ere long be encountered—viz., how this new work, so rapidly assuming great proportions, was to be carried on? The demands on his time were so serious as materially to interfere with the discharge of his duties as partner in the firm to which he

belonged ; and it became clear to him that he could not warrantably go on as he had been doing. After consideration, he was brought to the conclusion that it was his duty to enter in at the door which had opened before him. This accordingly he did in 1852. With the consent of his brothers, he withdrew from the active manage- ment of the business in which they were partners, retaining, at the same time, his pecuniary interest in it, that he might not only devote his whole time and energies to the work to which he felt himself called, but do so without money fee or reward. For some time Mr Drummond continued to work with tracts alone, issuing many new ones, and doing his best to discover and open up suitable lines of operation. During a few months of 1852 tens of thousands of the tracts were scattered among farm-servants and other labourers at fairs and feeing markets ; and, by correspondence with ministers and others, a system of distribution was organised in numerous country districts.

In accordance, however, with the uniform ex- perience of all such undertakings, the periodical soon followed the tract. Mr Drummond had been repeatedly urged by friends to start a periodical. Two in particular had sent him copies of "The American Messenger," suggesting he should either reprint the substance of it, or issue a broad-sheet of the same character. He did not move hastily, but ere long came to see that a periodical of some sort was not merely desirable in itself, but was becoming indis- pensable as a means of communication with the friends daily rising up in all parts of the king- dom. And "The American Messenger" seemed so thoroughly popular in character, and had proved so great a success (having at that time attained a circulation of 200,000 copies), that he thought he could not do better than make it his model. This accordingly he did ; and in March, 1853, the first number of "The British Messenger" was issued—the counterpart of "The American Messenger" in every respect ; alike in name, appearance, and the character of its articles.

The starting of the "Messenger" proved an important event in the history of the Enterprise, and by the interest thus excited, together with the admitted merits of the periodical itself, and the novelty of its form (being the first broad- sheet of the kind published in this country), a large circulation was speedily secured. It was

This is the original Depot used by Mr Peter Drummond at the commencement of the Tract Enterprise. in Messrs Wm Drummond & Sons' Seed premises & Agricultural Museum. King Street. in July. 1848.

The Original Depot.

King Street Depot.

soon found to answer in every way the purpose for which it was started, and by the appeals Mr Drummond had opportunity of making through its columns, friends were raised up to help in many ways, especially in providing funds necessary for gratuitous tract distribution. Mr Drummond continued for nearly four years to work the tracts and the "Messenger," being cheered by words of kindness and encouragement from Christian friends, to tne great mass of whom he was personally a stranger. In 1857 he commenced another now well-known publication of the Enterprise, viz., "The Gospel Trumpet." It was started specially as a large type religious paper for the aged and those who could only read with difficulty, and, although it followed the "Messenger," and had nothing whatever of sensational interest about it, it rose at a bound, 60,000 copies being printed monthly before the close of the first year.

The work, now thus well established, grew apace—the periodicals securing many friends for the tracts, and the tracts sending multitudes of readers to the periodicals. From the commencement, the Enterprise has been wrought in a revival spirit, and avowedly with the view of stirring up the people of God to pray and work for revival times. And when the revival in the later fifties did come the Enterprise shared in the blessing,—Christian people everywhere recognising in it a likely agent of revival work, and providing means for scattering its periodicals to an extent far beyond what had even before been reached. So large, indeed, was the amount of work now done, that the local post office required to be enlarged, and its staff increased, simply to meet the growing demands of the Enterprise. For the same reason Mr Drummond was constrained to seek larger premises for his operations. The place of business he had leased had become too small for the staff found needful, and it seemed to him that the Enterprise had so manifestly acquired the character of a public institution, that the most expedient course would be to erect a building as the centre of its operations. In March, 1862, the staff of the Enterprise entered on possession of the new premises, now the British Linen Company's Bank at foot of King Street. Mr Drummond at the same time made provision for handing over the whole property of the Enterprise to Trustees, with a view to its permanent maintenance as an evangelistic agency.

A third monthly publication, viz., "Good News," was begun in 1862. Its design was to supply reading of an evangelistic character, which should be sufficiently simple and pointed to be of use in general mission work, and also in Sabbath schools.

Upon the lamented death of Mr Drummond, which took place on 9th July, 1877, the body of Trustees entered on the management of the Enterprise. But the work was extending so rapidly that it soon outgrew the limits of the place in which it was being carried on, and it became evident for a second time that much larger premises must be secured. As there was no room for extending the building in King Street, the Trustees resolved to build elsewhere a Depot of such size as not only to meet existing requirements, but also to provide for increase in coming years. In 1887 the Depot in King Street was sold, and on the 6th of August of that year the foundation-stone of the new Depot in Dumbarton Road was laid. The ceremony was performed by the late Sir George Williams, of London, a well-known friend of all aggressive Christian work, in presence of a large company. The building, with nearly double the accommodation of its predecessor, completed, in May, 1888, the work of the Enterprise was transferred to its new home. And it need only be said further here that the wisdom, as well as the necessity, of the removal was shown in the still wider expansion of the operations of the Enterprise, in proportion as new opportunities were afforded for the prosecution of Gospel work at home and abroad.

Special mention must be made of the gratuitous circulation of its publications by the Stirling Tract Enterprise. This has formed a prominent feature in its work from the beginning. Grants are made to clergymen, missionaries, and open-air preachers, to Sabbath schools, temperance societies, etc. ; and in this way many millions of the papers have been circulated, chiefly amongst tne outcast and neglected in town and country, who are living in ignorance and in indifference to their eternal welfare, and whom it is difficult to reach through the ordinary means of grace. Of the good effected in this way, numerous and most encouraging testimonies have been given ; the blessing of God having manifestly accompanied the circulation of Scriptural truth. It may here be mentioned that numerous associations exist for the express purpose of dis-

Dumbarton Road Depot.

tributing religious tracts and publications, and thus acting as the pioneers of the Gospel to perishing sinners who might otherwise be left to live and die in ignorance of the Saviour. Furnishing as those do the active agents in such an important work, the Trustees are most anxious to be provided with the means of responding to applications coming to them from such quarters ; and they look to the liberality of the Christian public for help in this direction.

From the most recent catalogue of the publications—a closely-packed large size booklet of 72 pages—we note that there are upwards of one hundred separate volumes which have emanated specially from the Enterprise, some two thousand booklets, by such writers as the late Bishop Ryle, the Rev. George Everard, M.A., Bishop Moule, the Rev. P. B. Power, M.A., Major Whittle, Eva Travers Evered Poole, George Kelsey, Charles Cook, Rev. John M'Neill, William Thomson, H. K. Wood, William Luff, and others whose names are well known in the religious world. Of leaflets for inclosing in letters there are over two hundred, besides a great number of floral wall cards, text cards and mottoes, and other publications. Of the tracts in English, from one to sixteen pages, there are nearly three thousand, many of them on special subjects.

The gratuitous circulation of the "British Messenger," "Gospel Trumpet," "Good News," and Tracts of the Stirling Tract Enterprise, since its commencement, amounts to upwards of two hundred and fifty-one millions. The number in 1907 was over six millions. The Trustees are anxious to continue and greatly extend this gratuitous circulation, and they invite and would gladly welcome contributions of Christian friends to enable them to do so. Many applications could be more adequately responded to did funds allow.

The following quantities were given gratuitously during June, 1908 : —

20,587 "British Messenger,"	.....	£60	7	6
25,541 "Gospel Trumpet,"	....	34	15	5
53,648 "Good News," and				
497,628 Tracts, Small Books, and				
Tracts in Foreign Languages,	...	93	16	2
		£268	19	1
Amount of previous grants as reported in July "Messenger,"		116,594	6	5
		£116,883	5	6

"The Increase" (as the annual report is named) for 1907 gives the number of publications issued during the year ended 30th September as 12,291,531, and of publications given gratis as 6,940,682, valued at £2,914 3s 6d. The total issued at that date numbered 619,462,296 ; given gratuitously, 247,181,791, valued at £114,815 6s 11d, to meet which there had been contributed the sum of £91,004 17s 4½d.

A list of the evangelistic agencies in Great Britain which were helped, either by free grants or at reduced prices, during last year would require more space than we can afford. Suffice it to say that London, Glasgow, Edinburgh, Liverpool, Cardiff, Plymouth, Dublin, Belfast, etc., are included, besides hospitals, soldiers' homes, sailors' societies, town missions, Christian Endeavour, Y.M.C.A., Y.W.C.A., and other agencies of a varied character. But there is also a wide field abroad, Europe, Asia, Africa, and America appearing in the list as having received grants.

Mr Peter Drummond, who was in his 78th year when he died, had, as the result of failing health, retired five years before that to Edinburgh. Prior to his leaving Stirling, however, the inhabitants presented their distinguished citizen with his portrait, which was painted by Norman MacBeth, A.R.S.A., and bore the following inscription : "Presented to Mr Peter Drummond, Stirling, by his fellow-townsmen and friends, in token of their respect for his character, and in appreciation of his lifelong labours in the cause of Christian truth. 1873." This portrait is now in the Tract Depot. On Mr Drummond's death his remains were brought to Stirling and interred there, the funeral being a public one, and notable from the large number of mourners. Mr Drummond had seven children, all of whom have died except William, who resides in Edinburgh.

Since Mr Drummond's death the Stirling Tract Enterprise has been carried on by Trustees, in accordance with the founder's desire, and under their supervision the work has greatly increased. Much of that success has, however, been due to the late Mr John Macfarlane, who was connected with the work for over forty years, and was manager for a great part of the time. On his death some years ago Rev. Wm. Agnew, the editor, was also entrusted with the reins of management, and under his regime the Tract Enterprise continues to worthily fulfil its mission at home and abroad.

Robert Walls.

ROBERT WALLS & SONS, KERSE MILLS.

Than the ancient, honourable, and important occupation of miller, there is none more enshrined in song and story. It is bound up with the history of our country, and how many notable events from the birth to the death—generally by violence—of monarchs and others of high degree, are intimately associated with some mill throughout the land. In our own district, Beaton's Mill, near Whins of Milton, is an instance in point. And when one considers for a moment the important part mills played in every community in the olden days, and the fact that they were scattered all over the country, and formed, as it were, the central rallying point for the life of the community, where the news of the district and further afield would be discussed, it is apparent why the miller is such an outstanding personality, and the reason is clear for his being immortalised in the proverbs and annals of the people. Ever since corn was grown, the art of grinding or milling the grain has accompanied it, and that is from the earliest times. Many references to millstones are to be found in both the Old and New Testaments, and in Deuteronomy it is recorded that Moses issued the following command to the Israelites—"No man shall take the nether or the upper millstone in pledge, for he taketh a man's life in pledge." And it is interesting to note that the principles employed in the operation of crushing or grinding the corn when the world was young are followed to-day, though of course by other methods, and in a very much more scientific fashion. The earliest known form of grinding corn was by hand mill, which was a big stone worn hollow by the operations of rubbing. In this hollow the grain was put, and then crushed or ground by another stone being rubbed against it by hand, hence the expression, upper and nether millstone. Amongst savage tribes this is the method employed at the present day. The next step was the quern, or handmill, which is still in use in Shetland, the Faroe Isles, and other remote places. The quern consisted of two circular stones, scarcely different in form from a pair of modern millstones, except that the quern stones are small enough to permit of the upper one being turned by hand instead of driven by water, steam, or electric power. Nowadays even rotating millstones, weighing perhaps a ton and a half, between which the grain is crushed, are being superseded by metal discs, but at Kerse Mill, where the most up-to-date

milling machinery is to be seen at work, the big old circular millstones are still used for the manufacture of oatmeal. It may be a fetish, or it may be a fact, but the belief is entertained by the Messrs Walls, whose judgment is based on experience, that millstones give a better flavour to the meal than is produced by metal discs. It would serve no purpose to describe minutely in this article the various processes in oatmeal manufacture, because they would not be understood by the general reader, but a visit to the old establishment at Kerse Mill, and an "ocular demonstration" of the various operations employed in the conversion of oats into meal, is a very interesting experience. What impresses one most is the number of delicate operations carried out by the aid of machinery, and the little there is really left for man to do beyond the supervision of the mechanical forces he controls. This, however, is a duty both onerous and responsible. Machinery will do a lot of work—but it can do, and does, a lot of damage unless it is looked after and controlled by human beings equipped with the requisite knowledge.

What is, however, perhaps most significant to the visitor to Kerse Mills is the fact of there being no waste. Most, if not all, manufacturing processes have what is termed bye-products, and sometimes these can be disposed of as the "raw material" of other trades, whilst sometimes they cannot, with the result that they are of no use to anybody, and cause expense to get rid of. It is not so at Kerse Mills, where not only the husks and dust which cling to the oats in their natural state, and have to be cleared away, but also the ordinary "stour" of the mill, are marketable commodities. The husks mostly find their way to the Continent, where the foreigner has a use for them : the oat dust goes to Ireland, to be utilised in the feeding of young cattle ; and the "stour" or mill sweepings are a savoury mixture for the meals that home-fed pigs delight in.

Harking back to the historic associations of mills and millers, it is interesting to glance at some of the old laws affecting the trade. One of the most important of these was called "thirlage." In feudal times people having grain to grind were compelled to get this done at the mill connected with the estate off which they held their land, and there was no evading the obligation. Thirlage is now obsolete, but when in vogue it was, according to the law of Scotland, a right or servitude enjoyed by the proprietor of a mill over the neighbouring lands, whereby the owner or possessor of such lands was bound to carry corn grown thereon to be ground at the mill. The miller or owner of the mill was entitled to levy certain duties on the "suckeners," as the possessors of the lands within the area, or "sucken," were called, and these duties were termed "multures," being a proportion of the grain that was ground. Such multures got the name of "insucken," to distinguish them from "outsucken multures," which were similar payments made to the miller by strangers who were not bound to take their corn to the mill, but chose to do so. The right of "thirlage" was, however, extinguished if the mill got into ruin, or forty years' exemption from sending grain to it was permitted. In this connection it may also be mentioned that the miller's man was, if not legally, at least by custom, entitled to a share of the grain brought to the mill to be ground. His proportion was called the "gowpen"—that is, as much as he could lift in his two hands held together. Another interesting right the miller had if his premises were situated on the bank of a stream, was the use of the stream undiminished in volume, and should the other proprietors above him do anything to diminish his water supply, and thereby cause injury to the mill, the millowner had the right of an action at law against the offender. This right still exists, though that of thirlage has long ago disappeared.

As we have already indicated, the milling trade has, like other industries, undergone many changes during the last century. Up to about the beginning of the eighteenth century, and even later, the miller was simply a miller, and not a merchant as he is now. When the farmer had grain to grind, he brought it to the mill, and also brought with him fuel, in the shape of peats, to fire the kiln, to dry the grain, which part of the work he did himself, and afterwards, if it was oatmeal that was being manufactured, sifting it also himself with a hand sieve. The miller on his part simply attended to the grinding of the grain and exacting payment for his services by "muter" or "multure," that is, he kept about a fifteenth part of the meal, receiving no money whatever. In this connection a story was often told against the miller, that he wore a good wide open sleeve, and when feeling the meal, as it came from the stones, to see that it

was being properly ground, contrived to send a proportion of it into his sleeve, which went to feed the proverbial miller's fat horse or fat pig. We all know, however, that this was an unkind and false accusation against an honest and industrious class of men. In the Highlands the mills in many cases had no kiln, the people drying their grain over their own kitchen fire on a girdle before taking it to the mill. Even to this day this primitive system still survives in remote parts of Scotland, Mr Walls, sen., having had an instance brought under his notice not long ago. Gradually, however, a change took place, and the farmer brought his grain to the mill and left it—the miller doing all the work of drying, grinding, and sifting, and charging so much money per boll, giving the farmer his entire produce in return.

The baker also for a long time bought all his wheat and sent it to the mill to be made into flour. In some districts the bakers had mills of their own, and it will be well remembered amongst the older inhabitants of Stirling and district that up to about half-a-century ago Stirling bakers leased their own mill at Milton, where they made all their flour, or most of it. In course of time this system also stopped, and the miller became a merchant as well as a miller—buying the wheat and manufacturing flour, thereafter selling it to the baker. But flour-making in country mills—in Scotland more especially—is practically a thing of the past. Foreign wheat is now mostly used for making flour, and large mills have been erected at the ports of arrival, so that almost if not actually all the flour-milling in Scotland is carried on at seaport towns, and besides this a vast quantity of foreign flours are imported from every grain-growing part of the world. This does not apply to England, where many small country mills do a very flourishing little trade in flour-milling. This is explained in various ways. In the first place England gets more sun than Scotland, and is therefore better adapted for growing wheat, as wheat is a sun plant. The English miller can accordingly secure at his door good dry wheat fit to make excellent flour, either itself or mixed with foreign wheat, which he can get at less cost than the Scottish country miller, owing principally to the cheaper transit he has from the seaport in the shape of canals. Then, these English mills in the country are often driven with wind, a feature of the landscape when travelling, say, to London being the

2. Kerse Mills.

3. New Stores at Springkerse.

number of wind mills and canals which one sees. In Scotland, on the other hand, a large number of country mills, which a century ago or less were grinding merrily, now lie in ruins, and those which exist have had to turn their attention to the manufacture of oatmeal and feeding stuffs for horses, cattle, pigs, poultry, etc.

This is what has happened at Kerse Mills (illustration No. 2), where, up to about 50 years ago, flour-milling was the staple trade.

These mills, about a mile from Stirling, on the Polmaise estate, and driven by the waters of the historic Bannock, have been in existence from the sixteenth century at least, as a stone bearing that date is in the building. Almost a hundred years ago it was acquired by Messrs Paul & Walls, who were successively followed in 1839 by Mr James Walls of that firm, and in 1864 by Mr Robert Walls, his son, the present head of the firm of Robert Walls & Sons. The family originally came from Fifeshire to this district, and though there are now several branches here, "The Kingdom," and particularly that part adjoining the Firth of Forth, contain a good many more. This can be explained from the fact that the name Walls is of Scandinavian origin, and no doubt several of the old Norse sea rovers, who scourged the coasts of Scotland many centuries ago, settled in Fifeshire. Further support of that theory is found in the fact that both in Orkney and Shetland there is a parish called Walls, and long ago these two islands belonged to Denmark.

Mr Robert Walls, whose photograph we give above, is the oldest tenant on Polmaise estate, and is now under his fifth landlord. Mr Walls remembers many interesting events in the lives of the Murrays of Polmaise, and especially recalls with pleasure the occasion when the tenantry, on horseback, met the late Colonel John Murray at Kerse Mills on his return from the Crimean War, and accompanied him to the mansion-house at Old Polmaise, where the family were then in residence, and where that day the tenantry were sumptuously entertained.

On 1st January, 1865, the mills were burned down, all that was saved being one bag of wheat. That same year, however, they were rebuilt on a much larger scale, and fitted up with entirely new machinery, a change also being made in the driving power. Prior to the fire, the mills were driven by two large overshot wheels, 20 feet diameter, which were both destroyed by the fire. In their place a turbine was put in which did the work of the two large wheels, and also took up very much less space. This turbine was about the earliest introduced into this district, and was installed when this form of mechanical propulsion was much less talked about than is now the case. The turbine, it may be mentioned, worked until 1907, when it was replaced by one of a more modern type. This new wheel is no more than 21 inches in diameter, and to keep the mills up-to-date so many new machines have been added of recent years that one wonders how a wheel of such small dimensions can drive so heavy a load, but this it easily does.

Although doing a large and increasing business in grinding feeding stuffs for cattle, the principal business at Kerse Mills is the manufacture of oatmeal, and the Messrs Walls have a reputation for making first-class oatmeal, which is not confined to this country. Large quantities are certainly despatched daily to many parts of Scotland, but the firm also send a considerable amount of oatmeal to England and South Africa. But whilst this is the case, a great change has come over the public taste with regard to Scotland's former staple article of diet, and what our forefathers would have supped gratefully the present generation will not look at. This means that all foreign matter in the shape of other grains or small black seeds which grow amongst the oats have to be extracted, and for this purpose a very complete set of machinery has been erected at Kerse Mills. The grain used comes principally from the counties of Stirling, Perth, and Forfar, and these are three of the best oat-growing counties in Scotland, whilst Scotland is the best oat-growing country in the world, hence the finest of oats are used at Kerse Mills. Scotch oats, it appears, have a sweet, nutty flavour that no other oats have, the explanation perhaps being that, unlike wheat, oats are not fond of too much sun, and in no country on the face of the globe where grain grows do people see less of the heat-giving orb. Accordingly when we are inclined to grumble at our Scotch mists, drizzles, and grey skies, we may console ourselves by remembering that these go a long way towards making Scotland's famous oatmeal, and also our beautiful scenery, for there is no doubt that the wet weather we get has a great deal to do in giving the greenery and freshness to the landscape, which is one of its greatest charms.

It is a long time since it was said that Scotsmen were fed on two articles—oatmeal porridge

4. Port Street Store.

5. Craigforth Mill.

and the Shorter Catechism—although with regard to both one may nowadays well ask, "Stands Scotland where it did?" One doubts very much if these lines of our national bard—

"Now the supper crowns their simple board,
The halesome parritch—chief o' Scotia's food,"

are now applicable to us Scottish folk.

All medical men recommend oatmeal in some shape or form, more especially for bringing up children, and no parents who wish their offspring to develop well in brain, bone, and muscle should neglect this old Scottish diet. As an illustration, it may be mentioned that on one occasion a young Scottish student who had been well fed on oatmeal from childhood underwent a serious operation in London in connection with the bones of one of his legs. He amazed all around him by coming through it successfully, and when the professor who operated heard of his rapid and complete recovery, he exclaimed, "Another tribute to the properties of Scotch oatmeal." The day has, however, long ago passed when the Scottish University student got a week off in the spring to enable him to go home to replenish his meal pock, so that he could feed himself till the end of the session. The holiday—"Mealy Monday"—is still given, but the student does not now employ it in the fashion his prototype of a century ago did.

As already mentioned, a good trade in cattle feeding stuffs—maize meal, bean meal, etc.—is also done at Kerse Mills, and large quantities are manufactured and despatched daily to all parts of Stirlingshire and adjacent counties. Another specialty of the firm is their horse provender. About four years ago they erected a large and commodious store adjoining the railway at Springkerse (illustration No. 3), with a siding off the Caledonian system, which has proved a great convenience in the expeditious handling of their grain, and to these premises they removed this department of their business. The power used here is electricity, the current being got from the burgh municipal electric station across the railway, and here is prepared all the horse food, or "chop," as it is called in the trade. The firm also installed at the Springkerse Stores a very clever plant for the bruising, cleaning, and mixing of the various grains, which, along with cut hay, go to make "chop." It would be difficult to find a more complete and efficient plant for the preparation of horse provender, and the quality produced is such that the firm have a deservedly high reputation, locally and in the adjoining counties, for this article.

The Messrs Walls likewise manufacture specialties in poultry and chicken food, for which they have a large and growing demand.

Besides what they manufacture, the firm sell very large quantities of whole grain and feeding stuffs of all descriptions. They are wholesale buyers of grain direct from the ship's side at Glasgow or Leith, and also purchase heavily in Scotch grains in Stirling market and from neighbouring counties, and are thus in a position to distribute these at lowest prices over a wide area.

Illustration No. 4 shows the firm's town store and office, which takes the place of the old Kerse Mills Store, which was a landmark in Port Street for several generations.

Illustration No. 5 shows Craigforth Mill, which recently fell vacant, and has been acquired by the Messrs Walls, and which they expect will prove very useful, and enable them better to cope with their growing business.

The employees of this firm have gradually increased, and the best of relations exist between masters and men. Some of the latter have been at Kerse Mills for over ten, twenty, and thirty years, and one recently was presented with the "People's Journal" long-service medal for over 40 years' continuous service. He is still good for a fair day's work, and does it too.

BANNOCKBURN HOSIERY COMPANY.

The manufacture of hosiery goods is an industry that Stirling has only become acquainted with during the last twenty years, by the establishment in the town of the Bannockburn Hosiery Company's works, but the trade itself is an old and important one, and gives employment to many thousands of people in certain parts of the country. Nottingham and Leicester, in the English Midlands, are the chief centres of the hosiery manufacture in Britain, but it has extended into other counties, and has found a home on the Scottish Borders, Hawick being the principal seat. For many years the tweed trade has been the principal industry of the Border district, but the hosiery trade has made rapid strides, and is threatening to take the premier place. When that industry was founded, about 1771, the work was, of course, all done by hand, and it is not so many years ago since there were several hundreds of hand stockingmakers in the district, and now there are not five for every hundred there were then. Patent power frames and knitting machines are now largely in vogue, and this industry, which was pre-eminently a man's trade, has been invaded by the fair sex, who have completely swamped the men in the making of hosiery in the Borders. In connection with the tweed and hosiery trades, Archibald Dickson, along with George Beattie, began a hosiery factory at Denholm in 1783, and the house in which Dr Leyden, the famous Oriental scholar, was born, was used as the scouring-house. In 1815, when their stocking frames were valued at £570, they joined the firm of D. & A. Laing, at Hawick, which subsequently became the firm of Dickson & Laing, as at present. From 1786 or so, onwards, grants were made by the Board of Trustees for Manufactures to the hosiery, tweed, and other trades, in the shape of frames and money. In Stirling and district a good many years ago, when kilt and shawl tartans were manufactured, a Mr Johnstone, of St Ninians, did a considerable business in the making of kilt hose, but this trade has gradually decayed.

It is interesting to learn that no fewer than five thousand distinct articles are made in the trade which in its most limited sense refers to the manufacture of hose, but in the more general application comprises all knitted goods, whether made by hand or by machinery. In the present case we confine our article to that part of the industry carried on in Stirling by the Bannock-burn Hosiery Company, namely, the manufacture of plain hosiery. The use of hose or stockings originated in the cold countries of the North, and probably the first were made of skins, and later of cloth. Illuminations in ancient MSS. show that these nether garments were worn by the Anglo-Saxons and the Normans. The art of knitting was invented in Scotland, it is supposed, in the 15th century, and certain it is that knitted stockings found their way from Scotland to France. This led to the establishment of a guild of stocking-knitters, who chose as their patron saint St Fiaire of Scotland, who, however, was really an Irish monk of the 6th century, and the patron of gardeners. In 1589 William Lee, of Nottingham, entirely altered the hosiery trade by inventing the knitting or stocking frame, and although he did not live to enjoy much benefit from it, the machine, which was of wood, soon became a very important feeder to the commerce of Great Britain. Many improvements followed on Lee's invention, which, though driven by manual power, was a great advance on the ordinary hand-knitting by wires or pins, which had come down from the earliest times, and exists yet—as may often be witnessed in the spectacle of an industrious woman enjoying a gossip at her door whilst she plies the knitting wires.

But whilst knitting is an old trade, it is the youngest of all textile manufactures, and in this respect it is, compared with several others, quite modern. The first knitting machine, as distinct from the old stocking frame, which was, and is still, used at home, was only patented in 1816—just 92 years ago. Since then, however, there has been great progress, and improvement has succeeded improvement, until now there are few industries in which machinery plays a more important part. The highest type of specialised machinery is employed, and it practically does everything in the making of a stocking, the thread going in at one end and the finished article coming out at the other. There are, of course, different machines for different classes of goods, but all have this in common—they only require to be supervised by an attendant, to see that they are kept going, and they will do the work. As may be imagined, a mechanical agency of this wonderful description is a very delicate and complicated piece of engineering skill, and the best machine in existence at the present time consists of no fewer than 386 parts. All these are num-

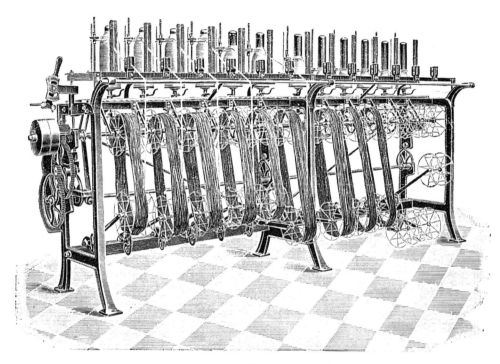

Hank-Winding Machine (James Foster, 41 Friargate, Preston).

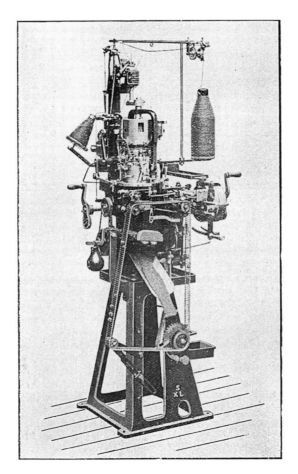

$\frac{S.}{X.L.}$ Fashioning Machine (William Spiers, Queen Street, Leicester).

The $\frac{S.}{X.L.}$ Machine has made a name for itself. One Operator with Six Machines has produced Men's Half-hose weekly as follows:—192 dozen, 194, 187, 191, 179, 184, 186.

bered and standardised, so that if one part breaks or gets out of order, a new one can be procured from the makers, and fitted into its place by anyone—not necessarily a mechanic—acquainted with the working of the machine. As showing the difference in production of one of these power-driven machines compared with hand labour, it may be stated that a woman could not knit a pair of stockings in a day, but a power-driven machine will turn out ten dozen pairs ready for wearing, whilst with the manually-turned stocking-frame only one dozen pair could be made in the same time. Prior to the introduction of machinery, there were stocking factories in operation on the same lines as the old hand-loom weaving shops, but when steam power came into vogue the trade got a great fillip, and has spread all over Europe and America, though Britain is still the chief centre of it. What machinery has done in the way of cheapening goods to the consumer may be gathered from the fact that, whilst in 1854 it cost six shillings to knit a dozen pairs of stockings by means of the hand-knitting frame, at present, by the power-driven machine, the cost for the same production does not exceed 1s 6d. As one girl can attend to four machines, turning out 40 dozen pairs in a day, it will be seen that the demand for stockings must be very great, but it has also to be kept in mind that but for the cheap production this demand would not exist, because if the public had to pay more for the goods a certain number at least would not be able to do so, and would have to be content with some inferior article.

As we have already stated, the production of stockings by mechanical means was introduced into Stirling twenty years ago, when the Bannockburn Hosiery Company, of which Mr Simon M'Leod is the principal, commenced opera-

tions in the Craigs district, but a few years ago the factory was removed to more commodious premises in the Abbey Road. Mr M'Leod has been connected with the trade since 1872, and though the Stirling establishment is not a very large one, the industry is developing, and will doubtless continue to do so, as there is a good field for it in this part of the country. Some of the best machines used in the trade are to be seen at the Abbey Road factory, and the output, which consists of stockings of all kinds, is manufactured for the wholesale trade entirely. The starting of the factory provided what was much needed in Stirling twenty years ago, and what is required yet, though not to the same extent, namely, employment for young girls of a clean, healthy, and interesting nature. The working conditions are excellent, and there is sufficient variety of occupation to prevent the employment becoming monotonous—which is a great advantage in itself. The girls can either sit or stand at their work, and also freely move about, and the benefit of this compared with having to remain in one posture for hours on end can easily be realised from a physical point of view. The usual age of the employees is from 14 to 17, though there are some older than that, and the wages are better than those generally earned in some other occupations by girls at that time of life. Mr M'Leod is very particular as to the class of girls he employs, and that a job in the "stocking factory" is coveted may be gathered from the fact that he has always more applications than he has vacancies, whilst he has never had a lassie from one household without getting another, if there were any more daughters available. Most of the employees remain in the service till they are married, and others have been with the Company for a good many years.

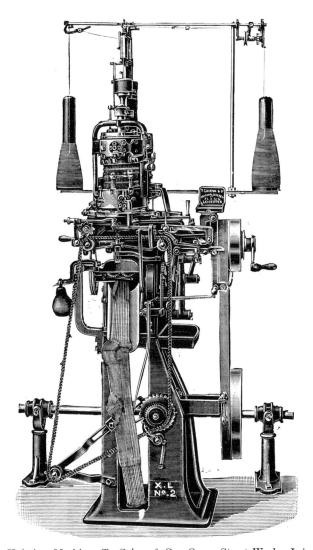

X.L. Knitting Machine (T. Grieve & Co., Queen Street Works, Leicester).

The "X.L." is the most up-to-date of all ribbed footwear machines, and inasmuch as it is fully automatic, reliable, and runs at a moderate rate of speed, it is difficult to imagine any but the most trifling advance in this type of machine in the future. The first machine for making knitted loops was invented in 1569 by William Lee, of Calverton, near Nottingham—referred to above—so that 350 years have passed before the machine under notice had reached its perfection.

James Johnston. Chairman.

James D. Smith, Engineer and Manager.

THE STIRLING GAS=LIGHT COMPANY, LIMITED.

This week we devote our article to one of the oldest industries of Stirling, and one which enters more largely into the lives of the citizens than any other, namely, the manufacture of gas. Like water, light is a necessity of existence, and whilst gas is not indispensable, some form of artificial illuminant is required to enable work to proceed when darkness has set in, for the time has long passed, if it ever existed, that "the night cometh when no man can work." In this highly civilised age work is carried on by night as well as day, and in enabling this to be done no modern agency has played a greater part than gas lighting. As everyone knows, or should know, it revolutionised the art of artificial illumination, which had hitherto been carried out by means of oil lamps and candles; but though it is nearly 120 years since these primitive methods of lighting were threatened with extinction by the newly discovered illuminant, they are still largely used for their original purpose all over the world, and continue to show a bold front to the giant that was expected to destroy them, even as gas is holding its own, and perhaps more than its own, against the modern electric light, which not so many years ago was in its turn expected by its advocates to render gas obsolete. All this goes to show that threatened industries, like threatened people, live long, particularly if they are fulfilling a useful part in the life of the community or the nation.

Into the comparative merits of gas and electricity, which formed a fruitful topic of discussion in Stirling some years ago, and was the cause of much heart-burning in connection with the proposed purchase by the municipality of the Gas Company's undertaking, we don't intend to enter at any length here. A good deal is, however, still heard as to the sanitary aspects of gas and electric lighting, and more especially with regard to the deterioration of the gas atmosphere by the former compared with the latter. Electricians say the electric light is absolutely clean, as it gives off no fumes, no smoke, and no soot, whilst all other artificial illuminants evolve unconsumed carbon particles, which settle on the ceilings and wall papers, and on anything exposed to their dirtying influence. When gas is in use, painting and redecorating has, it is also asserted, to be resorted to at least once in three years. But with the electric light, this period is lengthened almost indefinitely. To this gas engineers reply that electricians compare what (in a measure) has been, but ignore what actually exists to-day. They allude to conditions that existed in the days of the old wasteful and neglected flat-flame burner, and decline to recognise the changed conditions brought about by the incandescent gas-burner. They compare with the open luminous flame, and not the non-luminous flame of the bunsen burner. With the old-fashioned flat-flame burner, partly through the negligence of the consumer, gas was not always consumed properly. But as consumed in an incandescent burner, we have a complete change of conditions. In the case of the old open luminous flame, the carbon particles in the gas became incandescent, and emitted light. In the case of the incandescent gas-burner, that is not so. Here we have a busen or atmospheric flame; and it is a body in the shape of a mantle, that is introduced to that flame, is made incandescent by it, and so emits light. In such a flame combustion is as perfect as it can be, and no smoke, soot, or unconsumed carbon particles are given off, a fact which any householder can demonstrate by holding a white plate over the flame, and, notwithstanding that the plate is cool when put into that position, no carbon particles will be found deposited on it. Where there is a great up-current of heat from a large burner, and the ceilings are low-pitched, it is sometimes found that there is discoloration immediately above; but this is due not to carbon particles from the gas, but to the heat current carrying with it the dust that is contained in the air of the room. There is, so to speak, a constant purifying action going on in this way. There are several other claims made by advocates on both sides as to the superiority of their respective methods of lighting, but these are matters that the average man bothers himself very little about. In the aggregate he takes a broad view of the subject, and what appeals to him is the fact that whilst the electric light has the advantage of being more easily handled in the way of turning off and on, and is not liable to set fire to articles in its immediate vicinity, gas is a considerably cheaper illuminant, whilst giving a better, if not superior, light, and, judged by experience, less likely to cause inconvenience by a breakdown. Proof of the superiority of gas as a lighting agency is, not to go further afield, found in the fact that at the present time the principal lighting of the Edinburgh Exhibition is carried out by inverted incandescent burners on the high pressure system, and that the street lighting of most of the large cities on the Continent is conducted on the same lines. But to see what the inverted burner can do in this respect, we don't need to go outside Stirling. Since the Corporation electric lighting station was started, the gas lamps in most of the streets have been displaced by electric lighting ones, but at the village of the Raploch, where outer darkness reigned supreme for many years, we now find the best lit part of the town. This is accomplished by means of 22 gas lamps fitted up with inverted incandescent burners, and the blaze of light which now extends on a dark evening from the Drip Road to Dumbarton Road, is very noticeable to parties driving or walking in from the country. The reason the Raploch is thus honoured is because the electric cable has not been laid to it, and the Corporation had no other resource than to make use of gas for the public lighting of the village. In this connection it may be mentioned that the Gas Company offers to supply the Corporation with mantles for nothing, and not only that, but to maintain them also where gas is used for street lighting. For obvious reasons, however, the Corporation is not in a position to take advantage of this generosity. The town could be better and more cheaply lit by gas, but in that case a large proportion of the revenue of the municipal electric station would be lost, and consequently electricity has to be used as much as possible. Before leaving the subject of incandescent gas, it may not be without interest to mention here that the mantle, which is now such a familiar adjunct of the lighting of houses and business premises, was only invented twenty years ago, the discoverer being a German, Dr Aur Von Welsbach. The inverted mantle is, however, a much later idea, and in this case the improvement is an English patent. The inverted mantle has the advantage of being stronger than the old upright one, whilst giving an equal amount of light, and it also lends itself better to household and street illumination by throwing the light downwards. It is only within the last ten years that incandescent gas lighting has become anything like general in Stirling, and the inverted system did not come into vogue until half-a-dozen years ago.

But to come to the history of the Stirling Gas-Light Company. Gas was discovered in 1792 by the Scotsman, William Murdoch, whose bust has a place in the Valhalla at the Wallace Monument on the Abbey Craig, but it was thirty-four years later before the new illuminant was introduced to Stirling. In 1805 only three places in Glasgow were lit by gas, but after that the system rapidly gained favour throughout the country, and in June of 1825 a number of Stirling gentlemen, who had seen the light in Glasgow, called a public meeting to consider as to the establishment of a Gas Company for Stirling. The gathering was attended by the leading business men of the town, and it was resolved to form a company with a capital of £6000 in £10 shares, but it was also agreed that no one was to hold more than twenty shares "until after the townspeople had received the offer to subscribe." At the meeting £200 was subscribed, and very soon afterwards the whole of the shares were taken up. The Company having been duly formed, a site for the gas works was obtained where they still stand, and the project was energetically pushed forward, with the result that on 27th November, 1826, the streets of Stirling were lit for the first time with gas. Naturally the occasion was the cause of much interest, not only in Stirling but outside of it, and the town was crowded with people to view the first lighting. "This," a report of the time says, "turned out a success in every way, and rather astonished those who knew nothing about it (gas lighting), and quite delighted those who did." At that time there were two or three enterprising local shopkeepers with the advertising instinct well developed, and they took advantage of the introduction of the new illuminant to light up their premises in an attractive fashion. A shoemaker in Baker Street, we are told, showed a gas jet which issued from a spur fixed on the heel of a boot, whilst a tobacconist in King Street exhibited the bust of a negro with a cigar in his mouth, from which a jet of gas issued, "lengthening and shortening alternatively to suggest the act of smoking." The original area of the Gas Company's supply was practically the same as it is yet—Stirling, Bannockburn, Cambusbarron, and Causewayhead, but it was a long time before these villages took advantage of the new light. Even in Stirling people were slow in doing so, but this can scarcely be wondered at when it is stated that the price per thousand feet was 15s. There is a considerable difference between that

View of Generating House, Repairing Shop, and Gasholder.

Combined Charging and Discharging Machine.

and the present price—2s 10d. But there were other reasons than the cost to delay the progress of gas-lighting in Stirling. Eighty-three years ago, the people, according to a chronicler of the time, being "apprehensive of its reputed highly explosive qualities." Gradually, however, the light found its way into public favour, and we read in the "New Statistical Account of Scotland," published in 1845, that a number of shops and houses were now lit with gas, whilst some of the churches had also taken in the new light. At that time the price had been reduced to 6s 8d per thousand feet.

In 1845, however, a stirring period in the history of the Gas Company took place. Evidently there was some dissatisfaction with the price charged for gas, and the profits earned by the Company, and in the "Observer" of 27th February the following advertisement, dated 24th February, 1845, appeared:—

PROSPECTUS OF THE
STIRLING AND SUBURBAN GAS COY.

CAPITAL INCREASED TO £7,500,
IN 3,750 SHARES OF £2 EACH—DEPOSIT
2s 6d PER SHARE.

PROVISIONAL COMMITTEE.

Bailie Smith, Stirling.
Bailie Prentice, Stirling.
John Dick, Esq., of Craigengelt.
James Wilson, Esq., Manufacturer, Bannockburn.
William Hutton Forrest, Esq., Surgeon, Stirling.
William Wilson, Esq., Manufacturer, Bannockburn.
Patrick Connel, Esq., Banker, Stirling.
John Sawers, Esq., Banker, Stirling.
Martin Moubray Stevenson, Esq., Stirling.
John Wilson, Esq., Manufacturer, Bannockburn.
P. G. Morrison, Esq., Writer, Stirling.
William Knox, Esq., St Ninians.
William Rankin, Esq., Merchant, Stirling.
John Sawers, Esq., Writer, Stirling.
Robert Taylor, Esq., Soap Manufacturer, Stirling.
George Mouat, Esq., Manufacturer, Stirling.
Alexander L. Moodie, Esq., Surgeon, Stirling.
Patrick John Traquair, Esq., Merchant, Stirling.
James Smart, Esq., St Ninians.
James Chrystal, jun., Writer, Interim Secretary.

The reasons for the projection of the new Company were set forth as follows:—

There being only one Gas Company established in Stirling, the inhabitants have hitherto been obliged to pay a much higher price for that most useful article than is charged in most other towns, while no attempt has yet been made to supply the neighbouring important manufacturing and populous villages of Bannockburn and St Ninians. The present existing Company pays a large Dividend, and its Stock bears a high premium, while very considerable sums have from time to time been expended from the Profits in enlarging the Works. Stirling is rapidly extending, and the Projectors of the present undertaking, following the example of almost every other Town of any considerable extent, have resolved on establishing another Company with the view of affording the Inhabitants Gas at a cheaper rate and of better quality, and of supplying Bannockburn, St Ninians, and other neighbouring Villages.

In order to spread the benefits of the proposed Company among as wide a range as possible, and to induce Consumers of Gas to become Shareholders, it is proposed that the Shares shall be only £2 each, and in allocating these a preference will be given to the inhabitants of Stirling, Bannockburn, and St Ninians, etc.

The foregoing was not taken "lying down" by the existing Gas Company, as appears from the following spirited advertisement published in the "Observer" a fortnight later:—

STIRLING GAS-LIGHT COMPANY.

The Committee of Management of the Stirling Gas-Light Company observe that the promoters of the intended New Gas Company in Stirling have endeavoured to make the public believe that the Shareholders in the existing Company have been, and are, in the receipt of very high profits, and this forms the principal ground upon which they found their expectations of the new scheme being a very lucrative one. Such a supposition is altogether fallacious. For anything that the Committee of Management know other Gas Companies may be realising profits to the extent of 8, 10, and 12 per cent., but so far as regards the Stirling Gas Company they have not been so fortunate, for the fact as to them is that their profits on the average of the last ten years have just been Four and Three-quarters Per Cent. Per Annum on the amount of their capital. Even in the most trifling business, attended with little, if any, risk, such a profit would be deemed small ; but when it is taken into account that the manufacture of gas is considered so hazardous that their extensive and valuable range of buildings are uninsurable, the return that they receive for their capital must be admitted (their opponents themselves being judges) to be very far below what money invested under such circumstances should yield to them. But the best evidence that the Stirling Gas-Light Company is held to be no very paying concern is the value that their shares hold in the market. They cost the Shareholders £10 each—for many years £10 or guineas was the most that could be got for them, and in no instance have they been known to rise above £12.

Complaints have been made that the price of Gas charged by the Stirling Gas-Light Company is too high. They believe that the prices they are receiving are much the same as are received by other Gas Companies in towns of the same size. They say the same size, for it is altogether unfair to compare the prices in Stirling, with a population under 9000, to those in towns having double that number of inhabitants, and more so to places having ten or twenty times that number, where, from the great consumpt, gas can be produced at a much cheaper rate. The consumers will also keep in mind that the Company have for some time past been gradually reducing the rates of charge. Previous to the year before last (1843) the charge was 10s 6d per 1000 cubic feet, last year (1844) they reduced it again to 9s, and agreed at same time that in the month of May next it should be still further reduced to 8s. When it is taken into account that the purity and brilliancy of the Stirling Gas-Light are far superior to that of any other town in Scotland, the Committee have no hesitation in affirming that, at the latter rate, the public would be served with gas at a price really less than it is to be had for at any place whatever.

To meet, however, the wishes of many respectable consumers the Committee of Management have resolved to make an additional sacrifice in the hope that in some part at least their reduction in price will be met by an increased consumption. They have agreed that instead of postponing the reduction to 8s to the month of May, that it shall commence as at the term of Martinmas last, and further, that at Whitsunday another shilling shall be taken off, making the price from and after that date Seven Shillings per 1000 cubic feet. To a lower price they cannot possibly go. In Edinburgh, with a population of almost 170,000, the price is 6s 9d, and in Glasgow, whose inhabitants are nearly 300,000, the price is 6s 8d, so that comparing the one Gas with the other it will be found that the consumers in Stirling will be supplied at a rate considerably less in reality than those in these large cities, and that the profits enjoyed by the Company, far at the present time below the profits accruing to the Gas Companies of Edinburgh and Glasgow, will for the future be, by the present reduction, made small indeed.

Gas Works,

Stirling, March 6, 1845.

This statement of affairs did not, however, stave off the threatened opposition. The new Company went on with the allocation of their shares, and announced that they had been over applied for to the extent of £2000, whilst a newspaper correspondence also started. The anonymous writers asserted that the existing Company's works were ill-constructed, that the gas was poor, that the capital stock of the Company had not been paid up, that the profits earned were larger than admitted, and that these had been applied to the creation of a large sinking fund to renew the Works at the expense of the consumers— arguments that will be remembered were utilised half-a-century later in the great "Gas Fight" of 1896, which is still fresh in the memory of most of the inhabitants of Stirling. In 1845 a proposal was made by one of the newspaper correspondents that the Town Council should acquire the Gas Works on behalf of the town, but that came to nothing, as similar proposals did in 1874 and 1896, though in the interval Edinburgh and Glasgow municipalities, and a host of smaller ones throughout the country, took over their local Gas Company's undertakings.

To the attacks made upon them in 1845 the Stirling Gas Company offered a stout defence,

View of Retort Bench—Discharging Side.

Show-Room, Murray Place.

and dealing with their assailants, charged the latter with "showing a great lack of facts and of sound arguments, and at the same time calling names and making general charges." Further, the Company retorted "that the assertions made against them are in point of fact without foundation, and that as no right-minded person will pay much heed to such language, it may be permitted to pass without remark." An offer was further made to give proof of the Company's statements in regard to the relative prices of gas in different towns and other information, to anyone who cared to take the trouble to call at the Gas Works, "and after this it is to be trusted we shall hear no more of the excessive charges made and profits realised by the Stirling 'Monopolist' Company."

Whilst this was going on, a conference also took place with the promoters of the new Company, when an offer—of which there is no published record—was made by the existing Company, but apparently it was not satisfactory, as the new Company went on with their project, and in the course of the year 1845 advertised at different times that they had employed an engineer to plan their works, that a manager was to be engaged, that authority had been obtained from the Town Council to open the streets and lay pipes, and the erection of the new gas works would now be proceeded with "without delay." These various intimations the existing Company "countered" by advertising that their £10 shares would be reduced to £2 shares, and that 1500 shares of the value of £2 would be created, raising the capital to £6000, whilst in addition the price of gas would be reduced to 6s 8d, "being a cheaper rate than what gas is supplied at in any Town in Scotland of the same size as Stirling." A reduction of one-half of the rate charged to consumers for meters belonging to the Company was also intimated, and evidently these announcements made the new Company more amenable to terms, as the next reference to it is found in the following advertisement in the "Observer" of 5th February, 1846:—

STIRLING AND SUBURBAN GAS COMPANY.

Notice is hereby given, That in consequence of the amalgamation of the Stock of this Company with that of the Stirling Gas-Light Company, the full amount of the second call

of 20s per Share will not be required, and the same is hereby restricted to 8s 6d per Share.

By Order,

JAMES CHRYSTAL, Jr., Secy.

Port Street,

Stirling, 2nd February, 1846.

The reasons for the new opposition Company amalgamating with the existing one do not appear on record, but no doubt both sides were glad to arrive at a compromise, and very likely each would claim the victory. The new Company would be pleased at getting the price of gas reduced, and at securing shares on equal terms in the old Company, whilst the latter would no doubt be gratified at having staved off what might have proved a formidable opposition. In any case the share capital was increased to £12,400 by the amalgamation of the Companies, and the enterprise proceeded smoothly for many years, the business of the Company gradually increasing as the town and adjoining villages extended and increased in population.

There was some talk of the town acquiring the Gas Works in 1874, and they could have been got at that time for £25,000, but the Corporation of the day considered the figure too high, and the project dropped. In 1896 what appeared a more determined effort in the same direction took place. The public were again favourable to the acquisition of the Company, and affairs were so far amicably arranged that the Corporation and the Gas Company each appointed an arbiter to value the undertaking. Both were gas engineers of good standing, and the valuation of the Town Council's expert was, in round figures, £62,000, whilst that of the Gas Company's arbiter was £68,000. These figures amazed a large section of the public, who based their ideas of the worth of the undertaking on the works themselves, and not the commercial value of the business, and opposition was at once aroused. The flame was fanned by people who ought to have known, and did know, better, but who, for their own purposes played upon the ignorance of the citizens, and by insinuations against certain directors of the Gas Company, who were alleged to be desirous of palming off their "old, rotten Gas Works" on the town, succeeded in creating a ferment. During all this time the Town Council and the Gas Company carried out their honourable understanding with one another, and Sheriff Lees was appointed referee to decide between the two valuations that had been obtained. He found that the value of the works was £65,000, and the Town Council then went forward to Parliament with a Private Bill to acquire the undertaking. This step added fuel to the flames of opposition, and a defence fund was got up, and the measure opposed. The result of this was the defeat of the Bill, and there was great rejoicing amongst the opposition. Since then many of those who objected to the town acquiring the Gas Works have realised their mistake when they have seen the big profits earned since by the Gas Company, but the damage was done beyond recall. Not knowing what might be in front of them in the future, the Gas Company, very wisely, in their own interests, took steps to make their position secure. Hitherto they had been a private company, liable to be faced at any time by an opposition undertaking, or to have their works compulsorily acquired by the Corporation, and to get rid of these contingencies they promoted a Bill in Parliament to give them statutory powers—in other words, a monopoly which could not be interfered with by anybody. The Town Council —which was now composed of a majority of those who had opposed the acquisition of the works the year previously by the Corporation—opposed the measure, but, of course, they had little or nothing to go upon, seeing the town had declined to take over the undertaking, and the Company got their Bill.

With this, what may be termed a new epoch, started in the history of the Gas Company. The old manager, the late Mr Peter Watson, retired after 35 years' faithful service. He was one of the best gas engineers in Scotland in his day, and did a lot for the Stirling Gas Company, but that day was now past. In his time the manufacture of gas for lighting purposes practically represented the beginning and end of his profession, but a new era was dawning when he laid down the burden. The pressure of the competition of the electric light was beginning to be felt, the potentialities of gas were becoming manifest in directions that were undreamt of in his day, and the market price of residual products was soaring towards a value that made them a very considerable source of profit to gas companies. Mr Watson accordingly retired, and the Company set about finding a successor fitted to cope with the new condition of affairs. The history of the last eleven years proves how fortunate they were in their quest. Selkirk is a smaller place than Stirling, but from it they got a manager who is recognised as one of the leading men in his profession. Mr James D. Smith, like Mr Watson, belongs to a family of gas engineers, and under his management the Stirling Gas Works have been revolutionised, as well as re-constructed. Like sensible men, the Gas Company—which has always had during its 83 years of existence several of the best business "heads" in the community on its directorate—appreciated a good man when they got him, and with a free hand Mr Smith has worthily justified the confidence reposed in his abilities. Under his management the Works have been practically rebuilt, until now there is not a superior gas manufactory in Scotland. All this has been done without costing the shareholders a penny or curtailing the annual dividend one iota, and now the possession of shares in the Stirling Gas Company is not only far and away the finest and safest investment in the district, but is as good as can be found in Scotland. A few figures will easily demonstrate this. In 1825, the year of the formation of the Company, the share capital was £6200, which is less than the profit earned last year; now the capital is £82,000. Then in 1845 the annual make of gas was 4½ million cubic feet, last year it was 130 millions. Further, in 1846 the annual profit was £461, with the price of gas at 6s 8d per 1000 feet; last year the profits were £6500, with the price of gas 2s 10d. When Mr Smith came to Stirling, hand labour was the only kind employed at the works, now they are fitted up with machinery of the most efficient modern type, which is not only largely employed in the manufacture of gas, but in many other ways. Cookers, gas engines, penny-in-the-slot meters, incandescent burners, the manufacture of residual products—all were non-existent when Mr Smith took over the duties of manager eleven years ago. Now these are the great profit-producing assets of the Company. Last year the total gas consumers numbered 6476, and the huge sum of £4272 was collected from 2316 slot meters. The number of cookers in use is 2700, and this is a branch of the business which, along with gas fires, heating apparatus, and gas engines, is steadily increasing. And the end in this direction is not yet—not by a long way. When Stirling was full of amateur gas experts a dozen years ago, who prophesied the early demise of the old light in view of the advent of electricity, the late Lord Kelvin stated that there was a great future for gas. Did the local experts endorse this? Not they. "Oh," they remarked, "Lord Kelvin is only a scientist, and knows nothing about gas." They were quite right. He didn't know anything about gas—their kind of it—but he knew what he was talking about. He and some of the local experts are now in their graves, but his reputation lives, whilst they are forgotten. The history of the last dozen years has proved there was a great future for gas, and both the Stirling public and the Stirling Gas Company have got the advantage of it in the interval, though the former would have reaped a still greater benefit had they acquired the works when they had the opportunity.

As everybody knows, or should know, gas is produced by burning a certain kind of coal, and collecting and storing for use what may be called the fumes, and after certain processes the gas is then measured in a large station meter, and passes into the gasholders. From this the gas passes through a governor, where the pressure is regulated, and on leaving the governor it passes into the pipes to the consumers. In gas manufacture various bye-products are recovered, namely, coke, tar, and ammoniacal liquor. The coke is the residue left in the retorts after the carbonization process of the coal is over, and after being quenched with water is ready for the market. The tar is sold to the chemical manufacturers, who distil various oils from the same, the residue being pitch. The ammoniacal liquor is distilled in the Gas Works in a special plant designed for the manufacture of sulphate of ammonia, which latter, being used for agricultural purposes, finds a ready market in the district.

The Gas Company have a show-room in Murray Place where all the latest and best cooking, heating and lighting apparatus are kept in stock and on view. The following are a few specialities which may be seen or had at the show-room, namely:—Gas cookers, quick cookers, boiling rings, boiling tables, hot plates, gas fires and stands, gas fire burners, radiators, upright incandescent burners, inverted incandescent burners, inverted and upright mantles, pendants, hall lamps, brackets, high pressure lamps (for inside and outside lighting), automatic lighters, pneumatic switches, globes of every description, shades, plain and fancy; gas irons, copper kettles, steel stew pans, steel steamers, copper boilers, instantaneous heaters, etc., etc.

View of St Ninians Work.

Section of Dipping Process—St Ninians.

ST. NINIANS CANDLE WORK—D. M'DIARMID & SONS.

Humble as the candle is compared with gas and electricity, as a means of lighting it has a history, beside which that of these forms of artificial illuminants is but of yesterday. Candles and candelabra are alluded to as far back as the time of Job, which is a good many thousands of years ago, but gas and electricity are modern inventions, and from a comparative point of view very recent at that. Many references are to be found to candles in both the Old and New Testaments, and also to candlesticks and candelabra, but it would appear that the latter were contrivances for supporting oil lamps rather than receptacles for holding candles. But there is plenty of internal evidence in the Scriptures to show that, whilst lamps were used in several ways as a method of illumination, the candle was essentially an indoor light, and a portable as well as a stationary one. Job says, "How oft is the candle of the wicked put out," whilst in Luke there is the parable of the woman and the ten pieces of silver, and "if she lose one piece doth (she) not light a candle and sweep the house, and search diligently till she find it."

Candles seem always to have been associated with religious rites, and were early introduced with symbolical significance in Christian worship. They are still so employed in the Roman Catholic and Greek Churches, and in the Church of England too in connection with certain religious festivals. But the numerous superstitious notions associated with candles and their lights had in all countries a more remote origin than the advent of Christianity, and they may be regarded as relics of the once prevalent worship of the sun and of fire. Numerous omens were and are yet taken from them in various parts of the world by the superstitious. In Britain a portion of the tallow rising up against the wick of the candle was called a winding sheet, and looked upon as a sure omen of death in the family, whilst a bright spark from the candle denoted that the party directly opposite was to receive a letter. Then windy weather was prophesied from the waving of the flame of the candle without visible cause, and lights that appeared to spring up from the ground or issue from a house and traverse the road or air by invisible agency, were termed "corpse candles," the route they took indicating the road by which the corpse would be carried for burial. The size and colour of the light denoted whether the fated person was young or old. Candles were also supposed to be efficacious before birth and after

death in warding off evil spirits, which were assumed to be lying in wait to injure souls on entering or leaving the world. Then we have Candlemas in its ecclesiastical meaning, though it is now a certain defined date of the year when some rents have to be paid. But in the Roman Catholic Church it is a time when processions take place, and when the candles required in the observance of the ritual of that religion are consecrated for the ensuing year. This is an interesting survival of the Pagan times. Before the days of Christianity the Pagans of ancient Rome were wont, on what is now Candlemas Day, to burn candles to one of their gods, and an early Pope seeing it useless, on the introduction of the Christian faith, to try and abolish a custom of such long standing among the people, turned it to account in the interests of the new religion by enjoining Christians to make a similar offering of candles to the Virgin Mary, this duty at the same time being supposed to have the effect of frightening the devil and all evil spirits away from the persons who carried the candles, and from the houses where they were placed.

Contrasted with many other industries, that of candle making is a simple process. Little or no machinery is employed, hand labour supplying what motive power is required, and the principles and methods of manufacture are still very much on the lines of those practised from the earliest times. Of course there has been progress, and a great deal of it, a wax candle as regards light giving being no more like the old tallow dip with rush wick than the moon is to the sun, but in other respects there are many points of similarity. People still talk of candles as if they were the guttering tallow "dips" of evil odour and dim, smoky flame, which the prehistoric savage made by dipping partly peeled rushes into melted fat, but the illuminant of the present day is a much superior article, scientists and manufacturers having within the last hundred years brought the candle to its present state of perfection. Until 1823 candles had been made by simply coating a hank of yarn with tallow, but nowadays much more is required than that to produce the best quality of illuminant. Plaited cotton threads coated with a solution now furnish a wick that gives a brilliant, smokeless, or very nearly smokeless, light, which needs no snuffing or cutting away of the burnt portion ; and the paraffin wax, of which the candle is formed, being of a hard consistency, melts very gradually, leaving no

Wax Candle Making—Craigs.

Dip Candles Cooling—St Ninians.

smell. The first candles were purely composed of tallow, then beeswax, palm oil, and other ingredients formed the necessary composition, and now the best candle is made of paraffin wax. Candles are made to any size and weight, and there are many kinds, from nearly the height and circumference of cricket stumps, and which are mostly used in churches, down to the small, thin half a foot long illuminant employed in household purposes. And should anybody believe that the candle has become an anachronism, this notion will be rudely shattered on learning the vast range of candles makers are called upon to supply. Prices Company, London, which surpass every other firm, manufacture 130 specified classes, 60 different qualities, and unnumbered variations of material, colour, lighting power, and time of burning—altogether some two thousand kinds and degrees of candles. Some of the forms that ornamental candles take are very graceful, there being Corinthian and fluted columns among them, Cleopatra needles, &c., and a peep into a manufacturer's catalogue opens one's eyes to the large variety of designs that can be utilised in the production of this modest lighting agency. Without multiplying varieties, it may be stated that the kinds that are most largely used in this country are tallow candles, paraffin candles, self-fitting candles, and carriage candles. The tallow variety was once the household light, but oil lamps, gas, electricity, and last but not least, penny-in-the-slot meters have largely taken its place, and now the tallow "dip" is mostly employed by tradesmen. Plumbers, shipwrights, and miners make large use of the "dip," which, besides being cheaper than the other varieties, is softer in composition, and therefore more adhesive, so that it will stand up by itself when stuck in a piece of clay or on a stone or iron, when a little of the grease is melted to provide a foundation. Self-fitting candles are provided with moulded bases and tapering bottom ends, so that they will screw into any candlestick or socket, and remain upright. Carriage candles are those used as lamp lights for horsed conveyances, and it is interesting to know that they have proved superior to oil lamps, the flame of which is more liable to jerk and go out. Years ago carriage candles were always employed as table lights at the houses of the gentry, as at that time they were composed of beeswax, which was a hard substance, and gave a brilliant light. Latterly, however, these candles ceased to be used for house illumination, being driven out by the more modern variety made from a composition of distilled palm oil and other ingredients, the whole going by the name of "stearine." Paraffin wax candles are, however, the most popular, and have a much bigger sale in their various forms than the others. This is a graceful-looking illuminant, and, being made of a hard substance, burns brightly and gives forth no odour, there not being the least smell of oil about it. Besides their other qualities, all candles have to be made with due regard to the temperature they may have to be used in, but they are hardened to such an extent that a human being will begin to melt much sooner than they will. When it is stated that candles are manufactured to resist a heat of 130 degrees before beginning to melt by the action of the temperature, it will be seen that they can endure a great deal of warmth. And this is necessary, because if they were easily susceptible to heat, they would begin to "sweat" and "run," and would soon lose their circular form in hot countries.

And now a word as to the only local firm that manufactures candles—the Messrs M'Diarmid, St Ninians. Long ago when gas was a novelty and very dear, and many years before that, the industry of candle making was carried on in Stirling, but it is fully a generation since it ceased to exist. Apparently the manufacturers—there were several businesses of the kind—could not or would not advance with the times, and as a result their trade languished and disappeared. In the village of St Ninians, however, it has thriven for a long time, and continues in a prosperous condition. About the middle of last century the late Mr George Pitblado was a manufacturer of candles, and to him came as apprentice Mr Duncan M'Diarmid, who in due course succeeded his employer as head of the business. Mr M'Diarmid was a native of Braco, but when four years of age removed with his parents to Stirling in 1847. In 1855 he entered the service of Mr Pitblado, and remained with him in the capacity of apprentice and journeyman for twelve and a half years. In 1868 Mr Pitblado died, and Mr M'Diarmid took over the business, which at that time was a smaller one than is the case now. Mr M'Diarmid, however, was young and of a persevering, energetic nature, and he extended his trade connection so much that in a short time he found the old premises of his predecessor too small, and was compelled to erect new works for himself. This he did off the main street, and whilst the establishment was large enough at the time, it has had to be extended since. When Mr

M'Diarmid was with Mr Pitblado, tallow or "dip" candles were the only kind manufactured by that gentleman, but his successor developed a new branch by entering upon the manufacture of composite or "stearine" candles, and followed this up by engaging in the making of the paraffin wax variety as it became popular. Now that kind is, as we have previously remarked, far more largely used than other varieties, and as Mr M'Diarmid's business grew he had to look out for more room to carry it on. This could have been got in St Ninians, but, for various reasons, he deemed it better to look for a place in Stirling, and found it in the old tannery in the Craigs, a portion of which he acquired in 1894. Here he removed the paraffin candle making part of the business, the dip or tallow candle manufacture being retained in the old premises at St Ninians Mr M'Diarmid, who was a popular representative of St Ninians Ward in the Town Council for many years, died in 1897, but the business continues to be carried on by his three sons, Thomas, Duncan, and John, who all give close personal attention to the affairs of the firm, and deserve the success that has attended them since their father's death. The Messrs M'Diarmid confine their trade to the home market, and have a large connection all over Scotland, and also in the north of England. Altogether there are only a dozen or so candle manufacturing businesses in Scotland, and only one further north than Stirling, namely, Aberdeen. Most of the other firms confine themselves either to tallow or the wax variety of candle manufacture, but the Messrs M'Diarmid make both. And not only that, but they do a considerable business in making cooking fats, dog "cracklings," ship launching lubricant, miners' "fat," machinery grease, &c., whilst a large sale in soap is also carried on.

And, finally, let us glance at the process of candle making. As we have remarked in the earlier part of this article, the manufacture of this humble illuminant is conducted very much in accordance with ancient principles, and carried out by methods largely similar to those employed by our forefathers. This is particularly the case with respect to tallow candles; the paraffin wax variety are manufactured by a more scientific process. In neither instance, however, is machinery employed. Steam certainly is required, but it is for melting the tallow; not for driving engines, of which there are none to drive. The machines employed, and they are numerous, are really adjuncts to the hand labour. In making a dip candle, the first process is to cut up and melt the tallow, which is procured

from butchers. After the melting, the liquid tallow is taken to the dipping machines, from which strings of wicks are suspended on frames, and as the machine slowly revolves, each string of wicks as it comes round is dipped into the tallow and drawn up again. A portion of the tallow adheres to the wick, and takes on a circular form, and the dipping process is repeated time after time until the candle is made. Of course, care is taken after each dip that the embryo candle is cool enough, but not too cool before it gets another "duck" in the tallow, else the liquid would not adhere. The process is following the principle of rolling a snowball, the candle getting bigger and bigger by taking on more tallow with every dip that it gets. The making of a wax candle is, however, carried out on more elaborate lines. The paraffin wax, like the tallow, requires to be melted in coppers, and has also to be of a certain temperature according to the time of the year, but instead of being "dipped," the wax candle is produced by a block tin mould. Into this mould the melted wax finds its way from a trough, and the wick being also ready, a twist of a lever is given, and the candles pop up "ready made" and all complete, to wait for packing. In order to secure the melted wax being kept at the proper temperature, there is what may be termed a water jacket round the moulds. The production of one of these machines, though it is operated by hand, is at the rate of about a couple of thousand candles per day, and as there are a number of machines employed, it can be guessed that the output of work is a pretty large one in the course of the year. And it is not decreasing, but rather the reverse, candle manufacture being one of these industries which is looked upon by the uninitiated as being threatened with extinction long ago, but is more flourishing than ever it was, and is likely to remain so. And in connection with candle making there is no waste. Any bye products that there are come from the melted tallow, and these are fully used in other ways, but mostly in what we have already described as "cracklings," which are made up in the form of "cheese." These are greatly relished by dogs, hens, and other domestic animals and fowls, and as a food stuff for this purpose the "cracklings" have a ready sale. St Ninians Candle Work has many a visit from dogs who scent a succulent morsel, and enter the premises with a frank demeanour, the wag of their tail and the glance of their eye indicating as plainly as words would do that they hope to be hospitably entertained before leaving.

STIRLING PERAMBULATOR WORKS—M'EWEN & CO.

"To the health and happiness of dear children, to the gratification of tender mothers, and to the assistance of faithful nurses, these products of thought, love, and labour are respectfully devoted."—Simmons.

It is but right, proper, and in the nature of things, that "his majesty"—the baby—should command the attention of artificers in the various branches of mechanics. That this despotic personage has received this attention, by one kind of worker at least, with ungrudging devotion as regards thought, skill, material, and time, these lines and illustrations will amply demonstrate. For all this attention and thought that have been expended for his comfort and health, baby has a strange way of showing his gratitude. For this seeming ingratitude, however, he will be forgiven. The child is unable to look back, like people of mature years, and call to mind what the children of half a century ago had to put up with. Take, for instance, the infant of the present day, ensconsed in its softly padded couch, supported on carefully adjusted springs hung on leather straps with rubber-tyred wheels, and hood or canopy to protect the occupant of the perambulator from rain, wind, or sun, and compare the vehicle with the old-fashioned box on wheels which formed baby's coach of bygone days—in which, to save the child from being bumped and shaken, it had to be half-smothered in pillows—compare this with the elegant ones of to-day, and we shall have an idea of the progress man has made in catering for the little mite.

In regard to the early history of the child's carriage we are very much in the dark, we suppose because the contemporary writers deemed "his majesty" and his belongings unworthy of record. There is no ancient lore on the subject; no Scriptural or historic reference, no pen pictures, hieroglyphic writing, or sculptured representation of how the Israelites, the Babylonians, or the inhabitants of early Rome conveyed their children from place to place before they were able to walk, or if they were ever taken out for an "airing" in any form of baby carriage. Probably in the highly civilised communities of the ancients, when cities seem to have been laid out much as they are at the present day, some variety of child carriage would be in use, but no evidence of it has survived in any form. From time immemorial children have been carried in people's arms, slung on their backs, or other parts of the carrier's body, or deposited in baskets suspended from the back of a horse or bullock. Then there is also the prehistoric Glasgow form of carrying an infant in a shawl wrapped round the body of the carrier. It is, however, within the recollection of living man that children were taken for their constitutional in a low set carriage on four wheels, the front pair being pivoted or made to work on a swivel, the same as in a lorry. This carriage was generally built of wood balusters, and had a draw pole in front, through which a stick was passed for the fingers to grasp. In England this carriage was called a hop-wagon. Occasionally, too, about this date—half a century ago—one would see a miniature stagecoach or carriage perambulating the parks and country lanes, but these were somewhat rare, and were only used by families connected with the coach-building trade. The mothers and nurses of these days also seemed to be more careful than those of the present day, for infants were not wheeled in a carriage till they were six or even twelve months old.

In the early Sixties, this hop-wagon was superseded by an invention of Mr Burton, of New Oxford Street, London. This was the three-wheel perambulator, which forms one of the illustrations to this article. Of these there were several designs in wood and wicker, some having flat backs, and others round backs, and latterly some in which the body was made so that it could be reversed for the child to look from or to the nurse. The aim of this design was to shelter the child from wind or rain from any quarter, thus allowing the carriage to be used later in the season, and even winter. Not infrequently these three-wheel perambulators were made to seat two children side by side, an arrangement most inconvenient for pedestrians, who found the path blocked by these very wide carriages. These perambulators were generally run on wheels having wood spokes and flat iron rims, though on the better class wire spokes were demanded, and a year or two later rubber tyres could be had as a handsome extra. The fashion of this three-wheel enjoyed the remarkable life of about two decades, when a light French-made wicker body was introduced. This carriage was mounted on four wheels, fitted with a hood at one end, and was called a bassinette, which is also illustrated. The reversible hood, now so common on bassinettes, was first applied to these carriages by Charles Thomson, Newington Butts, London. About this time Messrs M'Ewen & Co., Stirling, brought out

Wm. Clark M'Ewen.

Abbey Road Works.

a new hood, which caused an unprecedented demand for their manufactures. It was not long before the above design of body was made in a variety of materials, wicker, wire, wood (some solid, some balusters, and some of laths), steel ribs, and paper mache being the principal, and the shapes were endless—from ordinary flat bottoms and ends to canoe landau, and even fantastic shaped ones. A notable improvement in the bassinette shaped carriage was invented by Mr Simmons, of London, in the form of a steering arrangement. In this invention the front wheels were pivoted, and a connecting rod from the handles operated the movement of the wheels. Another improvement about this time was made on this style of carriage by Messrs M'Ewen & Co. This improvement was their justly celebrated draught excluder. This draught excluder is still fitted by them, though now in a greatly improved form. A class of body that became very popular about this time was introduced by Messrs M'Ewen & Co., and was made of walnut three-ply veneer. These veneers were specially imported by this firm from America, and the bassinettes commanded a large sale This is not to be wondered at, when one meets these "veterans" still in active service. Another design by the same firm was built of yellow pine, and had either hand-painted panels planted on the sides, or had floral designs painted directly on the body. These were of exquisite taste, and were much in vogue at the time. Still another improvement was the employment of suspension springs in place of the ordinary under carriage springs, and many inventors were on the qui vive about this time. Messrs M'Ewen & Co., however, were able to hold their already increasing market with their improved hammock-hung bassinette.

A few years after the introduction of the bassinette a type of child's carriage was made with shafts and two wheels. This was first built of wood, with straight shafts, and was without any upholstery ; these were called mail-carts. The idea was for children to wheel one another in them, but apparently they soon got tired of the game. Anyhow, the mail-carts were soon required fully upholstered in various materials, and with hood. They were soon also made in various materials—notably cane. This latter lending itself admirably to every variety of artistic effect. One of the most successful of this class of mail-cart was one invented and patented by Messrs M'Ewen & Co. in 1895. This cart had a phenomenal sale all over the British Isles. and many

makers of children's carriages in England made them under license. The firm inform us that only last week they received a communication from a customer, who had sent one to the Continent recently, saying that the mail-cart was so much thought of that he believed the sales had not even yet reached vanishing point. As showing the continued popularity of this carriage, Messrs M'Ewen & Co. are still selling it in a variety of designs, but one in walnut is particularly dainty and attractive.

The latest form of child's vehicle, however, is that popularly known as the folding mail cart, and came on the market about six years ago. In its simplest form, this carriage is just a folding carpet-seated chair, mounted on wheels, but within the last two or three years dozens of designs have been placed before the public. Some of these designs are now very ingenious and elaborate, and one made by Messrs M'Ewen & Co. is completely furnished with upholstery and hood. We may mention in this connection that several inventors had turned their attention to an ordinary full-sized folding mail cart, but though several types had been placed before the public, none of them enjoyed a long or a large sale.

Having traced the history of the developments of the "voiture d' enfant," we would ask the reader to follow us in an imaginary visit of inspection to the works of Messrs M'Ewen & Co , where the manufacture of these carriages has been carried on by them for the last twenty-seven years. The business was established by Messrs Banks Bros. in 1861, and about the same time a department for the making of perambulators was opened by Messrs J. Buchanan & Co., coachbuilders. Glasgow. This department they, however, relinquished some little time after. Messrs M'Ewen & Co. bought Messrs Banks Bros. business in 1881, so that the present firm may justly claim to be the oldest established concern in Scotland devoted to the manufacture of children's carriages. From the first they spared no effort or expense to give effect to every suggested improvement, and to give value for money. These efforts are so far appreciated by the public that their manufactures find a ready sale all over Scotland, north of England, and in Ireland. The firm also enjoys the appreciation of a large clientele in India, Canada, South America, South Africa, Australia. and New Zealand, and every few weeks one may see consignments of their goods packed in close cases for foreign ports leave their works. One of the most prized awards to the firm was one

Old Perambulator.

First Bassinette.

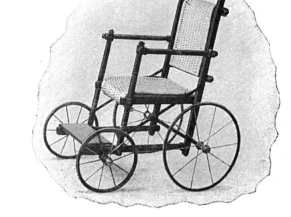

Latest Folding Mail Carts.

Latest Cane Mail Cart.

Up-to-Date Barouche.

received from the International Exhibition at Calcutta. This award was given for assortment and collection of model manufactures, especially designed for use in tropical climates. Abbey Road Works, the designation of Messrs M'Ewen & Co.'s premises, are situated on the river Forth, and extend to over two acres.

In this connection it may be mentioned that there are only some five perambulator manufacturing businesses in Scotland, the Stirling firm being the oldest. From the Abbey Road Works have emanated many improvements, which have been patented, and have been taken up by the trade all over the country.

In a perambulator factory the principal department is that in which the bodies are made, and is called the wood-working department. This department contains all the latest labour-saving machines, viz., circular and hand-saws, planing and spindle machines, turning lathes, sand papering and boring machines. The wood used is principally Russian white wood and American cypress, all of which is seasoned under cover, and without the aid of any artificial means. It is first held in stock some months as cut timber and then cut into the requisite shape for the bodies required; it is then allowed to season a second time, after which it is built up into the body of the carriage and receives a first coating of paint; then it is permitted to season a third time, so that it is just possible that wood is sometimes three, four, or even more years in stock before it goes out in its finished state. The wood stores are carefully planned, and have an abundance of light and air, so that any portion of the stock can be easily examined because of its careful classification. In this department, too, are made the bodies of the invalid carriages, which the firm despatch to all parts of the United Kingdom, besides rickshaws, which they send to South and East Africa. In a perambulator factory perhaps more than in any other work does system and order mean success. In Abbey Road Works there are six distinct departments, each under an experienced foreman.

We next inspect the spring and mount-making department; this department is popularly known as the smithy. It contains six hearths blown by fans, and completely fitted with Oliver hammers, bolt and rim-making accessories. In this department all the various springs, handles, and hood rods are made, as are also the mounting for the invalid carriages and rickshaws, which the firm

are frequently making. A special feature is the making of the rims for rubber-tyred wheels, as the firm make their own wheels.

From the smithy we pass to the wheel-making and engineering department. This department is replete with all the latest in drills, lathes (capstan and others), punches, buffs, and millers, and has, in addition, several novel special machines of the firm's own design and make. In this department may be seen the raw materials for the building up of the wheels, springs, and other metal fittings. One specially interesting machine is that for straightening the wires for wheel spokes and cutting them to the required length. A coil of wire is put to this machine, and it automatically takes up the wire, straightens and cuts it, without attention, till the coil is finished.

In the painting department is as much activity as in the others, and one sees here the bodies, springs, and other parts getting "colour." When varnished and sufficiently dry, bodies are handed to the next department, which is the upholstery or trimming department. This department is under the supervision of an experienced coach-trimmer, and the firm turn out all classes of work, from the cheap folding cart to the high-class article finished in velvet, with mountings of nickel plate, and ball-bearing wheels having tangent spokes.

Besides the baby carriages, the firm make a large range of invalid carriages in wood, wicker, etc., some having ball-bearing wheels and pneumatic tyres. The merlin chair, which we illustrate, is very popular, and is made much the same to-day as it was twenty years ago. Bath-chairs, as a type of these invalid carriages are called, were invented by John Heath of Bath rather before the middle of the eighteenth century, and many inventors came to the assistance with accessories to help the frail and convalescent to further appreciate the invention of Heath. The tyres claimed most attention, and improvements were made from time to time, notably among the workers being Reading, Scott, Mulliner, Carment, and others. M'Ewen & Co. have a great variety of embellishments and accessories suitable for their baby and invalid carriages, viz., rubber cloth hoods, stop joints (for allowing the hood to be kept half up when required), detachable and hinge shafts, umbrella holders, and canopies or awnings for summer use.

Rickshaws for tropical countries, delivery barrows for grocers, bakers, drapers, and others also claim their attention and skill. Perhaps some of our readers will remember that at the fire at Abbey Road Works a few years ago, some rickshaws, which were just ready for shipment to Africa, were destroyed.

The firm are continually improving and adding to their designs, and a fully illustrated catalogue is issued by them at the beginning of each year. "Edison was right when he said that man's ingenuity had not yet been exhausted. There will be, as the years pass by, endless improvements. tending to make human life (even that of children) more safe, healthy, comfortable, and refined."

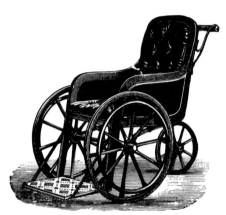

Oak Merlin, still as made 20 years ago.

In the Park.

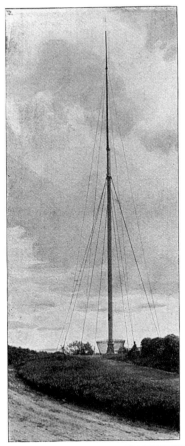

Alexander Calder.

MILTON MEAL MILLS—ALEXANDER CALDER.

Of all the cereals oats are the richest in flesh-forming substances and minerals, and stand second only to maize in the high percentage of fat. Scotch oatmeal is more coarsely ground than English oatmeal, but either kind is used in the making of porridge, brose, and oatcakes. Simply stripped of the husks, the grains are called groats or grits, and when crushed, are known as Emden groats. Occasionally the grains are rolled flat between heated rollers, which has the effect of partly cooking the starchy portions of the oatmeal, so that less cooking is necessary subsequently. This causes a change, also, in the fat of the grain, so that rolled oats keep longer without turning rancid than coarse oatmeal does. Porridge, oatcakes, brose, gruel, sowans, bladich, and budrum are each made from oatmeal, which also enters more or less largely into the preparation of other dishes.

Oats are cultivated extensively in all temperate climates, some sixty species being in use, these again being sub-divided into a large number of varieties, according to their several characteristics, the yield varying considerably, by reason of soil, etc., the weight per bushel also varying from 35 to 45 lbs., the meal product being about half the weight of the oats. The acreage of land under oats in Scotland last year was 951,011, and to this total Stirlingshire contributed 18,369 acres. The total produce of oats in Scotland in 1907 was 4,385,912 quarters, of which Stirlingshire produced 91,536 quarters; and the average yield per acre was—Scotland, 36.89 bushels: Stirlingshire, 39.87, as against 37.27 in 1906, and 38.72 in 1905. Ayrshire last year stood highest in extent of acreage, the number of acres under oats being 43,946, with a total produce of 243,412 quarters; the average yield per acre being 44.31 bushels, as against 48.01 in 1906, and 49.16 in 1905. The average of the ten years 1897-1906 was—Scotland, 36.38 bushels; Stirlingshire, 38.67; Ayrshire, 46.14.

Some years ago the milling industry was a much more extensive and important one locally than it is to-day, the number of meal mills in operation being greater, and the quantity of grain dealt with being considerably larger. The diminution has been brought about through various causes, some of these being the introduction of more modern machinery and equipments; the substitution of steam, and even electricity, as motive power in place of the cumbrous overhead—though very picturesque—water wheel; the transference to the larger centres of much of the marketing; as well as the combining of other industries with that of milling, this leading to the erection of more extensive premises, and necessity of greater facilities for railway transport. Some people go the length of asserting that the consumption of "parritch, Scotia's halesome fare," is not so great as it was a generation or two ago, and that this accounts in no small degree for paucity of trade amongst meal millers. Be that as it may. it is gratifying to know that a not inconsiderable portion of our population continue to pin their faith to the belief that oatmeal porridge is not only a wholesome article of diet, but one from which the body can derive a considerable amount of nutrition and other benefits. It is also a cheap food, and while in some quarters—particularly amongst a section of the poorer working classes—it is being discarded, its value seems to be becoming more appreciated amongst the wealthier.

Having thus entered somewhat minutely into the matter of oats generally, let us now turn to the processes by means of which the oatmeal is prepared for domestic consumpt. the methods here spoken of being those adopted by Mr Calder at Milton Mills. Mr Calder, it may be remarked, has now been engaged in the milling trade for forty years. He is a native of the parish of Chapel of Garioch, Aberdeenshire, and served his apprenticeship at Mill of Wartle, Rayne, and. after being engaged at other mills in Aberdeenshire, he came to Milton Mills some thirty-one years ago, for twenty-seven of which he was subtenant of Mr Muirhead, farmer. who held a lease of the mills, which form part of the estate of Sauchie, and are driven by water power, conveyed from the Bannock Burn by means of a lade diverted at Chartershall, and running through Milton Bog and dam. At the mills a number of operations besides that of meal milling are carried on, there being fitted up a threshing machine: pot barley stone or mill; a bruising machine, for the preparation of oats, barley, etc., for horse and cattle food; a breaking machine, for oats, Indian corn, beans, etc., also for feeding purposes.

Mr Calder contends that the oatmeal produced at Milton Mills—and which finds ready sale in Stirling and immediate vicinity—will compare favourably with any quality to be met with in Scotland save Midlothian, which, as is well

Milton Meal Mills.

known, holds premier place in general estimation. As he devotes his attention almost exclusively to the milling of oats for meal, it may readily be surmised that the necessary operations will receive the most careful supervision on the part of Mr Calder, and this, as already mentioned, finds return in the appreciation of his manufacture amongst his customers. In the milling of flour he does not engage, and, indeed, comparatively little of this is carried on now locally.

Having selected his oats, and taken delivery, the miller has to see to their being dried thoroughly before anything else is done, and at Milton Mills this operation is performed with the utmost care. The fuel made use of by Mr Calder for heating the kiln is anthracite coal from Millhall Colliery, and the grain is spread on perforated metal plates immediately over the heating chamber, and turned three times during the course of drying, so as to secure that it should be thoroughly dry to the core. After being cooled, the oats are conveyed to the shilling mill, where, after passing through riddles and sieves, in order to the removal of anything of an injurious nature that may have found its way amongst them, they are passed through the shilling stones, where the sid or husk is removed, and, passing on to scree, as it is called, all corn scree or dust is taken out. Next, passing through fanners, the sids or oathusks are separated from the groats, as the husked oats are now termed. Sometimes this operation is repeated, in order that every particle of dust or fibre may be removed, and the groats are passed on to a fine sieve, which ensures further separation. This operation is so performed that, by means of the employment of wires, any cereal other than groats, such as beans, peas, wheat, or barley, that may have been among the oats is prevented from going further. The groats are now ready for the grinding or meal stones, and when the grist (or size of meal particle) has been fixed, they are passed between the stones, and through a sieve, and then we have the oatmeal ready for delivery to the dealer.

It may be matter of interest to know that at Milton milling has been carried on for several centuries, Beaton's Mill (so termed from the fact that the then miller was named Beaton), about a hundred yards from Milton Mill, and rendered historic from its having been the scene of the murder of King James III., after the battle o Sauchie Burn in 1488. The foundation of the present cottage (erected in 1677) formed part of the original Beaton's Mill, and at the north gable is still to be seen the position of the water wheel, and water-worn stones may also be observed. The rising ground at the south end of the cottage is known as the Shilling Hill, and here, presumably, the groats and husks were spread out, the latter being operated upon by the wind and artificial aids in the process of separation. Although still retaining the name of Beaton's Mill, it is many a day since milling operations were carried on, the work being transferred to the building now occupied by Mr Calder.

Almost adjoining Beaton's Mill stands a building presently occupied by Mr Warner, wood worker and turner, which was formerly the property of the Stirling Incorporation of Bakers, and where the flour made use of by them was milled. This was discontinued, however, by them over thirty years ago.

King Street Warehouse.

Dumbarton Road Warehouse.

GRAHAM & MORTON, STIRLING AND FALKIRK.

Our notice this week in connection with the industries of Stirling is devoted to that of the old established and well-known firm of Graham & Morton. The business was founded as far back as 1830 by the late Mr William Graham, one of a Stirling family, in a small shop in Baker Street, but a few years later he built himself new premises in King Street, and it was in 1844 that Mr David Morton, then a young man (who had served his apprenticeship at Cupar-Fife, and is still alive and enjoying good health) came to him as an assistant. He was made a partner in 1861, and for the next ten years was instrumental in extending the business jointly with Mr Graham, the latter retiring therefrom in 1871. Although the designation of the firm remains the same, the partners (sons of Mr Morton) now are —Messrs Robert, David L., and Thomas M. Morton.

That the firm is a very enterprising one is well-known to the residents of Stirling and district, and the town has some reason to feel proud of being the headquarters of a business so widely connected and bearing such a respected name. But though now a large concern, with offshoots in many directions, it originated from a humble beginning, confined to one branch of trade— ironmongery. That of course is still a very important section of the business, but it is only one of the many departments that go to form the whole, and when "the man and the boy" who formed the staff of the first shop in Baker Street are contrasted with the 150 employees of to-day, it is immediately apparent that there must have been large developments. Some of these departures were made during the active regime of Mr David Morton, senior, but it is since the present head of the firm, Mr Robert Morton, assumed control that the chief progressive strides have been made. In Mr Morton, senior's, time upholstery was certainly carried on in a small way, but nothing approaching the scale of the firm's undertakings in that line nowadays, and other branches have been added that were unthought of a quarter of a century ago. In one particular, however, the old firm possessed a characteristic that is conspicuous by its absence now, and which only forms a kind of reminiscence. About forty years ago, when hand nail-making was the staple industry in St Ninians and Whins of Milton, Graham &

Morton employed between 20 and 30 nailmakers. The iron required was provided by the firm, and the operatives took it home and manufactured the nails, which were brought back to Graham & Morton, and sold by them to their customers. Many nails are still disposed of by the firm, but the days of the hand manufacturing industry have passed away, and machine made nails have superseded the old industry. A similar change has been witnessed in the production of furniture. For many centuries all requirements in this line were supplied by hand labour, and very fine work was produced under the old conditions, but here again machinery has supplanted the methods of the olden times, and all that survives of the original process is the beautiful specimens of hand carved furniture to be found in the residences of the old nobility and historic churches and castles. About thirty years ago furniture manufactories came into existence, and now machinery executes all classes of furnishing work in as perfect a fashion, and a thousand times more expeditiously than under the hand made system.

In their King Street premises the showrooms are devoted to the display of furnishing ironmongery, such as kitchen ranges, room grates and mantelpieces, the show of these comparing favourably with any city house. Large varieties of tiles, brass and iron bedsteads, cooking utensils, cutlery, travelling requisites of all kinds, brushes of every possible sort are also stocked here.

Special mention might be made of the silverplate room, where a finely selected stock is shown to the best advantage in airtight cases. All the best makers of sterling silver and electroplate are represented on the shelves of these cases, and customers must be difficult to please if they do not see many designs to satisfy them.

Large warehouses occupy the ground at the rear, right to the Back Walk, and they are filled with builders' and joiners' ironmongery, estate furnishings, dairy and farm utensils, domestic machinery, floorcloths and linoleums, etc. Specially constructed cellars, with fire-proof doors, are filled with oils of all sorts, methylated spirits, varnishes, and paints. Whilst accommodation is found for the making up and despatch of orders and the reception and unpacking of goods as they come from the various manufacturers, and the pricing of them.

The office work of the whole establishment is conducted at King Street, and gives employment to a large staff of clerks.

In Graham & Morton's ironmongery establishment will be found one of the largest and most varied stocks North of the Tweed. Workshops, fitted with machinery of various kinds, propelled by electric motor and gas engine, are under the charge of competent foremen, where railings and gates, fencing materials, etc., are produced. The repair and sharpening of lawn mowers is also extensively carried out. The firm's men are also conversant with the newest methods in heating by hot water, and are adepts in the building in of kitchen ranges, the tiling of interiors, etc. Amongst many specialties made are galvanised steel tanks for the conveyance by rail of live fish, the ideas for their construction having been supplied by the late Sir James R. Gibson Maitland, whose celebrated Howietoun Fisheries are in this neighbourhood. English and Irish Fisheries send to Graham & Morton for their tanks, as it is generally admitted that they are more carefully made, and stand the tear and wear of long railway journeys better, than other makes. Electricians are employed also for the erection of telephones, fitting up of bells and electric light. These premises were lit up by electricity 10 years before the town of Stirling adopted this form of artificial light.

But it is during the last 12 years that the greatest advance has been made by the firm. Although they have always done upholstery work, the complete house furnishing did not receive the attention it now does until they acquired the warehouses adjoining Drummond's Tract Depot at Dumbarton Road. They recognised that a warehouse where furniture of a reliable and up-to-date kind could be procured was much wanted in Stirling and district, and they have successfully catered for it. The necessity for keeping a large stock has been warranted in the support given by a wide circle of customer as goods are sent to all parts of the kingdom, and quantities are shipped abroad. The great variety of furniture kept at their Dumbarton Road warehouse (including a large reserve stock held at their factory) is such that the most cultured taste can be satisfied. A very interesting suite of specimen rooms is also shown, comprising hall, dining-room, drawing-room, and

bedroom. These are constantly being changed to show furniture belonging to different periods. In their carpet saloon, considered one of the best of its kind in Scotland, there are displayed Oriental and British carpets, art squares, tapestries and silks for draperies, besides curtains of every possible kind, as well as blankets and napery.

The display in the Dumbarton Road windows (the contents being constantly changed) of artistic furniture of reliable quality at moderate prices, attracts the attention of many more than the residents of Stirling and neighbourhood. The firm and their principal assistants make regular visits to London and other centres, and are thoroughly up-to-date in their purchases.

Ten years ago there came into the market the large mill at Burghmuir which had been used for carpet and tweed manufacturing, but owing to the death of the principal partner of Messrs John Paterson & Co., it was disposed of, and secured by Messrs Graham & Morton, and adapted to the wants of a thoroughly equipped cabinetmaking and upholstery business. With first-class men as "heads" of departments, they are enabled to turn out goods which will compare favourably with any other manufacturer. The buildings at Burghmuir enclose a square, in the centre of which is erected a large shed, where a stock of all classes of hard wood is kept, such as oak, mahogany, walnut, birch, teak, and pitch pine, as well as several kinds of soft wood. In the cabinet shop are many labour-saving machines for sawing, planing, moulding, etc., these being driven by gas engine power. The men are employed in making up sideboards, bedroom suites and beds, chair frames, mantelpieces, and fitments of various sorts. A specialty in this section is that of repairs to antique furniture, variety of inlays being kept for the treatment of old pieces. Although a large number of polishers are required by the firm for the various articles of furniture produced by themselves for sale, this department is largely taken advantage of by customers who wish their own work in marquetry, poker work, carving, etc., French polished.

The upholstery department is an important one, in which a large staff of skilled workmen are engaged in the making up of Chesterfield settees, lounge, easy chairs, etc., also in decorations and artistic draperies, which again give employment to a number of sewers (under an experienced forewoman), who are also employed in making

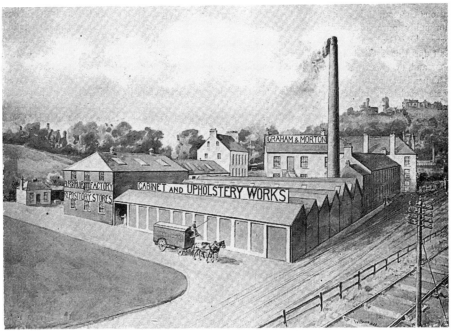

Burghmuir Factory, from the Railway.

One of G. & M.'s Furniture Vans.

up slip covers, window blinds, etc. In these days of discussions on insanitary bedding, and the revelations thereon, it is satisfactory to know where thoroughly pure and well made articles can be procured. Graham & Morton employ a special staff for this section of their upholstery department, and every care is exercised to provide only dependable material in the making up of mattresses, bolsters, pillows, etc. An important machine for the purpose of carpet-beating was introduced a few years ago, and the increasing demand for its services has shown how satisfactory the results have been.

Another department which has assumed large proportions is that of "goods on hire." Originating with the Stirlingshire Militia and Volunteers going into camp many years ago, a request was made that the officers' tents should be provided with equipment on hire, and this arrangement has been continued ever since. This led on to the catering for garden parties in the matter of marquees, tents, lawn chairs, &c. Householders and hotelkeepers requiring extra accommodation for guests have found it suitable to take advantage of Graham & Morton's hiring department.

One of the departments which has developed to a very large extent, and which requires a great amount of attention, is that of "removals." Having a number of special men, whose time is entirely devoted to the carrying out of this work, an amount of satisfaction is obtained by clients which is not possible where unskilled labour is employed. The plant for this purpose consists of 22 special vans, of various kinds, for road or rail. The haulage used is varied. We produce a photograph taken by a customer whilst one of Graham & Morton's vans, drawn by a steam motor, was passing through Kirriemuir.

The removal business has led to the firm acting as house agents, and they are always prepared to supply complete information regarding available houses to those in want of a residence. Whilst those families who find it necessary to store their furniture for a period are catered for by excellent storage accommodation in large warehouses, carefully ventilated, and where provision is made for heating by steam during winter weather.

About 18 months ago, owing to representations made to the firm that a branch establishment at Falkirk would meet with success, they secured part of a block in a prominent thoroughfare there, adapting it to the needs of a first-class furniture

warehouse, and they have the satisfaction now of that success being realised. The inhabitants of Falkirk, Grangemouth, and neighbourhood have shown their approval of the step taken by giving it a full measure of the support anticipated.

In conclusion, it is interesting to note that, were their various places of business put together into one building, it would bear favourable comparison with some of the important London houses. The floorage space alone amounts to 95.000 square feet, and the employees, many of whom have been with the firm for over 20 years, number 150.

The firm are delighted to show any desirous of looking over their premises, which are full of interest to most people, and are also pleased to forward illustrated catalogues, which give some idea of the extent of business undertaken.

A firm with so many ramifications as that of Graham & Morton must of necessity have a large clientile, and its customers are not only to be found over all the United Kingdom, but in many foreign climes. Business is done with the best families in the land, the firm sends furnishings to South Africa, and orders are executed for both the near and the Far East. Only recently goods were despatched to Constantinople, and also to far away Manchuria, which was made familiar to the British public as being the scene of the chief operations in the Russo-Japanese War a few years ago. With few exceptions, confined to the Metropolis and the more important cities, there is not a larger firm of the kind in the country than that of Graham & Morton, Stirling, and not one whose business connections range over a wider radius. And in one respect at least there is no firm that takes a more honoured place. We refer to the business training given to its apprentices. As everyone who takes any interest in the matter is aware, one of the great complaints regarding commercial and industrial training nowadays is the apprentice question. Under modern conditions there is great division and subdivision of labour; a department is a business in itself, and an apprentice is very often kept at one branch and gets no opportunity of acquiring a grasp of the whole elements of his trade. This charge cannot be laid at the door of Graham & Morton, Stirling. Every apprentice entering their service gets a thorough grounding in all the details of his business, even being put to a stool in the counting-house for a time, and it is his own fault if he leaves the establishment without a complete knowledge of the ironmongery trade. If he is willing he is encouraged in every way to make himself efficient by going through all the departments, and when he leaves to make his way in the world, the fact that he can claim to have been trained in the Stirling firm under notice is a valuable asset to him in the securing of employment. Graham & Morton maintain the happiest relations with their numerous servants, and many former "hands," who now occupy important commercial positions at home and abroad, look back with pleasure to the time they spent in the employment of "G. & M.," Stirling.

Falkirk Warehouse.

Smiths' Shop.

Machine Shop.

Peter Nacnab.

John C. Macnab.

LOCKHART AND MACNAB,

ELECTRICAL AND MECHANICAL ENGINEERS, STIRLING.

The subject of this week's sketch is the well-known firm of Lockhart & Macnab. The originators of this firm were Messrs J. & W. Grant, smiths and bellhangers, who started business in Broad Street in the year 1821. They removed from there some years later to Baker Street, and from thence to Murray Place, to a site now occupied by Messrs Virtue & Co.'s warehouses. On the demise of Mr Jas. Grant (the surviving partner), the business was taken over by Mr Alexander Lockhart and Mr Peter Macnab, and they shortly afterwards transferred their premises to the present site now occupied by the firm at 34-38 Craigs. Some years later Mr Lockhart died, and the business was carried on by Mr Macnab until 1906, at which time he retired, leaving his two sons, Mr Peter and Mr John Macnab, to carry on the business.

Whilst the firm was originally one that confined its operations to smith work pure and simple, it has changed with the changing needs of the times, and now the iron working element in the business takes secondary place to the modern electrical department. In not a few respects the electric has superseded the mechanical methods formerly used by smiths in various directions, but improved processes in the manipulation of iron have done more. The craft of the smith or worker in metals goes back to ancient times. Coppersmiths and silversmiths are referred to in the Bible, and the researches of antiquaries have proved that the knowledge of the art of working in iron was known to the Babylonians and Egyptians thousands of years ago. Certainly few relics of iron, as compared with bronze, have been found, but this is explained from tne fact that iron rusts more speedily, and a rare combination of favourable circumstances is required to preserve it intact. That being the case, the interesting question is raised of the uses the ancients made of the metal. Little remains to tell of the purposes for which they utilised it, but the fact that they did work in it suggests that they made use of iron in many ways of which we have no knowledge. Be that as it may, there are strong indications that Asia was in its iron age long before Europe, and Indian steel was greatly prized among the Greeks.

Though nations waxed and waned, the smith's craft came down the ages, and coming to this country, there is proof to show that iron was worked in Sussex by the Britons of Julius Cæsar's time. So far as is known the ancients had not the appliances of the present day, but that they could execute very fine work by their primitive methods of the hammer, the "block," and the forge is shown by the examples of their handicraft that are found in old historic buildings. Not to go outside our own burgh, the beautiful iron work round the Palace windows at Stirling Castle, made by the Sons of Vulcan in olden times, is a source of perplexity to present day tradesmen. It is all "hand done," and besides exhibiting the skill of the smiths of long ago, it must have been executed without the modern aids of punching, drilling, and shearing machines. These tools or implements are now indispensable to the trade, but they are creations of the last half-century or so. Up to that time the old methods were in use, with slight modification. The chief work of the smith up till then was the manufacture of locks and keys, the making of railings and gates, and the fitting up of bells for houses. Nowadays locks and keys are a branch of trade by themselves, and railings and gates, though still wrought by the smith to a furnished design, are now largely cast in foundries to specified patterns. As for the old mechanical wire-pulled bells, these are rapidly being superseded by the electric bell, where a button only requires to be pressed instead of a handle being pulled, as in the old style. In this connection it is interesting to relate that some mechanical bells which were fitted up eighty years ago by the firm of J. & W. Grant, and were in use for nearly fifty years, were overhauled and extended by Mr Peter Macnab shortly after starting business, and were only superseded recently by a complete installation of electric bells fitted up by the present firm.

The introduction of electric light for commercial purposes only dates back between twenty-five and thirty years, and was utilised at first for street illumination. The subsequent invention of incandescent or "glow" lamps ren-

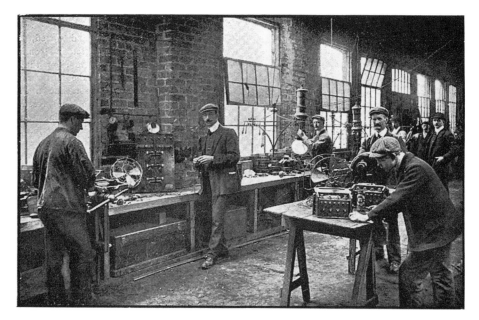

Electrical Department.

Electric Fittings Showroom.

dered electricity applicable as an illuminant for domestic purposes, and since then many improvements have followed, alike in regard to the use of the current for lighting and motive power. The last dozen years have witnessed the wide application of electricity in these directions, but the end is far from having been reached in this respect, and in the future this great natural force will be more largely employed than has yet been the case. So far as Stirling is concerned, the firm of Lockhart & Macnab, smiths, was the first to see the potentialities of the new era that was being ushered in, and with the introduction of the electric light into the town by the municipality, the firm struck out a "new line," and added to their business the important department of electrical contracting, which includes carrying out complete installations of power, lighting, heating, ventilating, etc. That the new departure of ten years ago has proved successful is shown by the large connection Messrs Lockhart & Macnab have built up in Stirling district and far beyond, and though the smith business is still extensively carried on, it is now secondary in importance to the electrical branch. More than that, it may be stated that the firm is the only private one in the district that has trained electricians on its staff.

Amongst others the following contracts have been executed by Messrs Lockhart & Macnab:— Drummond's Tract Depot (motors and lighting), also lighting into Messrs Virtue & Co.'s warehouses, Stirling Public Library, Royal Infirmary, light and power at Messrs D. & J. MacEwan, merchants; also power into Messrs Adam & Yates, cork factory, where an interesting electrically driven system of dust-extraction may be seen. The following churches were lighted throughout by the firm—Allan Park U.F., South U.F., St Mary's Roman Catholic, and the Peter Memorial Church, the fittings of which were executed in wrought-iron and copper by the firm, from special designs supplied by the late Mr Stevenson, architect, London. Messrs Lockhart & Macnab have a running contract with the Electric Supply Corporation of London to carry out all installation work required at Dollar, and have executed practically all the lighting there. A large number of contracts have likewise been carried out at Alloa by the firm, including the West U.F. Church, New Liberal Club, Burgh Chambers and

Court-House, Station Hotel, also the extensive warehouses and offices of Messrs John Paton, Son, & Co., Ltd., etc. They have also carried out motor wiring contracts at Kilncraigs, Alloa, aggregating 300 horse-power, and lighted up a large woollen factory at Peterhead. The firm make a speciality of mansion-house work, including wiring, supply and erection of fittings, accumulators, and generating plant, and have lately carried out complete contracts at Kippenross House, Leckie House, and a large extension of lighting, bells, and telephones at Kinloch Castle, Isle of Rum, and lighting and bells at Auchentroig mansion. At the new "Observer" Printing Works, Stirling, an up-to-date system of wiring and controlling has been erected by the firm for the motor installation, consisting of about 40 horse-power. Electric motive power is now universally used in modern factories and workshops, the old system of power transmission through shafting being practically obsolete. Electricity is also now extensively used for domestic purposes, and the following are several of the uses to which it is applied, viz.:—Cooking, heating, dish-washing, boot-brushing, ironing, hair-dressing, massage, and last, but not least, lighting. The greater or lesser brilliancy of the light from illuminants such as gas, oil, and candles depends on the greater or less amount of oxyge1 (which is the one ingredient in the atmosphere necessary to sustain life) which they abstract from the air. In the production of light these forms of illuminants use up oxygen; furthermore, in combination with hydrogen in the burning flame, and with carbon (the particles of which, whe1 raised to incandescence, give out light, forming at the same time a vapour which is dispersed through the air, condensed in the form of water, and deposited on the walls, ceilings, carpets, books, pictures, etc.), carbonic acid gas is also formed and inhaled to the detriment of health. One gas jet in a room will consume more pure air in one hour than five human beings, hence the desirability of electric light.

Since the invention of the carbon-filament lamp by Edison, many improvements have been made (especially during the last five or six years) in lamp construction and efficiency, the latest being the Psram Yungsten lamp, its efficiency being rated at 1.2 watts per candle-power, as against 3.5 watts of the carbon-filament lamp. This remarkable economy in consumption (practically

70 per cent.) now brings the use of electric light within the reach of all.

But whilst the firm also employ a large staff of fitters, smiths, and sheet-iron workers for the manufacture of shop sunshades, grills, ornamental gates, sign-brackets, etc., likewise for overhauling and repairing of all classes of weighing-machinery, from weighbridges down to apothecaries' scales. The workshop is 130 feet long by 30 feet wide, and the machinery is electrically driven. To show the good feeling that exists between employers and employees, it is interesting to note that the average period of service of the men is about fifteen years.

VIRTUE & COMPANY,

IRONMONGERS AND FURNISHERS, STIRLING.

The business that comes under notice this week is not only among the oldest in the town, but also one of the largest and most flourishing. The firm of Virtue & Co., as it at present exists, represents an old established concern, though since its foundation it has not enjoyed an unbroken line of family succession in regard to its principals as some other local businesses have done. In the historic aspect we have to go back to the year 1841, when the business was started by Bailie John Christie, who was an ironmonger purely and simply, and never dreamt of the changes that have since taken place in connection with the enterprise which owed its inception to him. There are many yet in Stirling who remember well of the Bailie, but there are even more to whom his name is but an indistinct memory, or who never heard of him, and in these circumstances the following biographical sketch of one who played a prominent part in his day in the public life of Stirling may prove interesting. Drysdale's "Old Faces of Stirling" says : —

Born in Stirling in 1817, the eldest of a family of ten, after receiving a sound education he (Bailie Christie) entered the service of Mr William Graham, who had his ironmongery shop at the foot of Bank Street. He was a most ingenious youth, and his reading was not only of an omniverous character, but it may actually be said that he devoured books, and applied himself with indomitable courage and industry to the study of the various sciences. The construction of a microscope was a feat which gave him immense gratification. Phrenology was another of his studies, and his acquaintance with this subject pointed him out as a suitable assistant when, by permission of the head of the Crown, a cast was taken of Allan Mair, the last person executed in Stirling.

The limits of Stirling being too small for Mr Christie, he got employment in Walsall, Staffordshire, where, an election taking place, and he being an earnest worker in the cause of reform, he wrought hard for that party, having Mr Cobden and Mr John Bright among his colleagues. Returning to Stirling in 1841, Mr Christie commenced business in a shop which stood where Messrs W. & A.

Johnston, King Street, have their drapery establishment, removing in 1854 to handsome and commodious premises in Murray Place, which had not till then a single shop with any pretensions to beauty, and with only a few decent buildings.

Mr Christie first stood for the Town Council in 1856, and was returned third on the poll, there being no wards at that time. In 1861 he resigned his seat, having to go to Australia on business, but in 1863 he was again returned to the Council, and afterwards promoted to the Magistracy. To Mr Christie is due a great part of the credit for the restoration of Cambuskenneth Abbey Tower, as also the alterations on the Guild Hall. His acts of kindness were many, most of them only known to himself ; he was always ready with advice or assistance, and it was one of his gentle traits that he took no offence when his counsel was not followed. In private life he was the most entertaining of companions. He died 1st December, 1881.

In King Street Bailie Christie's business so prospered that extension of premises became a necessity, and that was why he removed to 14 Murray Place. That was 54 years ago—a lifetime and more in many cases—but when one looks at the still commodious and fine shop and warehouse, and compares it with its modern neighbours, one can readily see that in these early days, when there were not so many fine premises in Stirling as there are now, the building in Murray Place must have appeared an exceedingly handsome one to the townspeople. Even yet Messrs Virtue & Co.'s property is well to the front of premises more recently modernised ; and it exists without alteration from the period when it was specially designed for the hardware trade. When he removed from King Street to Murray Place, Bailie Christie assumed his brother James as partner, and the firm was known as J. & J. Christie until they retired from business, which both did about the same time.

In 1869 the business was disposed of to Messrs George Virtue and Duncan Ferguson. The former belonged to Causewayhead, and the latter was a Stirling man, and had been an apprentice with J. & J. Christie. The new firm of Virtue &

Ironmongery Warehouse, 14 Murray Place.

Ferguson carried on the business under that title for ten years, when the latter retired, and Mr Virtue became the sole partner. In 1876 he had purchased the premises which had formerly been rented by the firm.

Twenty years later, in 1889, saw a further change in the proprietorship of the business, when Mr Virtue decided to retire and enjoy a well-earned leisure. Negotiations were then entered into and concluded between him and Messrs M'Cririck, Watson, and Meiklejohn, three young ironmongers well-known in the town of Stirling, who had had a local training, and assumed possession and control of the business. With such an influx of young and increased energy, it was natural that the steady old concern should show new life, and prove itself capable of extension. This is what happened. A new chapter in hardware seemed to be opened, and the business increased by strides. Under the new regime trading was pushed further afield, representatives worked up the country, and the surrounding districts were made tributary to the rising firm. Connections were established in Kinross-shire, Clackmannanshire, Perthshire, Argyllshire, and Stirlingshire, and are maintained and strengthened up to the present time.

Still following the fortunes of the establishment as it has been, we find the hand of time working changes. In 1893 Mr M'Cririck was struck down by fatal and lingering illness, and died several years after, while Mr Watson was also carried off in the prime of manhood in 1898. This left Mr Meiklejohn sole surviving partner, and since then the business has been conducted solely under his supervision, and also under the old firm name of Virtue & Co.

While the business still embodies its original characteristics as an ironmongery establishment, this still being one of its leading features, its present composition shows a great contrast to its small beginnings in 1841. New departments have been added, and the firm is now as wide in repute in respect of house furnishings and removals as it is in the field of hardware. A remarkable feature of the trade of Stirling is the development of house furnishing. The older cabinet-making shops of the town have nearly all ceased to exist. In the present aspect of things Virtue & Co. claim to take a lead. They were quick to recognise that the days of the provincial cabinet-maker, like the weaver, were numbered, and that

the great city factories had now assumed control of supply. Securing premises in the rear and adjacent to their warehouse at 14 Murray Place, and putting themselves in touch with the leading factories in the West of Scotland and England, they started a new line of business, which has had a remarkable development, but we shall leave details to the treatment of the particular department.

The business as at present existing is conducted under four distinct sections, and each section must give in its own account at the end of each financial year.

First, Ironmongery or Hardware.—This, the parent department of the business, is conducted in the old premises, 14 Murray Place, a front view of which is given.

In addition to the retail branch, a large business is done wholesale throughout the country. While the great bulk of merchandise is sent per rail, the immediate vicinity, to within a radius of ten miles, is served weekly, and sometimes more frequently, as occasion may demand, by the firm's own vans, which deliver orders free of charge. Virtue & Co. have the patronage of all classes of the community. They number amongst their clientele the principal estates in the counties mentioned, and have an extensive connection throughout the country amongst hotels, hydropathics, and public institutions.

On the ground floor, to the left, as we enter is the Builders' Department, showing row after row of shelves from floor to ceiling, and laden with innumerable parcels, each bearing outside a sample of what is inside. Here are products of Birmingham in particular, the chief producer of brassfoundry, and here is brassfoundry of every conceivable description—mountings of great variety in pattern and many grades of vertu, suitable for every requirement in the building and cabinet trade. This department also embraces locks, and one can hardly name a kind or size of lock that the firm does not keep on hand, and bearing in mind the immense variety and different sizes in which these are required, we get some conception of the stock carried. How many packets of screws are on the shelves we had better not risk a guess. They are too numerous.

On the right we have the Cutlery and Electro-Plate Department. Here we find the chief industries of Sheffield represented. One of the

Furnishing Warehouse, 26-30 Murray Place.

Section of Drawing-Room Furniture.

large front windows is always devoted to the display of plate, and forms a great attraction. In this the firm do a large business, providing goods from the best manufacturers. The articles are kept in air-tight wall cases, and form an interesting and important corner. A great portion of plate is sold for wedding presents. The mind seems to run instinctively to this class of article in considering what to give as a gift. The stock is too varied for detail, but mention may be made of tea and coffee sets, silver trays and salvers, cake baskets, epergnes, entree dishes, candle-sticks, etc. Here is also an array of cutlery representative of the best forges of Sheffield. The firm make a speciality of cutlery, and are particular to mention the quality. All table cutlery is warranted Sheffield make. The pick of their quality, bearing the trade-mark "True," is made from hand-forged double shear steel, and is a perfect example of the cutler's handicraft. The handles are composed of finest ivory, an article which is a very important factor in ruling the market price of cutlery, of which it forms a part, the supply of first-class ivory seeming to be a diminishing quantity year after year. But cutlery of reliable make is also to be had at extremely low prices to meet more modest wants. Forks, instead of being an exact counterpart of the knife, are now almost exclusively supplied in nickel-silver and electro-plate. As against Sheffield manufacture there is the German product, and we only mention this in connection with razors, for which the Germans have a just reputation, more particularly in hollow-ground. There are pocket knives galore—the schoolboy's delight—and scissors, from the fine embroidery to the large cutting ones used by tailors and dressmakers; butchers' knives and steels, and bootmakers' knives, are some of the various kinds.

In the rear of this spacious saloon, in a central position, are shown modern examples of kitchen ranges on the open and close fire principle, conspicuous among which is the "Sunbeam" patent, and for which the firm is famous. A range of high grade, it is the daily pleasure of the mistress (or her cook) of many a household. Here, it may be opportune to mention, that the building-in of ranges is of the utmost importance, and Virtue & Co.'s men are acknowledged experts in this branch. They receive orders frequently for the attendance of their "range doctor" to put right a fickle cooker or cure an obdurately smokey vent. Alongside these is shown various sizes of a useful

kitchen labour-saving appliance—the knife-cleaner—suitable for family, hotel, and institution use. To the right the wall shelves are devoted to carpenters' tools, such as planes, edge tools, saws, braces, etc. Opposite these is an array of ordinary pots and saucepans, not particularly attractive as mere looks go, but most useful and indispensable articles, and for which there is a steady demand. But these are only a fraction of the large reserve stock stored in other premises. There, too, are galvanised buckets, and black and galvanised coal scuttles, all waiting a call to duty, use and abuse.

We may now turn downstairs or upstairs, but we shall elect to go up in search of the light. This is practically a replica of the floor we have left. It is splendidly lit by a continuous frontage of windows, and in the rear from the dome-shaped roof. In the windows referred to, and on an extensive platform, are arranged a large selection of oil lamps. The season for these is just starting, and the firm have already got delivery of a large stock. Where do they all go to? That is the wonder. In the days of electricity and gas the demand for this older method of lighting might be considered as in decline, but not so; and when the firm inform us that alone they dispose of some two thousand barrels of burning oil in a year, there is absolute proof that an enormous number of lamps must still be required. Although the country claims a large portion, still among townspeople the oil lamp has many supporters. The lamp trade is an important one with Virtue & Co. In connection with it the firm require to stock an immense quantity of glass, and at the beginning of a season the large quantity of cases containing this make a heavy demand on available space. These number thousands of dozens, and of course they cannot be squeezed into a corner. The main sources of supply are Saxony and Austria, from which countries the lamp glasses are shipped direct, and each country is an indication of the quality of glass.

We reproduce a photograph showing a corner of this flat devoted to grates and chimney-pieces, fenders or kerbs, and fire-brasses. The ironmonger, like the draper, is troubled with changes of fashion. The transition may not be so quick, but it is there. Grates must be shown in a variety of designs, but they change in character. Stock must display the characteristic of the times. Here we have a fine display of modern

Corner of Grate and Chimney-Piece Department.

Removal Van Ready for the Road.

fire-places, fine finished grates, and interiors, all in iron, brass and copper-mounted, and all brass. No fireplace is complete without tiles, and the department is overflowing with a wonderful variety of every conceivable shade of colour. There is in fact a tendency of these glazed and unglazed tiles, with their brethren bricks, to displace the iron fitment altogether, and take sole possession of the fireplace. They lend themselves well to variety of design and colour, and are very effective when carefully built-in by an experienced man. There are chimney-pieces in oak, walnut, and mahogany. Many of these are made in the firm's own factory, where it has special facilities for manufacturing these at the lowest cost, and carrying out clients' own designs. This department also represents much that is distinctly household hardware. There are coal boxes in wood and japanned steel, carpet sweepers—the Bissell and Ewbank—sponge and hip baths, toilet cans, wash-hand basins and stands, enamel ware of every kind. Trays, tin and copper goods in daily requisition for cooking and baking, such as jelly and pudding mouldings, cake and biscuit tins, pastry cutters, etc. Here, too, travelling requisites occupy a large space, and these include portmanteaux, overlands, brief, Gladstone, and kit bags in leading sizes. Brushes are plentiful, and brushes require careful buying, so much inferior material being often used in their manufacture. The firm is particular of the quality of their brushes, which include hearth and long brooms, bannisters, scrubbers, hair and cloth brushes, tooth and plate brushes, paint brushes, and other varieties in first-class quality.

In the basement, or third flat of this building, are stocked oils, such as linseed, colza, castor, whale, sperm, and paraffin oil, all of absolute purity, as well as paints, while apart we have heavier hardware, such as shovels, spades, and manure forks. These are but classifications, and under such there is the same apparently extensive variety, which makes an ironmonger's stock, such as Virtue's, a bewildering thing. Here are tons of fencing wire, plain and barbed.

Leaving this building by a passage shelved with cast-iron gratings, we enter a large store adjacent. In face of us we have a perfect stock of manilla binder twine, put up into trusses for farmers' present harvest use. Much has already gone out, and this too will disappear before the grain is all cut down. This is imported from America. The firm has supplied the same brand for years, and

it always brings back the old customers. Here too are many tons of galvanised and corrugated iron, so much used for iron roofing, and the firm are in a position to despatch large quantities at short notice. Shelves are filled from end to end, and from floor to ceiling, with hardware, such as saucepans, pots, and kettles, and equally prominent are tin goods. Milk pitchers of different sizes and kinds, suitable for dairy and carrying purposes, and also oil jars in all sizes. Space is valuable, and it is all utilised, so even among the rafters there are hay-forks and rakes, and also van shafts.

Only the low flat is devoted to hardware, and that above is part of the furnishing department, containing general stock of suites and bedsteads. It was this building which was so completely gutted by fire some twelve years ago.

Reference has already been made to the firm's introduction of house furnishing as a branch of their trade. This for some years was mainly confined to the sale of furniture and carpets, which were stocked in the upper flat of the building referred to in last paragraph. This was more or less an inconvenience, but the firm had to bide its time, and this time arrived three years ago on the expiry of leases which had been granted to the then tenants of their property at 26-30 Murray Place. With this opportunity Virtue & Co. themselves entered into occupancy of the premises. Some alterations were required to adapt them to their requirements. They had been let as three distinct shops, and it was necessary to throw the whole into one to give a spacious saloon, a necessity for the proper display of furniture. The frontage was also altered, giving one plate-glass window of about 30 feet, and other two of 10 feet each. Here in these magnificent windows, always tastily dressed and arranged, are brought before the passing public a changing show of the latest in furniture, bedsteads, upholstered goods, curtains, and draperies. Inside there is an ample stock for the most fastidious to choose from, all well laid out and neatly arranged.

We show a reproduction from a photograph of a portion of the showroom devoted to drawing-room furniture. There are drawing-room suites in beautiful frames of Chippendale and Sheraton design, upholstered in dainty fabrics, cabinets to match, occasional chairs in great variety, and writing bureaux. These suites are upholstered in their own factory. They carry a large range of upholstering materials in tapestry and silk, from which clients can choose to suit their own particular fancy in colouring. Turning, we are confronted by dining-room furniture, comprising large and massive sideboards in oak, made, as it is evident to anyone, from the finest selected timber, nicely figured, accompanied by an equally fine array of suites covered in leather, velvets, and morocco to match. Here too are mahogany sideboards and chairs, after the Queen period, to please the eye of the connoisseur. We are now face to face with an imposing number of bedroom suites, but we are assured this is not half the stock. It is only a selection of the best. We have them in plain and inlaid mahogany, plain and inlaid oak, satin and American walnut, and white enamel, with artistically carved panels and pediments, or the more severe lines of Sheraton. Before us is one in chaste "Adam" design, the wardrobe being 5 feet wide, which would make a bedroom as recherche as could be desired, and would make happy the bride about to assume the duties of housekeeping.

Proceeding downstairs, we come to the basement, where again there are bedroom and dining-room suites, hall furniture, and comfortable lounge chairs of the firm's own upholstering. The chief feature of this section is floor-coverings. Here are floorcloths and linoleums, plain, printed, and inlaid, the last of which is a rapidly increasing selling line, on account of its wearing quality, the pattern never becoming obliterated. Kirkcaldy is the chief source of supply for this popular material, but the best English houses also provide their quota. There are piles of carpets, embracing Scotch, Art, Brussels, Wiltons, Axminsters, and Orientals. This is a section which has developed with strides, and Virtue & Co. are a recognised carpet house. There is abundance to select from in every kind.

Hard wearing Scotch and Brussels, velvety pile Axminsters in exquisite colours and designs, and things wondrous from the Orient.

The Furniture Factory.—This is situated in Forth Street, and connected with their warehouse with private telephone. This is an indispensable adjunct of their furnishing section, and it gives them greatly increased facilities. Here is a permanent staff of cabinetmakers, upholsterers, and French polishers, but the factory is not equal to the full supply of the firm's requirements in furniture, and they make up particular lines in bedroom furniture in cypress, oak, walnut, and mahogany, for which they always have in hand a plentiful supply of seasoned timber. The factory is equipped with modern machinery of the latest description for cutting up timber, fret-sawing, and moulding. The power is derived from electric motors, of which there are two, driven by current from the Corporation Station, and they are found very satisfactory. The firm's men are always at call for every description of jobbing, such as laying linoleums and carpets. Here also are undertaken the cutting, sewing, and making of blinds and carpets, and chair slips, mattress-making, and every description of upholstery work.

Removals are another addition of recent years. The firm had heavy vans specially constructed, and these are engaged in an ever increasing trade. Their vans are well-known all over Scotland, and have travelled over both England and Ireland. This work is carried out by their own experienced men, and they have received many congratulations for the speedy, well-organised, and careful execution of the work. It is work requiring careful calculation in estimating, and watchful arrangement in carrying out. Associated with this is the storage of furniture in suitable premises.

THOS. MENZIES & CO.,

DRAPERS AND MILLINERS, STIRLING.

Our notice this week in connection with the industries of Stirling is devoted to that of the well-known firm of Thomas Menzies & Co., which is the oldest drapery firm in the town that has descended from father to son, as every other one which was in existence when it started has either passed away or changed in name beyond recognition. The business was founded in 1861 by the late ex-Bailie Thomas Menzies, in company with Mr Melrose, under the firm name of Menzies & Melrose, in the front portion of the present warehouse in King Street. After three very prosperous years, and in order to meet the ever-growing demands for space, they purchased a number of properties immediately in the rear of their warehouse, and erected thereon the present large and well-lit saloon, of which the accompanying photograph gives a very good representation. The firm prospered so much that in a few years they acquired another drapery concern in the town of Peebles, which Mr Melrose subsequently took into his own hands, leaving his partner in full and exclusive control of the Stirling business. Mr Menzies, it may be stated here, was, like a good many others who have founded businesses in Stirling, not a native of the town. He belonged to an old family connected with the Blackford district, and as a young lad went to Paisley to learn the drapery trade. His apprenticeship over, he came to Stirling to be an assistant with Messrs W. & A. Johnston, drapers, King Street, and after serving that firm a few years proceeded to Manchester to gain wider experience. In Cottonopolis he "foregathered" with Mr Melrose, and, both being desirous of striking out on their own account, they fixed upon Stirling as a suitable centre in which to start business. Mr Melrose is still alive in Peebles, but ex-Bailie Menzies, who found time to serve the public as a Town Councillor for over a decade, died fully a year ago, and the head of the firm is now his son, Mr James Menzies, who was associated with his father several years before the latter's death.

As in all other trades, there have been great changes in the drapery and millinery lines of business since the time of the foundation of the firm of Thomas Menzies & Co. To be a milliner nowadays is synonymous with being an artist. It requires an expert to combine the various colourings and materials into a harmonious whole,

and also taking into consideration its suitability for the lady who is to wear it. When ex-Bailie Menzies commenced business there were no Paris models, and no fashion magazines giving the latest Continental styles in dressmaking and millinery, by means of which the most out-of-the-world hamlet can now keep itself abreast of the times. In the sixties ladies came in and bought an untrimmed straw or felt hat, a few yards of ribbon, and some other odds and ends, and the whole was sent down to a woman who made a "speciality" of trimming hats, mostly in one and only style of her own, which was not a very serious operation. Everyone has heard of the church parade in Hyde Park, London, on Sundays, after the forenoon places of worship come out, when in fine weather ladies promenade through Hyde Park clothed in all their best plumage, to admire, and sometimes envy, and be admired, but in this connection it may not be so generally known in Stirling that about the middle of last century, when all the churches were, with one exception—Viewfield—on the hill, that the local ladies of the period had their after church parade. This took place on the high Back Walk, from the Guildhall past the Ladies' Rock, and round the outside of the cemetery back to Broad Street. Clad in their crinoline skirts of those days, it would be a difficult matter to get past two ladies abreast on the narrow road. The days of the crinoline have passed away, and the vagaries of fashion have been many since then, and we should think the ladies of 50 or 60 years ago would be as much surprised at the directoire dresses worn by our modern leaders of fashion, as the present day public were to see a young lady walking up Bond Street, London, not long ago, dressed in all the glory of her great grandmother's crinoline dress.

With reference to the working hours of shop assistants there has been as great a change as in anything else in the drapery business. In the pioneer days of the firm's existence there was no early Saturday closing, no Factory Acts which compel the workrooms to be cleared at a certain hour, and no monthly holidays. Ex-Bailie Menzies was one of the earliest advocates of the 5 o'clock Saturday closing movement in Stirling, and although there was great opposition, he along with several of his fellow-merchants made up

The late ex-Bailie Thomas Menzies.

James Menzies.

Front Warehouse, King Street.

their minds to shut on Saturdays at 5 p.m., instead of keeping open in many cases until midnight was nearly striking. The Factory Acts, which were passed to do away with the positive sweating labour demanded in some workrooms, did not cause any inconvenience to Thomas Menzies & Co., as they always made it a point to treat their workroom "hands" in the most generous spirit, the proof of which lies in the fact that they have had girls in their employment for years, many of them only leaving to enter the matrimonial state. Regarding apprentices, a large number of young men have learned their trade with the firm, who make a special point of giving them every opportunity of acquiring a knowledge of all departments, and do not confine them to a single one, as is often the case in many warehouses. It is a frequent pleasure to the firm to have visits from their former lads, many of whom have gone abroad, and "look up" the old place when on a visit home, and to learn how well they have prospered in the battle of life, and to hear them say that no little part of their success is due to the thorough training in their business they received at 36 King Street.

With the keen competition nowadays the old type of commercial traveller is also fast dying out. In the olden days the commercial gentleman's visit was eagerly looked forward to, like that of an old friend, and he was warmly welcomed on his appearance, and always knew his order was ready awaiting him. Nowadays, with the bustle of business, and perhaps ten to twenty travellers calling per day, all keen for orders, they must show the best value at the keenest price before they can make an entry in their order book.

Window-dressing is another thing which has leapt into importance in the drapery trade especially. Formerly the merchant had his regular customers, who knew what they wanted, and that it was kept in stock, and never thought of going anywhere else for the article. Now it is almost impossible to stock every new item that is put on the market, and unless it is shown in the window nobody knows it is to be found inside. Thomas Menzies & Co. have often been complimented on their artistic window-dressing, and no later than last week notice was taken in the press of the splendid show of clan tartans of all descriptions, the display being described as being equal to, if not surpassing, the best city houses.

Referring to regular customers, it may be in-

teresting, as showing the good feeling existing between the firm and their numerous clientele, to state that they supplied the wedding trousseaux to many of the mothers of the young ladies who are now in turn getting theirs. This is the best evidence that could be provided that the goods supplied and the attention given have been appreciated.

Returning to the firm, steady and sustained progress marked its operations from the time ex-Bailie Menzies became sole partner, and some years after, when the stock and goodwill of the Drummond Tartan Warehouse Co., Stirling, came into the market, he was the purchaser. The firm who owned the Tartan Warehouse, it may be mentioned, commanded almost a world-wide reputation for Scotch homespun tweeds for ladies' and gent.'s wear, clan tartans, table linens, sheetings, towellings, real Shetland hand-knitted goods, and these are still a very important feature of the business of Thomas Menzies & Co. Among other orders in this connection that the firm have had the honour of supplying was a complete Highland outfit to Prince Kalubha, brother of H.H. the Rao of Cutch—an Indian principality on the Bombay coast—when staying at Ballater, where he had greatly admired the picturesque dress of the Scottish Highlander.

When the late Mr William Crawford, china merchant, built the Arcade leading from King Street to Murray Place, it was found necessary by Thomas Menzies & Co. to take in one of the large halls, which is contiguous to their warehouse, to still further increase the space devoted to their mantle, carpet, and linoleum departments, and also provide fitting rooms and millinery workrooms. About six years ago ex-Bailie Menzies, who had now the assistance of his son, Mr James, in the active management of the business, decided upon entirely remodelling the front of the warehouse, in order to keep abreast of the times, and, entrusting the operations to one of the leading specialists of this work in the kingdom, the firm have now a splendid show space, as both windows have been fitted up with the latest appliances and fittings for displaying goods to the best advantage. The only drawback is that the windows are too inadequate to give a proper indication of the large and varied stock carried inside, which the accompanying photographs may provide some idea of. At the same time the various departments were re-arranged and the warehouse was fitted through-

Part View of Main Saloon.

Mantle Saloon.

out with electric light, in order to meet modern requirements.

Large as the local clientele is, Thomas Menzies & Co.'s business is not confined to Stirling and district only, as they have many customers writing for goods from all over the British Isles and many parts of the civilized world. Post orders are a very valuable adjunct to the business nowadays, and owing to the facilities of the parcel post, and the personal care displayed in the execution of same, these orders are increasing every year.

Dressmaking and millinery have always been very strong departments with the firm, and the ladies in charge pay periodical visits to Paris and London, in order to visit the creators of fashion and purchase models for the approaching seasons. The large dressmaking workrooms of Thomas Menzies & Co. comprise two large flats at the top of the warehouse, with perfect ventilation and cleanliness. The millinery workroom is situated in the Arcade, and both are pronounced by the Sanitary Inspector as excellent for the purpose they are used for.

Even thirty or forty years ago business was conducted in a very different manner to what it is now. In the Dress Department, for instance, there were only some half-dozen standard makes of materials, such as cashmeres, merinoes, winceys, etc., and the same with silks, the regulation wedding dress for a bride at the time mentioned being of stiff coloured faille silk. Nowadays their name is legion, and to suit the varied tastes of their numerous customers, the firm require to purchase fabrics from innumerable home and foreign manufacturers, and show a range of high-class materials seldom met with outside large city warehouses. The same may be said of their ready-made Mantle and Costume Department, which is a special feature of their business, and where may be found the very latest novelties as they appear during the season. All that was shown in this department forty or fifty years ago were some ungainly dolmans, and the inevitable "Paisley Plaid," without which no bride's trousseau was then considered complete. Now is to be seen a charming collection of garments adaptable to all ages and figures, at prices to suit everyone, including matrons' black

silk, cloth, and plush mantles, capes and jackets, exquisite designs in perfect cut and finished tailor-made costumes, real Scotch tweed travelling coats and capes, misses' coats and costumes, etc. With the coming of the motor, garments capable of defying the elements are a necessary adjunct, and ladies will find in this department such a collection of tweed coats, fur-lined, leather-lined, and fur-trimmed; also in all fur and leather, from which they can hardly fail to find something suitable.

The fashion for fur garments is largely on the increase, but in place of the seal jacket, which was a sine qua non some years ago, ladies have now quite a variety of fashionable furs to choose from in sable, sable squirrel, grey squirrel, electric seal, mole, musquash, mink, Persian lamb, caracul, etc., etc., in styles suitable both for young and old. The dyeing and finishing of furs have advanced to such perfection within the last few years that ladies will do well to purchase their furs from a reliable firm, as otherwise they may find to their cost that they have only got an imitation of what they asked for. The remodelling and renovating of furs and fur garments is another branch of this business, and Thomas Menzies & Co. are always pleased to advise ladies as to the best manner in which alterations may be made, and give estimates for same free. It is better to put these alterations in hand as soon as possible, to prevent delay in execution when the crush of the season comes on.

The firm have also an extensive connection among the Highland hotel-keepers all around Loch Lomond, Perthshire, on to Oban, and as far north as Stornoway, whom they supply with all kinds of household furnishings. The leading manufacturers from whom Thomas Menzies & Co. purchase their goods confine themselves to the firm for this district, so that ladies may not fear meeting a friend dressed exactly alike, as Thomas Menzies & Co. take special care to purchase only one garment of any pronounced style, and if sold in this district do not repeat it. They have the entree to all the most up-to-date manufacturers in Paris and London, and naturally the goods shown in their warehouse bear the hall-mark of fashion and good taste.

Millinery and Underclothing Saloon.

Carpet and House Furnishing Department.

G. R. Jenkins.

G. R. JENKINS,

DRAPER, MILLINER, AND DRESSMAKER, STIRLING.

Stirling has a great reputation for its up-to-date and fine business warehouses, and commercial men, who travel all over Scotland, say that no provincial town can boast of such an array of fine shops as are to be seen in the "City of the Rock." Prominent amongst these are the drapers, or, as they are sometimes called, soft goods merchants.

In the olden time, when there was less variety and change of fashion, fine window displays were not so much required, or thought of, but of late years quite a craze has sprung up for fine frontages and window space, and the result has been quite a transformation, as far as Stirling is concerned. No effort is spared, either in money or labour, in making the show windows attractive, and that the merchants in Stirling have succeeded is proved by the general opinion so frequently expressed, that the drapery shops in Stirling cannot be surpassed in the provinces, and, in fact, by few cities.

Amongst the first to recognise the importance of window display was Mr G. R. Jenkins, whose up-to-date warehouse is the subject of this week's article.

Although the name has been changed, this is one of the old-established businesses in Stirling, having been founded by the late Mr Thomas Peacock nearly sixty years ago. In 1882 the business was sold to Messrs Inglis & Smith, who had established themselves further up the town, and in this same year Mr G. R. Jenkins commenced his apprenticeship with Messrs Inglis & Smith. After serving his "time" with this firm, Mr Jenkins, with the view of furthering his knowledge of the business, spent some years in London. Later he returned to Scotland, and received an important appointment in the leading drapery warehouse in Dundee, a position which be held till he acquired his present business from Mr William Inglis, son of his previous employer, this taking place in the year 1900.

Since then the premises have been thoroughly modernised inside and out, and the result is a finely equipped and up-to-date general drapery store, that will stand comparison with any city house of similar dimensions. The warehouse is wrought on the departmental system, there being ten different departments, all dealing with their own special business as if it were a separate concern.

On the ground floor, as you enter, you have, to the right, the Lace, Ribbon, and Smallware Department, and on the left Gloves and Hosiery and the Art Needlework Department. These are generally classed as the fancy goods, and as they embrace such a variety of little articles that need quick selling, are placed near to the door for convenience of customers. Along a short passage, lined with a great quantity of pieces of floor-cloths and linoleums, you reach the spacious department devoted to the sale of carpets, linoleums, and household linens. This department has been much improved by the increased light which the alterations effected. The old firm had a great reputation for sound and reliable household goods, and the present proprietor takes a pride in keeping up, here at least, the old traditions. At the further end of the Household Section is the department devoted to the sale of men's underwear, etc.

Retracing our steps, and ascending a broad and easy new stairway, we arrive at the spacious and splendidly lighted saloon devoted on the one side to dress materials and silks, and on the other to the Print Department, which embraces printed flannels, delaines, muslins, flannelettes, molletins, etc., while the centre portion of the saloon holds the umbrella and fur stock—the latter a most important branch of business, and comprising a large and well-selected stock.

Turning from here we enter the Millinery, Mantle, Blouse, and Ladies' Underclothing Saloon, which is completely divided off from the others. A very high roof and abundance of daylight is here, giving the apartment a cheerful appearance. The walls are tastefully done in green, with a deep, telling frieze, and throughout the room is an abundance of large mirrors—a very essential item in an up-to-date ladies' emporium. Branching off this portion, and situated in another building, are the dressmakers' fitting and main workrooms.

There are in all about fifty "hands" employed in the warehouse. Electric light is used throughout the entire establishment, and just now the new Osram lamps have been introduced, and alterations made which should make the premises

Section of Millinery and Mantle Saloon.

Dress and Costume Department.

second to none, so far as artificial lighting is concerned. Gas is used exclusively for heating purposes, in the form of the latest radiators, and gives most satisfactory results. The latest gas heating arrangements are also used for the heating of workroom irons in a brick-lined chamber specially made for same. The office and cash desk are together on the ground floor, and we notice the telephone, typewriter, duplicators, and every up-to-date notion there.

The proximity to Glasgow and Edinburgh puts the Stirling merchants on their mettle, and it is satisfactory to learn that men like Mr G. R. Jenkins are able to retain their customers' orders, even when they move to such centres. Commercial men, who should know, state that Stirling is one of the keenest cutting places in the country for prices, and as this fact is corroborated by customers, who have migrated to the large cities, it is small wonder that a big volume of business is transacted by such an enterprising firm as the subject of this article. The wonder is that a few people are still found foolish enough to go further afield for what is done better at their own door.

In a business so influenced by fashion it is essential that frequent visits be paid to the leading centres of fashion. Mr Jenkins and his principal lady superintendents have just returned from London, and the warehouse is tastefully "dressed" with all that is considered "correct wear" in the most up-to-date and fashionable circles. Indeed, to walk through the spacious saloons on a show day, one is inclined to forget that it is Stirling, and imagine themselves transported to Regent Street or Oxford Circus.

We find ourselves looking enviously at most handsome fur coats in squirrel, caracul, beaver, and sealskin ; while the selection of cosy-looking fur-lined cloth coats, with rich fur collars and cuffs, are very inviting, and suggest extreme comfort. It is interesting to know that although garments are here for the long purses, wonderful value is to be had for 60s.

The neckwear in fur is simply bewildering, and exhibits a wonderful variety in shape and almost every kind of fur—sable, stone and baum marten, kolinski, beaver, nutria, squirrel, marmot, fitch, Persian lamb, caracul, oppossum, fox, ermine, skunk, etc., etc. Real sable requires a full purse, but we were astonished to see a special lot of handsome necklets, in kolinski, so beautifully tinted that one would require to be an expert to say they were not sable, and offered at a figure within the reach of people who are not of the wealthy class.

From the furs we turn to look at the handsome cloth coats, and it is pleasing to note that the fashion is for the best make of real Scotch tweeds, a fabric that can hold its own the world over. Whilst there are the better and dressier coats in abundance, very special value is offered at prices within the reach of all. Very smart ready-to-wear costumes in freizes, striped tweeds, faced cloths, etc., also attract more than passing attention.

The millinery is simply exquisite, and we cannot help noticing that the hats are large, although we are pleased to see many modified styles. The real artist makes the hat to suit the wearer, and does not endeavour to find the person to suit the hat. Here seems to be such variety that any one should be easily suited.

Attracted by a large pile of neat boxes, we are informed that this is a special consignment of a wonderful bargain in blouses. Six dozen seems a lot of one kind of silk blouse, but the quantity will be too small, we think, after inspection. It is a cream Japanese silk shirt, tucked and veined right down the front and also behind, with double collar of silk, very full shape and beautifully finished, the smartest of half-guinea blouses, it is to be sold for 7s 11d, and can only be had from G. R. Jenkins. A large variety of blouses, it may be added, is held in stock.

Passing a fine display of moirette and silk underskirts, our attention is drawn to the new directoire skirt, which, fitting perfectly at top, springs out to great fulness at the hem, and is very graceful.

A great choice of materials and silks are displayed at the dress counter. Pretty soft satins, fabrics for the new directoire style, and an enormous variety of costume materials—checks, stripes, plain materials, and combinations of check and plain fabrics—in all the newest colourings, meet the eye.

The Dress and Costume-Making Department is already very busy, and we learn that garments are turned out complete from two to twenty guineas. A splendid lot of new friezes and check tweeds are here in a pile, ready to be made to measure and to fit perfectly. It takes a lot of work to keep about 30 girls employed, but except for the usual holidays, they are always kept busy—dress and costume-making being one of the strongest features in this up-to-date concern.

Household Linen Department.

Section of Front Shop.

For those who make their own blouses there is much to attract them to the counter, where printed delaines, flannels, winceys, and flannelettes are sold. G. R. Jenkins has first choice from one or two of the best printers in the trade, and buys direct, and a fine taste is shown in design and colourings. Here also we see those cosy pyrenese wools and molleton cloths for dressing gowns and jackets, in very rich warm colours and striking designs. One very smart cloth, and quite inexpensive, was an exact reproduction from an old Paisley shawl.

Coming to the Carpet and Household Department, every preparation has been made to cope with a brisk demand for flannels, blankets, quilts, etc., for the coming winter. The difference in values from last year is all in favour of the purchaser, whose pound note should buy more, and better value, than last year.

Dorcas and charitable societies are catered for at keenest wholesale prices, and G. R. J. supplies a great number of such institutions. Besides the keen cutting of prices, the secret of success lies in supplying thoroughly sound and good wearing materials. In this section we see a wonderful lot of carpets—not so many as there were, for they are selling freely—but still a wonderful little stock of them, and going at less than makers' prices. Hard lines on the maker, but money must be had, sometimes even at great sacrifice, and realisations are bound to take place. This was the case here, and the most beautiful art carpet squares, in all sizes and pretty art colourings, are being offered at nearly half-price. The goods are perfect, and it must be satisfactory to the people of Stirling that enterprise has secured such a plum or chance for them.

Coming to the lighter and daintier goods, we see in the very fully equipped Art Needlework Department enough to occupy the attention of lovers of needlework for months. Here is a great bundle of traced white cable goods, in the form of table centres, tray cloths, nightdress cases, comb bags, duchesse sets, sideboard and tea cloths, etc., and a host of lovely mats. Alongside these are many finer examples of traced, commenced, and finished work. One particular lot of fine Japanese drawn-thread linen tea cloths takes the eye, and the work is so elaborate and fine that we are certain no lady would like to do the work for twice the money that is asked. Smart hose, pretty belts, gloves of every kind, and for every occasion, and dainty linen collars and pretty neckwear are here.

In the Lace Department there is a great revival of frillings, and scores of boxes are here, and each box contains a frilling quite different from any other, and you begin to wonder where all the variety can come from in a simple frilling for the neck, but it is here all the same.

There is a corner devoted to all the little patent articles that crop up week by week, and G. R. J. is always ready to secure the latest. Patent neck supports, dress fasteners, hairpins, combs, etc., etc., that make for comfort and convenience, while to speak in detail of the lovely ribbons and real laces would require a column to itself alone.

Special shows are being advertised, and every lady who likes an up-to-date store, where there is the greatest liberty to walk through, and no pressure to buy, should make it a point to visit G. R. Jenkins on one of his special show days, or any other day for that matter.

Front View of Premises.

Alexander Galbraith (Principal).

Cecil Galbraith (Son).

COWBROUGH & MERCER,

FAMILY GROCERS AND WINE MERCHANTS, STIRLING.

This week our article deals with a firm in the grocery trade, which, although not the oldest business of the kind in Stirling, has the distinction of being the second in seniority. Many changes have been seen in the "City of the Rock," and outside of it, since Cowbrough & M'Nab—which was the original name of the firm—opened their shop in Port Street, 69 years ago. At that time, and for a number of years afterwards, Broad Street was the commercial and professional centre of the town, and most of the business men resided in the vicinity. Even then, however, indications were not wanting that a change was in progress. The old thatched houses which occupied the south side of King Street, and were a prominent feature of Port Street and Murray Place, were gradually disappearing, to give way to the modern establishments, which compare favourably at the present day with those of the best shops in Edinburgh or Glasgow, and Cowbrough & M'Nab were among the first to recognise the trend of events, which became accelerated later, and left Broad Street in the condition that we now find it in regard to the business of the town. The advertisement setting forth the advent of the new firm appeared in the "Observer" of 4th July, 1839, and was as follows:—

NEW GROCERY WAREHOUSE,
WRIGHT'S BUILDINGS, PORT STREET, STIRLING.

COWBROUGH & M'NAB

Respectfully intimate to their Friends and the Public that they have opened the above commodious premises with a Stock of every article in the Grocery Line, carefully selected in the first markets under every advantage.

C. & M. were for the last eight years in the establishment of Messrs D. & J. MacEwen & Co., and had every opportunity for becoming intimately acquainted with the markets, and they feel confident that their Stock, into which no inferior articles will be admitted, particularly their Tea, Coffee, Sugar, etc., etc., will on trial give satisfaction to consumers.

The Wine and Spirit Departments are to be added to the establishment about Martinmas next, and C. & M. hope, by a steady attention to business and moderate prices, to merit a share of the patronage of the public.

Stirling, 27th June, 1839.

As Mr M'Nab only remained in the business a few years, nothing more need be said respecting him, but Mr Cowbrough, who belonged to a farming family long connected with the Polmaise estate, became a well-known local man, who held an honoured position in the community, and the following account of his life, extracted from Drysdale's "Old Faces of Stirling" may prove interesting:—

Mr James Cowbrough was the second son of Mr Henry Cowbrough, Dykes Farm, was born 31st December, 1816, and, after leaving school, served apprenticeship as a grocer with Messrs D. & J. MacEwen & Co., Port Street, continuing in their employment until 1839, when, along with Mr D. M'Nab, he commenced business in a small way in a part of the premises in the same street now occupied by the firm of Cowbrough & Mercer. The business rapidly became a prosperous one, and by and bye branches were opened in Baker Street and Wallace Street, as well as in Bridge of Allan and Callander, Mr Cowbrough devoting himself most assiduously to its interests for the long period of forty-five years, until failing health compelled him, about a year before his death, to retire from active participation in its affairs.

Notwithstanding the claims of his extensive and, at the time, steadily growing business, Mr Cowbrough found opportunity to devote himself to public affairs, in 1855 being Dean of the Guildry, and from the same year until 1858 occupying the position of Dean of Guild in the Town Council. He also devoted not a little attention to educational matters, and from the passing of the Education Act until his death was a member of both the Burgh and Landward School Boards, although for some little time previous to his decease he was unable to attend the meetings. Another educational agency which received attention and support from Mr Cowbrough, as well as other leading

Shop Front, Port Street.

Wallace Street Branch.

merchants, was what was known as the Boys' Charity Evening School, by means of which not a few lads were enabled to better equip themselves for the battle of life.

Being a man of probity and acknowledged business ability, Mr Cowbrough's services were frequently requisitioned as a testamentary trustee, these being given most ungrudgingly, and with considerable benefit to the interests concerned.

A devoted adherent of the Free Church, Mr Cowbrough for many years held office in the Free North as an elder, and was also treasurer to the congregation, both during the ministry of the late Dr. Beith and the Rev. Mr Chalmers. The religious welfare of the youth of Cambuskenneth had also in him an ardent friend, his interest therein being manifested by his bequest of the sum of £100, the annual proceeds from which were to be expended in the purchase of gift-books for the children attending the Sabbath School there, "of which," he stated, "I have had the honour and privilege of being superintendent for twenty-three years;" this bequest to continue to be paid "so long as the school shall continue under the care of the Free North Church."

Mr Cowbrough was a genial friend, ever ready to serve his fellows, and very general regret was expressed at his demise, his funeral being attended with every mark of public respect, the shops on the route of the cortege to Stirling Cemetery being closed.

Mr Cowbrough, who remained a bachelor all his life, and died in 1885, was, it may also be mentioned, an indentured apprentice of Messrs D. & J. MacEwen, grocers, and as such, instead of getting any wages, his people had to pay a premium to his employers to learn him his business. In return, under this system, which was general at that date, the employer had to lodge, feed, and clothe the lad, and, in fact, practically enrol him as one of his own family, severe penalties having to be paid if the indenture was broken without justifiable cause by either side. This kind of apprenticeship is now obsolete, but it is a moot point whether it was not a better one for both master and apprentice, than the modern practice of paying a lad a few shillings weekly as a wage, and having nothing further to do with his supervision and training.

The premises in which Cowbrough & M'Nab commenced business are still occupied by the firm, there having been no change of quarters in these 69 years, but, of course, the property has been modernised to meet the needs of the times. At first the shop was a small one, with a single window, and steps up from the street at the door, but all this has long ago been altered. The establishment is now a fine commodious one, with two large windows, and the premises have been largely extended internally by blasting out the solid rock to the rear, thereby giving much more shop space, and also making provision for extensive cellars. When the firm started operations, the grocery trade was on a much more restricted scale than is now the case, and business was done very differently. In the olden days a grocer, practically speaking, existed for the purpose of supplying luxuries to the better classes of the people—better in regard to purchasing powers if nothing else. The principal commodities then kept were tea, coffee, sugar, syrups, confections, tobacco, wines, condiments of various kinds, dried fruits, rice, etc., and even pins. The provision trade, which is now such an important branch of a grocer's business, was then only in its infancy. At that time everything in the food line was produced at home. There was no importation of Danish butter, foreign eggs, or American tinned goods; no flour from foreign wheat, and no Canadian apples or bananas from the West Indies. All the butter, cheese, and bacon were made or cured by the farmers' wives in the district, and the grocer had to go into the country to buy these articles. There were no highly-burnished Government stamped weights in these days, and after the cheese or butter was bought, it was put on a hanging scale out of doors at the farm, and weighted with boulders or stones collected from some adjoining dyke, and weighing as nearly as possible the 22 lb. stone—the tron. On the other hand, foreign produce in the form of tea, coffee, etc., was procured through what would now be termed commission agents. The commercial traveller of the present day, who may be seen hanging round the shop door of any firm in the town, waiting his turn to interview the principal or buyer to see if he can get an order, was an unknown personage at the time of which we speak. All that was required by the local grocer was procured through the instrumentality of some wholesale firm in Edinburgh or Glasgow, and despatched to Stir-

Interior View of Shop.

Spirit Cellar.

ling by carriers' carts, or canal boats as far as possible, and driven for the remainder of the distance. With most people then it was a compulsory case of plain living, owing to the low wages earned by working-men, and the high prices of what are now regularly used foodstuffs by the working classes. Tea and coffee were rarities to them, and would be rarities yet, if the same prices were charged nowadays as ruled 69 years ago. As good tea as anybody wants can now be purchased at 2s per lb., but in 1839 it cost between five and six shillings; sugar, which is now 2d per lb., was then 7d; coffee, which was then 3s per lb., is now 1s 6d; and ground rice, which cost 7d per lb. in 1839, can now be got for 2½d. The prices of other commodities have fallen in proportion, wines—and particularly whisky—being the only things that show an increase. They are now nearly double the price they were 69 years ago, this being due to the heavy Government duties imposed, but, of course, the raising of the Imperial revenue in this way permits of the reduction of the taxes on the food of the people, and brings us nearer the ideal of a free breakfast table. What the taking off of the duties on the food of the nation means, can be better grasped if one sets himself to imagine the breakfast table of a thrifty working class family one hundred years ago in contrast with that of to-day. Then everything was produced and made at home; now nearly everything is of foreign origin. For instance, the flour used in the bread may be Canadian, American, or Hungarian; the butter may be Danish, Canadian, Australian, or Russian; the eggs may be Irish, Danish, or Canadian; the bacon may be English, Irish, Danish, or Canadian; the tea may be from India, Ceylon, or China; the coffee may be from Mysore, Brazil, Mocha, or Costa Rica; the marmalade from Spain. In order, therefore, to provide for the requirements of the consumers of the present age, a successful merchant has to take into account the produce of almost every country in the world, and these can only be procured at the cheap rates now prevailing by having no taxation on imports.

Even in regard to some of the commodities we have mentioned, fashion has greatly altered. For instance, half-a-century ago there was scarcely such a thing as fresh butter. This was because, owing to the want of railway and other expeditious methods of communication, the butter could not be easily got to the market, and preserving

agencies being little known, it was salted and placed in tubs till the grocer came round to buy. People in want of tobacco don't generally go to a grocer's nowadays, but long ago they had to do so, because there were then no tobacconists' shops as we have now. The same thing applies with respect to pins. These are not articles which are much sold by grocers of the present day, but half-a-century ago the humble pin was neither so easily nor so cheaply got as it is now, and the grocer did a good trade in them. Then in regard to sugar, it could not, half-a-century ago, be procured in the fine granulated form that is the case now. It was then imported in the form of loaves, which were in shape something like a shrapnel shell, each loaf being wrapped up in thick blue paper. When the loaf sugar had to be sold in small quantities it had to be cut into pieces with a hand knife or some similar utensil. Except for preserving purposes, and for what is called piping or ornamental work on bridescakes and shortbread, loaf sugar is now very little used, though it is only recently that some of the old county families gave it up. They got the loaves of sugar chopped up, and were under the belief that it was better than the other and more popular kinds. Crystallised sugar is another variety that is rarely seen nowadays, but it is still used to a considerable extent in some of the mining districts of the country. Granulated sugar came into vogue in the late Seventies or early Eighties, and lump, or tea, sugar followed.

In the old coaching days, before the introduction of railways, Stirling, besides being the centre of a wide and prosperous agricultural district, was the depot on which the inhabitants of West Stirlingshire and West Perthshire depended for their supplies. During the first half and well on in the second half of the nineteenth century, Broad Street was the great rendezvous for buyers and sellers from all parts of the surrounding country, and before the Butter Market was erected by the Town Council, it was crowded on market days with farmers' wives and daughters exposing for sale their butter, eggs, poultry, etc. The only available system of conveying goods to and from the outlying villages and the Highlands was by means of the local carriers, whose principal location was on both sides of King Street.

That is now a thing of the past, and now not only town residents, but country people also, can, and do, get their supplies without moving across their doorsteps. Delivery vans and message boys

Another View of Spirit Cellar.

Wine Cellar.

have worked the revolution, and the grocer who is to hold his own against the fierce competition of the present age, must not emulate his "forbears" and sit contentedly in his shop waiting for his customers to call, but must go to them at their own homes if he wishes to retain their connection. Then the merchant of 60 or 70 years ago troubled little about the smartness of his business premises, and never dreamt of the expensive advertising methods of to-day. His success depended largely on his own character, his personal connection, his ability to accommodate his customers with a liberal amount of credit, and of course, the quality and reputation of his goods—still important considerations. The advance of science and education has revolutionised the system and rules of business which were then in vogue. The slow and expensive communication by letters has given place to the penny postage, the halfpenny post-card, the telegraph, and the telephone ; the stage coach has been ousted by the steam engine ; the system of transit by carriers has disappeared with the advent of railway trains and motors ; the old-fashioned dip candles and the oil lamp have been superseded by gas and electricity ; and the quill pen, which did service a century ago, has its functions now more efficiently and expeditiously discharged by type-writing machines.

Coming back to the firm of Cowbrough & Mercer, it may be explained that the second name was added in the Seventies, when Mr Robert Mercer, who was then foreman shopman to Mr Cowbrough, was assumed as a partner, and the title of the firm, which had been Cowbrough & Co. ever since one of the two founders of it—Mr M'Nab—left, was altered to its present name. At Mr Cowbrough's death in 1885, Mr Mercer became sole partner, and, like his predecessor, took a leading part in public life, being in turn a Town Councillor, Bailie, and Dean of Guild. Mr Mercer died some years ago, and the business was latterly purchased by the present principal, Mr Alexander Galbraith. He, like the founders of the firm, got most of his training in the service of Messrs D. & J. MacEwen, than which there is no better educational centre in Scotland for those acquiring a knowledge of the grocery trade, and, like Mr Cowbrough, Mr Galbraith has worthily upheld the reputation of his business alma mater. During all the years that Cowbrough & Mercer have been in existence, the firm has borne a first-class name in the trade, whilst known by the public as a fine old family business, and it is still maintaining that high character. But whilst it is doing so, it has been undergoing alterations and developments. Formerly the firm's operations were confined to the standard grocery "lines"—provisions, groceries, and feeding stuffs—but with the advent of Mr Galbraith at the head of affairs, changes have been made, which, whilst not altering the ramifications of the business in regard to its traditionary aspects, have partaken of the nature of a very marked new departure. We refer particularly to the addition of the green fruit, vegetable, and cut flower branch, which has become one of the most outstanding features of the business. In this new "line"—to use a trade term—we find history repeating itself, as it sometimes does in commercial, as well as other matters. Thirty years ago the fruit trade in Scotland was a comparatively small one, and was almost entirely in the hands of grocery firms, but for some reason or other they latterly practically gave up this department, and turned their attention to what was then an alluring article—Danish butter—along with other provisions, such as cheese and bacon. There was no margarine in those days. Owing to several causes Danish butter, and the other articles mentioned above, are not the profit-making "lines" that they used to be, and recently the green fruit and vegetable trade, along with cut flowers, has been re-introduced into the grocery business in various parts of the country. This new feature is, however, only in its infancy yet, but it has been long enough in existence for the originator of the new departure in Stirling—Mr Galbraith, of Cowbrough & Mercer—to be paid the compliment of imitation by some of his brethren in trade. That the innovation has "caught on" has been shown by the interest and appreciation the public display, and by the success that has attended it, and in this item alone Mr Galbraith has demonstrated that the merchants of Stirling are gifted with the business acumen to discern what the public want, and to supply it almost before the mass of the people are aware of their own desires in this direction. The new departure is but another instance of the ability of the local shopkeepers to keep abreast of the times, and to show what hardly needs to be demonstrated—though there are people foolish or ignorant enough to think and say otherwise—that the merchants and shops of the "City of the Rock" are equal to those to be found in the best streets of the large cities, and far ahead of most provincial towns, and also that what cannot be got in Stirling which will favourably compare both in regard to quality and price with other places, is practically unattainable.

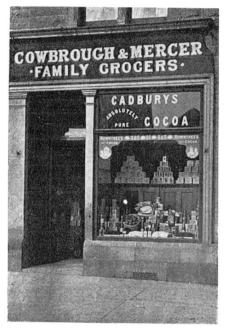

Forth Crescent Branch.

ROBERT FOSTER, PLASTERER, STIRLING.

The industry—or rather craft—we deal with this week, that of plastering, will to the ordinary man appear a very humble one, devoid of the higher branches of skill associated with many other trades. Everybody has witnessed at one time or another the plasterer laying a pavement, harling a house front, or covering the walls of a building with what resembles a coating of another kind of mortar after the masons have done their work, and this is generally looked upon as the sum total of the former's business. No greater mistake could be made, however. The operations we have mentioned are merely the simple externals of the plasterer's art, and also the roughest forms of it. The elements of the craft have a much more artistic conception than that. Plastering in its higher branches is numbered among the fine arts, and the craft has a history that goes far back into the dawn of civilisation. It is one of the earliest instances of man's power of inductive reasoning, for when men built they plastered, at first, like the birds and the beavers, with mud, but they soon found out a lasting and more comfortable method of making their dwellings wind and water tight, and at the same time decorating them. Inquiry into the art takes us back to the dawn of social life, until its origin becomes mythical and prehistoric. Into that dim, obscure period we cannot penetrate far enough to see clearly, but the most distant glimpses we can obtain into it show us that man had very early attained almost to perfection in compounding material for plastering; in fact, so far as is yet known, some of the earliest plastering that has remained to us excels in its scientific composition that which is used at the present day. The Pyramids of Egypt contain plaster work executed at least four thousand years ago, and this, where wilful violence has not disturbed it, still exists in perfection, outvying in durability the very rock it covers, where this rock is not protected by its shield of plaster. Dr Flinders Petrie, the eminent Egyptologist, shows, in his work on the Pyramids and Temples of Gizeh, how serviceable and intelligent a co-operator with the painter, the sculptor, and the architect, was the plasterer of these early days, and that to his care and skill we owe almost all we know of the history of these distant times and their art. Indeed, the plasterer's tools still remain, showing that the technical processes in the trade at that time were practically the same as those now in use. Machinery the Ancients did

not possess, or, if they did, nothing remains to show it, and there is abundance of reason to believe that their work took a much longer time to accomplish than is the case at the present day, but for beauty, allied to durability, it is to be feared that the modern methods are not equal to those of the craftsmen of the early ages. This, however, is not the fault of the present-day plasterer, it is the result of one of the most noticeable features of our time in all departments of industry and trade; the desire for cheapness and rapidity of production. These are fatal to development of the higher branches of all arts and crafts. If one desires to become acquainted with plaster work in its finer aspects, he has only to glance at the drawings and photographs of the exquisite decorations on the walls and ceilings of Egyptian and Grecian temples, and the ornamentation in the old Italian and Venetian palaces and historic country mansions in England and Scotland, to realise in some measure the artistic temperament and executive ability of the craftsmen of long ago. There is yet extant a piece of Egyptian plaster pavement executed fourteen hundred years before the birth of Christ, and there are many more recent examples of floral and frieze work and bas reliefs in stucco or Plaster of Paris discovered in Rome, and of the time of the first century of the Christian era. In England, in the 15th century, plasterers became the supreme decorators of houses, and usurped the province of both the painter and the sculptor. They were formed into a Guild in 1501, in the reign of Henry VII., when they got a charter, and at that time were the highest paid craftsmen, getting 11d per day, whilst joiners and painters received 6d and 7d.

Nowadays the plasterer does not hold the pre-eminent position amongst other tradesmen—in regard to wages at least—that he did in the past, but his trade is still a very important one, and is likely to remain so. As in the case of others, however, it has changed, and is still changing, though its original features and methods remain. Decorative work yet plays an important part in it, but not to the same extent as formerly. In Stirling and district there was, about thirty years ago, a good deal of ornamentation in plaster executed on the walls and ceilings of private houses and public buildings, but in more recently erected properties this has been largely replaced by painting and papier-mache decoration in colours. This is another outcome of the desire

Robert Foster.

for cheapness whilst striving to get the effect of the more durable and artistic decoration. The Arcade Hall and the Albert Hall afford another example of the change that is taking place, the former having much more florid ornamental plaster work about it than the latter, where the plaster decoration is of a quieter and more classic description.

Mr Robert Foster, the head of the business under notice this week, belongs on the maternal side to an old Doune family—the Gentles'. There are few, if any, of them in the district now, but for generations back they were associated with the slating trade of Kilmadock and neighbouring parishes. Mr Foster's maternal grandfather was a master slater in Stirling, and his father was a member of a farming family, which came to Stirling—where they had relatives—when he was young. In 1850 James Foster was apprenticed to Mr John Craigie, plasterer, who was a well-known Stirling man in his day, and executed the plaster work of most of the older villas in the West End of the town, among the last jobs he did being the Smitn Institute. Mr Craigie had two sons, who, however, were never associated with him in his business. Both were bred as plasterers, but wishing a bigger field, they went to Edinburgh when young men, and entered on a very successful trade career there, whilst their father conducted his own undertaking by himself till 1872, when he retired. For some years before that Mr James Foster had been his foreman, and on his employer's retirement he took up the business, assuming as his partner Mr Alexander Walls. The partnership, however, only lasted for some years, and Mr Foster then conducted business on his own behalf. He early acquired a reputation as a good tradesman, and had a wide connection, his firm executing a number of important jobs. Chief among these were the Callander Hydropathic, the Albert Halls, Stirling; Bannockburn House, and a number of villas in Stirling. Mr Foster was a member of the Water Commission during the time when the important work of constructing the big reservoir at Touch—No. 4—was entered into, and it is interesting to relate that it was due to his advice that the Commissioners resolved to construct the 80 feet deep well there of concrete—a building material that was only coming into use then, and the advantages of which Mr Foster was among the first to recognise.

Mr James Foster died in 1888, and was succeeded by his son Robert, who had been asso-ciated in the business with him for some years previously. During the twenty years that have elapsed since the latter became the head of the firm, the plastering trade has changed considerably in some of its ramifications. As we have already stated, the decorative element is not so conspicuous as was once the case, though this work is still a considerable branch, but apart from ordinary household plastering, the use of cement and concrete has greatly increased for several purposes for which stone and brick were formerly utilised, namely, stair steps and landings, concrete or granolithic pavements, window-sills and lintels, and "harling," or rough casting, the fronts of buildings. In this way the plasterer now does work that used to be confined to masons, and so skilfully are the operations carried out, that only an expert could tell the difference between the imitation hewn stone of a house front that has been cemented, and the real article. In Stirling there are several examples of this feature of the plasterer's craft, but in England and Ireland, and also on the Continent and America, where neither stone nor brick is so easily or cheaply got as in Stirling, cement is much more largely used in the erection of buildings. Cement, indeed, can be employed nowadays for many of the purposes for which iron and wood are utilised, and is also cheaper and more durable. For instance, who would think of telegraph poles, factory chimneys, and drain pipes composed of concrete, but such are in existence, and are rapidly becoming more numerous, whilst as for pipes of this material, they are to be found in this district, Mr Foster having two years ago been entrusted with the contract to supply pipes for enclosing part of the Raploch Burn, near Stirling, the pipes—about 200 in number, and $2\frac{1}{2}$ feet diameter each—being made of concrete. These pipes are half the cost of fireclay ones, and also much cheaper than iron.

We have referred to cement, concrete, and granolithic, and most people look upon these as synonymous terms descriptive of one and the same article, but this is a mistake. There are various kinds of cement, which is an adhesive substance employed for the purpose of uniting solid bodies, and the variety now almost exclusively used in the plastering trade is known by the name of Portland cement. It was patented in 1824, by a Leeds bricklayer, and got its name from its resemblance in colour to Portland stone, even as Roman cement, which was a discovery of the year 1796, got that title because of its

Yard and Workshops, Linden Avenue.

similarity in hue to the mortar found in old Roman buildings. The Ancients were acquainted with cement too, but none of the previous cements combined the strength and durability of Portland, which resists the ravages of all climates, and is equally suitable for building purposes above and below water. Portland cement is a mixture of chalk and clay, reduced to mud, then dried, and burned to a "clinker," which latter is ground into a powder—all these operations being carried out by machinery. Other cements are made in much the same way, though the ingredients may be a little different. Concrete, on the other hand, is a mixture of broken stones or gravel and sand, bound together by cement, whilst granolithic is cement mixed with granite chips. Plaster of Paris, or stucco, is practically manufactured by the same process as cement, but as stucco is used for decorative work, it is composed of the finest of white chalk, burned and ground into a powder. In regard to the ornamental part of the plasterer's craft, the beautiful results attained are the outcome of what is termed "modelling" in the trade. Without entering into technicalities, it may be stated that the modeller is the higher craftsman, who works to designs supplied by the architect, and after these are prepared in a particular kind of clay, a plaster mould is taken off, and from this the ornament is made in stucco ready for placing in the building where it is wanted. Modelling is a trade by itself, and if the master plasterer has not one of these craftsmen in his employment, he can forward the design to the modeller, even as a commission is given to an engraver. The other two branches of the trade are plain plastering and cement working.

Stirling has always had a good reputation for the quality of the work done by its plastering firms, and outside architects have frequently complimented them on this, particularly the granolithic branch, the result being that local tradesmen have not only held their own, but have secured contracts against the competition of city firms. Since he went into the business, Mr R. Foster has worthily upheld the name and fame of his native town in this respect, and has been entrusted with a number of important contracts, among which the following may be mentioned— alterations and additions on the Trossachs Hotel— a fine job in ornamental work ; the plaster and cement work at the Ordnance Stores, Forthside, Stirling ; additions to the mansion-house of Keir, including a billiard-room and dining-room—which

was another fine undertaking in decorative plastering ; the concrete foundations for the new gasholder at Stirling Gasworks, and the platforms at Stirling Station ; alterations at Braco Castle ; the concrete work in connection with a new water supply for Keir House and grounds ; Stirling High School additions (Spittal Street frontage) ; Peter Memorial Church, Stirling ; Fever Hospital at Bannockburn ; plaster and cement work at Auchentroig mansion-house, Buchlyvie ; Ardchullery Shooting Lodge and offices, Callander ; workmen's houses at Polmaise and Fallin Collieries ; plaster and tile work at new Elementary High School, Stirling.

One of the most interesting, and at the same time unusual, commissions Mr Foster has had entrusted to him was that placed in his hands a few years ago by Sir John Stirling Maxwell, Bart., of Pollok. This was nothing more nor less than taking plaster casts of ancient Celtic sepulchral carved monuments in Govan Churchyard. There were about eighty of these, including a big stone coffin, and the job, which was executed to the satisfaction of Sir John, took three months to carry through. Last, but not least, among the contracts we will mention is that under H.M. Office of Works for the plaster and cement work for Stirling Castle and other Government buildings in the district. This contract Mr Foster got a year ago.

Soon after beginning business, he found his trade connection developing so rapidly that larger space for workshops, etc., became necessary, and the result was the removal, in 1900, of his establishment from Thistle Street to Linden Avenue. That district of the town—which, for the sake of readers at a distance who possibly do not know the locality of Stirling's newer streets, it may be interesting to state is the carse feuing ground, situated between what is known as the Burnside and old Wester Livilands House—owes a good deal to Mr Foster's enterprise. He was one of the first to build on it, and has erected four villas, which are a refreshing departure from the typical style of architecture to be found in the same class of property in other parts of the burgh. Linden Avenue is private feuing ground, over which the Town Council has no power, and the result is freedom from the restrictions that gall many persons able and willing to build on lands under the control of the Corporation, but who object to be tied down to conventional ideas in regard to architectural design. Mr Foster's Linden

Interior of Casting Shop, Linden Avenue.

Ornamental Plaster Ceiling in Dining-Room,
Keir House.

Avenue properties are constructed of brick, cement harled, with concrete block dressings, and since they were erected others in a similar style of architecture have been built on the outskirts of the town in different directions. In conclusion, we may also state that for the purpose of his concrete work Mr Foster has leased the sand and gravel pits at Chapelcroft and Birkhill, Cambusbarron, from both of which the very best material is got for that class of work.

Imitation Stone (in Cement) Dining-Room Fireplace in Local Residence.

Business Premises—Street View.

WILLIAM CARSON & SON, PAINTERS, STIRLING.

The art of the decorator is a very old one. Architecture, sculpture, and painting flourished on the banks of the Nile 2000 years before the dawn of the Christian era, and even at that remote period had attained a development that excites our wonder and admiration. So far as we know, the Egyptians were the first to use brilliant colours on their buildings, and they, centuries later, largely influenced the art of Assyrians, Greeks, and Romans, who found in the examples from the land of the Pharaohs a storehouse whence they drew their inspirations. But the love of the beautiful is not confined to civilised nations ; in every savage tribe through all the world's history we find a keen desire for ornament, which shows itself in all manner of ways. The naked savage gratifies his personal vanity and strives to improve his appearance by tattooing his body in curious designs. It is not enough for him that his hatchet be sharp, his shield tough ; that his canoe shall float, and his hut protect him from the elements. He must decorate all these, and turn them into objects of beauty. So he carves his weapon with intricate patterns ; beats his spear into elegant shape, and maybe inlays copper into its iron ; his canoe is moulded to a graceful curve, and his hut adorned with mats woven from dyed bark or fibre in simple but effective diaper. All this may be done with more or less refinement, but showing the instinctive inborn love of beautiful things with which the Creator has endowed all mankind.

But it is only when we come to more modern times that the house painter's craft claims our closer attention. In our own country, until the reign of Queen Elizabeth, there was not much scope for the painter, but about the beginning of the 16th century a great many mansion houses and castles for the nobility and gentry were built up and down the land. The walls of the principal apartments of these buildings were mostly covered with tapestry, which had then been brought to its greatest perfection, and which was very costly. Some of these are still to be found in our great houses, and are much prized, and now almost priceless ; but they have had their day. There must, however, at this time have been a certain amount of painter work done in those houses which it would be difficult now to describe, but it is certain that for many years to come the patrons of the craft would only be found amongst the wealthiest classes. Our country has been gradually advancing in all forms of prosperity, and especially so as we come nearer our own day. Our middle and lower classes are now able to enjoy many advantages which not so long ago were the prerogative of the rich. There has been specially a great advance in the good taste of the people, and there is now a growing desire for a more artistic treatment of our homes. We are no longer satisfied if they are clean—they must be beautiful. A white ceiling and an oil painted wall coloured in some glaring way is not sufficient. It is recognised that a house, whether it be a lordly mansion or a humble cottage, should present to the eye a pleasing harmonious whole, and that the colouring of its hangings and carpets, its walls and furniture should all tone and blend together.

Science has come to the aid of the decorator. The chemist and the paint manufacturer now supply him with many colours and other materials which a generation ago were unknown, and which enable a workman to produce effects with comparative ease that not long ago were impossible. Less than 20 years ago a painter's stock consisted mainly of white lead, oil, turps, patent drier, varnish and colouring materials. It is vastly different to-day, and the list must be greatly extended. Strange names, not to be found in any dictionary, appeal to him—"Velure," "Duresco," "Permadure," and a host of such words are familiar to the decorator, however mysterious they may be to an ordinary mortal. These names suggest new processes, and promise desirable results. Sanitary considerations are not forgotten, and now we have a whole class of paints manufactured that disinfect while they beautify. If we turn for a moment to the matter of wall coverings, we are no less surprised at the variety than the richness of the materials at the disposal of the decorator. Prominent amongst these are "Fabricona," "Lincrusta Walton," "Anaglypta," "Tekko," and many others more or less expensive, and all of them capable of an infinite variety of decorative treatment. While the well-to-do are thus catered for, the wants of the humbler classes are not neglected. It no longer follows that because an article is cheap it must be nasty or vulgar. Thanks to improved machinery, increased production, and a greatly increased knowledge of the principles of art as applied to manufacture, wall papers can now be had in the most perfect taste at a very small cost, and it must be a poor home indeed that cannot afford the few pence necessary to brighten its walls.

View of Showroom.

The firm of William Carson & Son was established in Stirling over 65 years ago. The late William Carson was born in Edinburgh in 1807. He served his apprenticeship with Chalmers, of George Street, where he early distinguished himself as a grainer of woods and marbles. The painting trade has undergone many changes since those days. Imitation of wood or marble is now in disfavour, and in aesthetic circles entirely taboo. At that time the art of graining was only beginning to be understood and cultivated, and the late Mr Carson devoted much care and study to it. He brought it to great perfection, and being naturally gifted with a fine taste for and appreciation of the beautiful, his work was greatly admired and much sought after both far and near. It quickly became the fashion of the day to paint most of the principal woodwork of good houses in imitation of oak or other costly woods, and in particular it was customary to paint ceilings, cornices, walls, and woodwork of all important dining-rooms in imitation of oak. Mr Carson did many of these jobs with his own hand most artistically, and so well have they resisted the ravages of time, and the daily tear and wear of life, that many of them in this neighbourhood and far beyond it remain unto this day. Such rooms are generally treated with much consideration by their owners, and justly so, for they could hardly be repeated now. Chalmers had more than a local reputation, and his workmen were sent all over the country. Of railways, of course, there was none at that time, and many a cold night was spent on the top of the London coach. Mr Carson used to tell of one adventurous trip, when he and a number of others were shipped from Leith in a specially chartered sloop, with all their painting materials on board, for Darnaway Castle on the Moray Firth. A week was spent tossing about on the North Sea before the weary sea-sick craftsmen regained terra firma. The hours of labour were also long, and the pay small in those days— the best workmen not earning over 17s per week. Such were the good old times!

Paperhangings are now in general use, and can be had at prices to suit every purse and every taste, and to them we owe a great deal of the brightness and comfort of our homes. Sixty years ago they were only beginning to be introduced, and were hardly known unless amongst the wealthier classes. They were printed in 6 feet long sheets, and very expensive. An old man and his wife used to do all the paperhanging in Chalmers' shop for several years: the wife pasting the sheets, while her guid man hung them on the wall.

The late Mr Carson died in 1876, and since then the business has been carried on by his son, Mr David R. Carson, now sole partner of the firm.

Six years ago the premises of William Carson & Son in Port Street were rebuilt in the English domestic style, and they now form a very pleasing addition to the architecture of the locality. Their paperhanging showroom (on the first floor) is large and well lighted, and well adapted for the display of all classes of goods, of which a large stock is kept. This firm have all along been noted for high-class workmanship, and that position is maintained to the present day. They have a large staff of experienced and capable tradesmen, whose work is scattered over a very wide district. Nothing is known of labour troubles; on the contrary, the most harmonious relations have always existed between master and man. This will be apparent when it is seen that the average length of service among the older hands works out at 24 years. One respected workman has served 43 years, another 35, while several range from 30 to 20 years.

Painters used to have rather a bad name, and doubtless there are still some "weeds" among them, but there seems to be a great improvement, and the trade, we feel sure, will now compare favourably with any. A firm that can be certain of every man promptly turning up every morning to his work is in an enviable position, and that obtains here. Long may such a happy state of affairs continue! These are days of rush and hurry; the old-fashioned slow ways of doing things are over, still W. Carson & Son are determined that their reputation shall not suffer, and are resolved to maintain the high standard of their work under all circumstances.

Robert Frater.

ROBERT FRATER, PLUMBER, STIRLING.

The plumber—who was originally, as he is still, a worker in lead—derives his name from the term lead, which has its equivalent in the Latin word "plumbum." Lead is one of the metals which has been known and used from very early times, and articles made from it by the ancient Romans —some of them inscribed and dated—such as water pipes, water tanks, weights, rings, and small ornamental cylinders are still preserved. During the excavation at Pompeii in 1860 lead pipes and other examples of plumbing work were unearthed, which showed that the workmanship, even two thousand years ago, must have been of a high order. In this country, however, sanitation in connection with housing accommodation, as we know it now, was very little heard of even as late as sixty years ago. In the better class dwellings certainly there was some attempt at drainage arrangements, etc., but in the houses of the ordinary working class there was nothing of this. The open "siever" on the street to carry away refuse, the earth closet and the "midden," located in the garden or "yaird," were conspicuous features then, and public baths or private baths were practically unknown. All these have we become familiar with since then, and the art of plumbing has progressed accordingly. The methods of working in this trade have, however, almost completely changed during the last thirty to thirty-five years. The serious illness of the present King, then Prince of Wales, in 1872, which was traced to defective drainage, was among the first causes of a thorough investigation into what was then the slip-shod and dangerous method of carrying out plumbing and drainage systems. For years after 1872, the systems of plumber work and sanitation as applied to buildings were in a state of constant change and improvement. Questions relating to the trade received the attention and assistance of scientists, and now one might almost say—although the last word has not by any means been said—that plumbing work and sanitation have as nearly as possible reached perfection. The older class of plumbers have had, in the transition of the trade, to adapt themselves to very much altered circumstances. Formerly nearly all the work was made and put together in the shop or "on the job." Soldered pipes, made, presumably, much in the same way as those of the old Romans, have for many years been replaced by machine-made solid pipes. Nearly everything that a plumber requires is bought ready for fitting, and the work now consists to a greater extent in putting together materials such as water-closets, baths, and wash-hand basins supplied by manufacturers. The "working" and putting in of lead pipes, sheet lead, and other metals is still as important a branch as ever, but the newer methods of doing this necessitate a wider knowledge of sanitary principles than was expected of the older race of plumbers. The trade, however, is not by any means confined to the use of lead alone. Copper, zinc, tin, and iron, in the form of sheets and pipes, enter largely into the requirements and equipment of a plumbing business, and in the better class of work copper piping is used to a great extent. Then the old system of concealing pipes behind plaster and boarding has in large measure been superseded by the better method of exposing the pipes and giving easy access for repair when required. For this purpose copper pipes lend themselves very readily. Much of the comfort of a house depends on the efficiency and stability with which the plumber does his work, but when good and substantial materials are used. and well protected from frost, the danger and discomfort are reduced to a minimum.

Drainage work in connection with buildings is now almost entirely in the hands of the plumber. Formerly any unskilled labourer was considered to be quite qualified to do this class of work, but the attention of the house proprietor and the tenant are now so much directed to the drains that a high grade of efficiency is required The substitution of cast-iron for fire-clay pipes inside and outside of buildings, the improved methods of workmanship, and the compulsory testing of work by certificated sanitary inspectors have practically revolutionised this class of work, and drains, properly laid, are found to remain practically perfect for years after they have been completed. The Police Act now requires that every house drain connected with a public sewer shall have an intercepting trap placed between the house and the sewer. This trap serves the purpose of cutting off the connection between the house and the sewer, so that if any imperfection exists in the house drainage the intercepting trap will prevent the air from the public sewer entering the house. The ventilation and trapping of drains and soil pipes, if properly carried out, should entirely prevent the escape of sewer gas into a building. It is not possible in this article

Section of Brass-Finishing Shop.

Part of Plumbers' Workshop.

to particularise in regard to the choice of fittings. Glazed fireclay and earthenware fittings of all kinds, cheap and expensive, are now in such common use that mention of them is almost unnecessary. Scotland has a large share of the manufacture of this class of goods, and it is satisfactory to know that at home one can be supplied with the best article on the market. Among other changes that have taken place in the improvement in the plumbing trade must be mentioned those which benefit the modern apprentice. Schools, taught and superintended by competent certificated teachers, are now established in all important centres, and the apprentice plumber who cares to study and qualify has advantages in the way of practical and theoretical instruction that were not enjoyed by his older predecessors.

The firm of Robert Frater was established in Stirling in 1851 by the present proprietor's father, who belonged to Edinburgh, and who died in 1873. While plumbing, gas-fitting, and sanitary work form the principal parts of the business, brass-founding and brass-finishing have also always been carried on. The plumbing and brass-finishing trades are in some branches so closely allied that it would be difficult to conduct advantageously a plumbing business of any extent without also employing brass-finishers. During the existence of the firm large contracts in connection with every class of buildings have been completed. Among others that deserve mention are—Extensive buildings at Larbert Asylum, Dollarbeg mansion-house, near Dollar, with its water supply; Auchentroig mansion-house, near Buchlyvie; Fever Hospitals at Stirling and Bannockburn; Government Store Buildings at Stirling; and Doune waterworks and water supply. Mr Frater is also at present the Government contractor for plumber work, gas-fitting, and cast-iron drainage work at Stirling Castle, and the other departments of H.M. Office of Works in Stirling.

William Gourlay.

WILLIAM GOURLAY, BUILDER, STIRLING.

Of all the arts or crafts that we have dealt with in this series of articles none has a greater record of years behind it than building, and in no department of human industry do we find one which has left its visible records impressed to so great an extent on the world's surface or which has changed so little in its methods of working during the passage of the centuries. In many trades the use of machinery has worked a revolution, but in building with stone and lime, or with brick, the means employed are very similar to those used by not only our forefathers, but by the Ancients. Mechanical power we certainly find utilised nowadays in steam cranes for hoisting purposes, and also for sawing freestone in blocks and planing or polishing the much harder marble and granite, but when we have mentioned these, we have comprehended practically all the departments of the building trade in which hand labour has been superseded by machinery, though it may be remarked that the supersession is by no means universal.

The antiquity of the building trade goes without saying. From the time of the erection of the Tower of Babel, mentioned in the eleventh chapter of Genesis, the Scriptures have frequent references to building and builders, but probably the art existed long before the time of its first mention in the Bible, as the world, according to geologists, was old even then. But whether or not this be the case, it is the fact that from the earliest period of which history tells, building has assumed various forms according to the necessity of mankind and the materials readily at their disposal. In ancient Egypt, Greece, and Italy, building in stone attained to a high state of perfection, and in this connection, down to the present day, it may be said that the greatest progress in the art is only made where stone of a manageable kind is conveniently at command. On the other hand, where brick is resorted to, there the allied arts of architecture and building, as regards domestic accommodation and elegance of style, are on a poor scale. Two of the noted nations of antiquity, Assyria and Babylonia, though reaching a high stage of civilisation, made little or no use of stone in their buildings—probably because brick was more easily got—and the result is that they have left no enduring monuments like the Pyramids and temples of Egypt, though in the form of inscribed bricks, which have been found buried in

the sands, much has been revealed of the lives of these peoples, who were the first-class Powers of their day thousands of years ago. The ancient examples of masonry, i.e., the art of construction in stone, are amongst the most magnificent specimens of the building craft. Not to go further back, or even outside Europe for proof, we find that emphasised in the temples of Greece, the amphitheatre of Rome, or the beautiful old Gothic churches and baronial castles in our own country, and there is no doubt that the Ancients, though they did not possess a knowledge of all the modern methods for erecting buildings, had nothing to learn from the builders of the present day so far as workmanship is concerned. No nation has excelled the ancient Egyptians in the erection of stone work, whether we consider the size of the materials used or the unequalled exactness with which they are fitted together. The Egyptians did not use mortar in their important structures such as the Pyramids, the joints being carefully "rubbed" and fitted. The masonry of the Greeks and Romans very closely resembled that of the present day. Following that, the early mediæval masonry was of very bad construction, but the art gradually improved again with the advance of Gothic architecture, particularly in church building, which was mainly carried out by bands of skilled artisans, who travelled about Europe as their services were required, and who, in consequence, were called freemasons, from whom the well-known society of that name derives its origin.

But whilst the builder has by his skill to be able to erect out of stone and lime what expresses the ideas of the architect in regard to certain forms and outlines, still the builder cannot be expected, any more than the architect, to become an expert craftsman in all trades, though he must have a general knowledge of them, and should be familiar with the capacities of workmen in various trades, and the amount of work that may reasonably be expected of them. The builder may be called upon to erect buildings varying greatly in the purpose for which they are to be used, and of course ought to be conversant with the system of construction peculiar to the work in hand. He should share with the architect the desire for the production of a sound and well-constructed building, and from a business point of view it should be his just and reasonable expectation to execute such work with

Clydesdale Bank.

a fair profit to himself. Though these interests may to some extent clash, his efforts should be directed to securing his profits by fair prices, good management and supervision, rather than by the introduction of inferior materials, the employment of indifferent workmanship, or any other unworthy means. Whether he does this on every occasion is another matter, but speaking generally the builder has no reason to fear comparison with other tradesmen in respect to the manner in which he carries out the commissions entrusted to him.

Coming to the subject of this notice—Mr Wm. Gourlay, builder, Stirling—he is one of the comparatively few natives of the town whom we find at the head of its business enterprises, and who has also taken an active part in its municipal administration. During his 46 years' connection with the mason trade, he has seen a good many changes in it. For one thing stone has been largely displaced by concrete for steps, stair landings, and pavement, but the former material is coming into use again, it being considered that a concrete surface, after being worn, becomes more slippery, and accordingly more dangerous than stone to walk upon. Attempts have also been made to introduce concrete blocks for building purposes in this district, but this so far has not been successful. The foundations of buildings, which were formerly of large flat stones and lime, are, however, now laid of cement concrete, which is not only more satisfactory as a foundation, but also cheaper. Then damp courses, which were formerly of slate, are now laid of Caithness pavement, asphalt, or lead, which is an improvement, likewise along with iron columns. Brick has to a great extent taken the place of stone in the erection of buildings, the demand for a cheaper article being to a large extent responsible for this. The result is that houses and other erections are erected at considerably less cost than would be the case were all the buildings of stone, but they are not likely to stand so long as those built of the latter material. However, we are not like our forefathers: they built for posterity, we do it for the present. Few of the ordinary business premises and modern villa residences, where brick enters into their composition, will be standing a hundred years hence. When Mr Gourlay went to learn the trade, the hours that were worked were longer and the wages paid lower than they are to-day. In 1862 masons' wages were 5d per hour in a 57 hours' week.

Now the wages are 8½d per hour with a 51 hours' week. It was in 1865 that the 51 hours came into operation, and there has been no alteration since. In 1862 labourers got 3d per hour, now they get 6d. The wages of masons are regulated by the state of the building trade in the country, and locally they have reached as high as 11d per hour, and fallen as low as 6d, within the last thirty years, but 8½d per hour has been the standard for the last few years.

As we have already stated, Mr Gourlay began his apprenticeship in 1862, when he entered the employment of Mr James Paterson, who was then the leading builder in the district. He erected many of the principal buildings in Stirling, including British Linen Company's Bank, King Street (the old Tract Depot), the Pyramid at Cemetery, Waugh's building and "Toy" Baird's premises in Murray Place, Allan Park Church, the first houses in Wallace Street, and several of the original villas in Victoria Place and Southfield. When Mr Paterson died, his business died with him: nobody taking it over as a going concern.

As a journeyman, Mr Gourlay worked at the County Buildings and the Smith Institute, Stirling, and at the erection of the Earl of Mar and Kellie's residence at Alloa, and afterwards gained further experience in Edinburgh and Glasgow. He also wrought two seasons in America, spending some time in Boston and at Chicago, at the re-building of the latter city after its destruction by fire in the early Seventies. Returning home he and a friend commenced business in Stirling in 1876, under the firm name of Gourlay & Bringans, builders, but two years later the partnership was dissolved, and since then Mr Gourlay has carried on the business on his own account. For the last thirty-two years he has done his share as a builder in improving the residential and business quarters of the town and district, the following being among the outstanding contracts he has executed:—Additions to Ochtertyre mansion-house, erection of Clydesdale Bank Buildings; Deroran, Springwood, and Batterflats residences, Polmaise Road; Spittal Street addition to Stirling High School; additions to Auchentroig mansion-house, Buchlyvie; "Stirling Observer" new buildings, Craigs; Messrs Macdonald, Fraser, & Co.'s new auction mart; Stirling Public Halls, Dumbarton Road; Allan Park new buildings (Port Street end);

"Deroran," Polmaise Road.

Stirling Public Halls.

Robertson & Macfarlane's, grocers, old property in Port Street; Mr Jas. Young's suite of shops, houses, and offices, Barnton Street, and a number of villas and tenements in various parts of the town.

Whilst Mr Gourlay has given careful attention to his own business, he has not forgotten the claims of citizenship, and the administration of the public affairs of his native town has also reaped the benefit of his services. He has been a member of the Town Council for eighteen years, and besides filling the office of convener of several committees, he has served as a Magistrate, and at present is a Police Judge. In addition to the foregoing, he is an elder in the Erskine U.F. Church, from which it will be seen that if the Bailie has had his share of public honour, he has also borne his part in the heat and the toil of the day.

Allan Park Buildings.

The Founder of the Business,
Ex-Bailie Robert Lawson, of Annfield, Stirling.

LAWSONS LIMITED.

Than Lawsons Limited there are few businesses in Scotland better known or with wider ramifications, and it is the only commercial undertaking originating in Stirling that has spread its arms far and wide and yet retains its headquarters in the place of its birth—the old "City of the Rock." The business was founded in 1856—52 years ago—but Stirling cannot claim the founder as a native, though he has been long one of its leading citizens. Ex-Bailie Robert Lawson, J.P., of Annfield, belongs to Fifeshire, was of humble parentage, and knew what it was to do a full day's work by the time he was in his teens. But though not born with a silver spoon in his mouth, nor having a college education, the founder of Lawsons Limited had a full graduation course in the hard school of life at an early age, and looking to the strenuous career he has had in building up a business of the dimensions of the one that bears his name, it is a striking testimony to his physical and mental energy, as well as his tact and perseverance, that he is still hale and hearty, and able to take an active interest in the undertaking. To very few men is it given to celebrate their business jubilee and still continue in harness. Ministers, of course, reach their fiftieth anniversary oftener than other people, but the members of the cloth lead a prosaic, unruffled existence compared with business men, most of whom have either retired voluntarily or compulsorily from the worries of a strenuous life long before half-a-century has passed over their heads. Ex-Bailie Lawson, however, is one of the exceptions that proved the rule, as he celebrated his jubilee two years ago last June, when he was the recipient of gifts from the directors of the Company and the employees, and received many congratulations. On that occasion the Bailie might have been tempted to dwell in a self-complimentary vein on his career, and the success that had attended it, and he could well have been forgiven had he done so, but though a self-made man in every sense of the term, the strain of strong commonsense, which has been a characteristic of his private and public actions, once more asserted itself. He claimed the possession of no particular qualities in himself that made for success, but modestly remarked that it was easier to obtain a business footing fifty years ago than is the case nowadays. "A man of tact, energy, and perseverance," he said, "had then probably a better chance of success than occurs in these later days, when competition is so rampant, and the battle of life is waged so furiously."

The enterprise to which ex-Bailie Lawson addressed himself, more than half-a-century ago, is indicated by the sub-title of the firm, "The Trades Clothing and Furnishing House." His aim was to cater for the personal and household requirements of the industrial classes. Phenomenal success has attended his efforts, the business having long since expanded beyond the confines of the town and county of Stirling, and is now established and flourishing in all the populous centres of Scotland. The staff numbers six hundred, and many of them have long years of service, showing that the relationship between master and man is of a mutually appreciative kind. All this has arisen from the modest start made by ex-Bailie Lawson 52 years ago in Stirling. The methods of carrying on the business are very much the same as they were then. All the difference is, that it has marched with the times, and is now a triumph of organisation, as it would need to be, looking to the widespread nature of its operations. Lawsons Limited is a commercial enterprise of which the founder has every reason to feel proud, but like all active business men, he has found time to serve the public, and also to engage in recreative pursuits. Thanks to the business abilities of his sons, the Bailie was relieved of a good deal of labour at an age when he could enjoy a respite from it, and he utilised his leisure by serving the community of Stirling as a Town Councillor and Magistrate for several terms. He has likewise taken an active interest in church affairs, and is Vice-Preses of the Allan Park U.F. congregation, of which he was one of the founders 45 years ago. In politics the Bailie has always been a staunch Liberal, and is at present an hon. president of Stirling Burgh Liberal Association. A capital bowler, he was for many years a member of Stirling Bowling Club. As a draughts player there are not many better in Stirling, and he can also put up a good game at chess and billiards—from all of which it will be seen that the founder of Lawsons Limited has not made business his only consideration in this world, but has played his part worthily in other connections, which help to make up the sum total of existence. But to come back again to the story of the firm.

After successive changes of the premises from

Baker Street Premises, Stirling, Furnishings Department.

Spittal Street Frontage, Furnishings Department, Stirling.

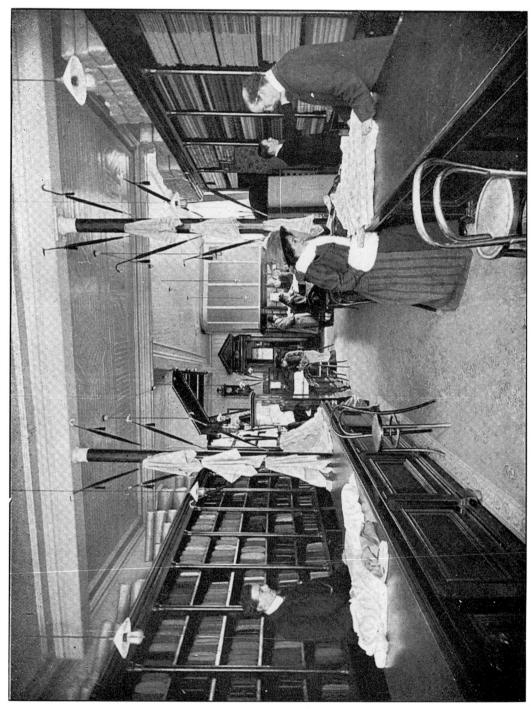

Front Shop, Drapery Department, Baker Street, Stirling.

Carpet and Linoleum Saloon, Baker Street, Stirling.

Port Street to Barnton Street and to Friars Street, all occasioned by increasing demands for space, the Stirling business finally settled in its present extensive premises in Baker Street in the year 1865. Here are situated the general drapery, clothing and outfitting departments, and work rooms, while on the opposite side of the street, at No. 25, in a large block with frontage both to Baker Street and Spittal Street, is carried on the house furnishing branch. This building was specially erected in 1899, and the furniture show rooms, with the carpet and linoleum saloon, are of exceptionally spacious dimensions. The total floor space of both premises is 21,000 square feet.

In the development of his business Bailie Robert Lawson was ably seconded by his sons. One of them, Mr William, took a leading part in the management. His organising abilities were of a high order, and the business derived great impetus from his well directed energy, until his lamented demise in 1906. Mr James, also well-known in Stirling, an officer in the local Rifle Volunteers, passed away suddenly ten years previously.

In 1877, a branch was established in Glasgow at Stockwell Street. A migration for increased space was called for in 1894, when the substantial five-storey block at the corner of Argyle Street and James Watt Street was acquired. This warehouse has a street frontage of 132 feet, with 12 shop windows for showing goods, and is fitted with both passenger and goods lifts to all floors. Here a large staff is accommodated, and from this centre the operations of the firm are conducted in the City, and embrace as well the counties of Lanark, Renfrew, Ayr, and Dumbarton.

In 1884 a warehouse was opened in Elm Row, Leith Walk, Edinburgh, which, outgrowing its shell in 1890, found a habitat in George IV. Bridge. Chambers Street was the next move, and in 1900 a further change was made to large new premises in Hill Place, Nicholson Street. The floor space here extends to 31,000 square feet, and from this warehouse the wants of customers in the Capital City and in the Border counties, the Lothians, and Fifeshire, are supplied. The special feature of this centre is the mantle and millinery saloon, an apartment of noble proportions, lighted by an arched glass roof, and reached by a single flight staircase from the entrance floor.

In 1872 Bailie Lawson's brother, the late Bailie James Lawson, of Newport, and a Justice of the Peace in Dundee, started business in Dundee on the same lines, and on a foundation already laid down from Stirling. Here, assisted by his four sons, he built up a prosperous trade, which in 1898 necessitated the erection of the large warehouse with frontage to Whitehall and back elevation to Dock Street and the River Tay. Spacious accommodation is here provided for the following departments—Tailoring, ready-mades, millinery, mantles, dressmaking, drapery, and furniture. The floor space extends to 45,000 square feet.

In 1883 Bailie James Lawson acquired premises at 190 George Street, Aberdeen. These have since been altered and greatly enlarged on several occasions. The floor space is now 30,000 square feet.

In 1900 the consolidation of the northern businesses in Aberdeen and Dundee with the southern businesses in Stirling, Edinburgh, and Glasgow, was effected with a paid-up capital of £267,500.

Bailie James Lawson died shortly after this consummation. He was a man of great business ability and of undeviating integrity, and throughout his life a strenuous supporter of the Temperance cause. In his earlier years he was secretary in Glasgow of the Abstainers' Union, and the inception of the popular Saturday evening concerts, which have been held for such a long series of years under its auspices, was due to him. His eldest son, William, retired from the management of the Aberdeen branch, and settled in Brighton in 1898, where he is a member of the Corporation. His youngest son, David, adopted the medical profession, and practised for some years in Bath. He was one of the first to appreciate the open-air method of combating the ravages of phthisis, and is the head of the well-known sanatorium at Banchory for the treatment of consumptives, known as Nordrach-on-Dee.

The Board of Directors, as at present constituted, is as follows:—Robert Lawson, J.P., Stirling, chairman; Robert Lawson, Dundee, managing director; Robert Lawson, jun., Edinburgh; Daniel Lawson, J.P., Dundee; Robert William Lawson, Stirling; Hugh M. Dunn, Glasgow; James Gray, Aberdeen; William B. Inglis, Dundee; and William Manners, Stirling.

Glasgow Branch.

The Late Bailie James Lawson, Newport.

Dundee Branch.

Wm. Aitken, founder of the business.

ST NINIANS BAKERY—WILLIAM AITKEN.

Of all the callings or trades practised by mankind, the art of bread-baking is one of the oldest, and it is certainly the earliest of which we read. The words, bread and baking, occur in many places in the Old Testament, though, of course, bread-making as first practised was a purely domestic industry, conducted both as to preparing the grain and making the bread by the females of the household. To a large extent this is still the case—at least so far as the baking is concerned—in all countries, but more particularly in primitive or less civilised communities. When the art developed into a distinct trade, however, which it did very early in the world's history, there is abundant evidence to show that it became a profession for the male sex. We all know the story of how Joseph was sold by his brethren and carried off into Egypt, and when he was resident in the establishment of Pharoah, the chief baker there, as recorded in Genesis, obtained a somewhat unenviable notoriety. Among such a clever people as the Jews baking soon became developed as a trade after they settled down as an organised nation, and the leaven process in the manufacture of bread was fully understood. In the writings of the prophet Hosea there is evidence that the baker had ceased to be a mere domestic, and there is also some proof of the fact that the baking carried on at that far off time—some thousands of years ago—was in its essential features like that practised up to the period of the introduction of machinery which has taken place within the last forty or fifty years.

All down the ages the baking craft stands out prominently. The ruins of Pompeii and other ancient cities have provided evidence which goes to show that there were public bakeries to which the poorer people took their bread to be baked, or from which they obtained ready-made supplies, and even yet in our own country, the custom prevails in some places of housewives sending dishes to the baker to be covered, or certain kinds of bread to be "fired." In ancient Rome baking was a distinct profession, and there was a Bakers' Guild or College from which neither the bakers nor their children were permitted to withdraw. The position of the Brotherhood was high in the State, and one of them was elected to the Senate. More than that, the bakers were the only craftsmen who were freemen of the City, all other trades being conducted by slaves, which was the great blot on the political organisation of the former Mistress of the World. But though the bakers of ancient Rome were held in high repute, and enjoyed privileges not given to other craftsmen, they were also subject to particular restrictions, not being permitted to visit entertainments or mix freely with their fellow-citizens in their various societies. There was a reason for this. In these days poison was a handy and very effective method of getting rid of an enemy or other obnoxious person, and in their own interests the ruling classes took precautions to prevent their bread supply being tampered with.

Regarding the kind of bread baked in the olden days, it is interesting to note that in Rome they had many varieties, the names of which, like our own sorts, were names of association, rather than description. Wheat from different parts of the then known world was then, as now, the favourite material for bread-making, and the old Romans, like the modern Britons, had a distinct weakness for white bread. Indeed the appreciation of good bread was a point of culture among the Romans, and between the various cities and towns the keenest rivalry seems to have existed as to which produced the best bread, whilst the same rivalry in the matter of quality existed among the individual bakers. Though the fact is not recorded, there is every reason to think that the bakers of the time of which we write would have exhibitions and competitions as the members of the trade have nowadays, in order to pit their products and skill against one another. The wheaten loaf is early mentioned, and in the writings of the time referring to the craft, a clear distinction is drawn between bread and cakes. Probably the first author on bread-making, or at least the first of whom there is any record, was Chrysippus of Tyana, a city of Cappadocia, an important Roman province in Asia Minor, who wrote a treatise on the art of bread-making about 240 years before the birth of Christ, and a god or goddess was set up in its honour.

But to leave the pages of antiquity, and to come down to more modern, though still far off times, we find that in England a Bakers' Guild was established in the reign of Edward the First (1042), and similar associations, called Incorporations, were afterwards instituted in various burghs in Scotland, our own town of Stirling included, the "baxters" or bakers being one of the Societies included in the Seven Incorporated Trades. For hundreds of years these Guilds exercised great power in the regulations of their respective trades, and though their special privi-

Thos. Aitken, present proprietor.

leges have long since been swept away in the march of modern ideas, they still exist as charitable bodies, fulfilling a benevolent purpose in providing pensions for members in need of them from the funds accruing from the investments left by the Incorporations of the olden days. For many hundreds of years in this country the price of nearly everything was regulated by law, and the bakers did not escape the enactments. Indeed it is only since 1822—86 years ago—that the bread assize, as it was called, was abolished. By this assize not only was the price of bread regulated, but the allowance given to the master baker, for materials used, and the wages of assistants, were fixed. Five hundred years ago, the wage allowed for a journeyman was threepence, this princely remuneration being much the same as other tradesmen received. Care was also taken that the master baker should not wax too fat, though in spite of all restrictions some of them prospered exceedingly well. These enactments were passed for the purpose of keeping the price of bread low, so that there should be no riots in times of drought or famine, which were more or less frequent when no grain was brought from over the sea, and the whole nation was dependent on the home crop. In these days, too, there was what was termed "assize bread" and "priced bread," and in one or two respects these archaic enactments have left their mark on the trade down to the present day. In regard to priced bread, the weight had always to remain the same, though the price might be altered, and we see the enactment still surviving in the common 4 lb. loaf, the weight of which continues the same, though the price to the consumer may rise or fall. Assize bread, on the other hand, was what would now be termed fancy bread, and here the price had to remain fixed, though the weight might be altered. In Australia and America these two systems are still in vogue. In the former the fixed weight system is rigidly enforced, whilst in America the price is fixed and the weights are changed. In Britain the baker is now permitted to sell at any price and weight he thinks fit, the only reservation being that he must sell the household loaf by weight. What his punishment would be were he not to do so we are not aware, but long ago bakers were subject to severe penalties for breaches of the law. For instance, it is recorded that when people in England were in the habit of taking their bread to be baked, the baker was sometimes inclined to "pinch" off a portion of the customer's dough,

and in one case an offender in this respect was caught, and for his crime was put into the pillory, and a girdle of dough hung round his neck.

In the baking trade, it is generally supposed that the supply of bread by vans to country and also town customers is a modern institution, but whilst this may be the case in several respects, it is not so in all particulars. History records that some hundreds of years ago both in Scotland and England, country bakers were in the habit of conveying their bread to the towns on certain days, and exposing it for sale in the public marketplace, and in order to protect themselves, the town bakers got a law passed compelling their country brethren to give more weight of bread than the town bakers for the same price, to make up for the heavier rents and taxes the latter had to pay.

There are several bakery firms in Stirling which have been established for many years, and in the matter of descent from father to son in direct line, that of William Aitken, St Ninians Bakery, is the oldest. It was in 1858—exactly half a century ago—that the business was started, the founder being the late Mr William Aitken, father of the present head of the undertaking. Mr William Aitken was a native of Bannockburn, and a member of a family long resident in the district, and whose name is a familiar one in different trades. Mr Aitken served his apprenticeship to the baking in his native village, and the trade was very different then in some of its conditions to what it is now. In Mr Aitken's time apprentices were bound by indenture to their masters, and resided with them, whilst journeymen were housed in bothies, the same as ploughmen are at the present day, in many parts of the country. The journeymen got their "keep" and a certain sum as wages, but it was not paid weekly. This bothy system existed until about forty years ago. Soon after his "time" was out, and not many months after his marriage Mr Aitken sustained the accident which caused him to be a little lame all his days. He was travelling by railway to see the first show held in Glasgow of the Highland and Agricultural Society—the carriages in these days being little better than modern trucks—and there was a collision at Cowlairs. Several persons were killed, and Mr Aitken was among the injured. His leg was broken, and the limb not being properly set, he ever afterwards suffered from lameness. This affliction prevented him pursuing his trade as an operative baker, and for some time after his acci-

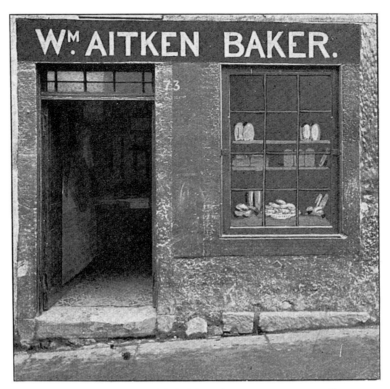

Original Premises.

Present Premises.

Flour Store.

Part of Bakehouse.

dent he acted as clerk to the late ex-Bailie Millar, baker, Stirling. Leaving this employment fifty years ago, Mr Aitken started business on his own account as a baker in the village of St Ninians, and how well the undertaking has prospered is apparent by its progress. Mr Aitken began operations in a small shop and bakehouse with one oven, and before he died the output was quadrupled. The business during the fifty years of existence has only been housed in two places; first the small bakehouse in the southern end of the village, which was only occupied for three years, and since then the present premises at the north end, which have been several times enlarged as necessity demanded. The late Mr William Aitken was a cannie-going, yet shrewd, far-seeing man, and he quickly built up a capital business, which supplied bread not only to the immediate neighbourhood, but by means of delivery vans had a connection over a wide district, from Thornhill and Kippen on the west, to Dunmore and Airth on the east. This connection still remains, and has been added to under the regime of the present head of the firm. On the death of Mr William Aitken in 1899, the business descended to his two sons, James and Thomas, who had been associated with him, but the partnership was dissolved by the death of the former in 1906, since which time Thomas has had sole control.

The founder of the St Ninians Bakery was an enterprising man, who had an up-to-date establishment, and his example has been followed by the present head of the firm, there being fewer better equipped bakeries outside the large cities and towns. When Mr Thomas Aitken began his apprenticeship, the old methods were in several important particulars giving place to the new. Machinery was coming into use, and it has in a number of ways revolutionised the trade, notably in the matter of specialising some of the branches of it. Formerly an operative baker was expected to do all classes of work connected with the turning out of bread, biscuits, and cakes, but nowadays there are in different parts of the country large bakeries which make a specialty of loaves or biscuits, in the production of which machinery plays the principal part. Even yet, however, in certain particulars there is a good deal in the baking trade which is better done by hand labour than machinery, but the latter is a great help in the matter of cleanliness and rapid production. In some of these machine bakeries the flour and liquid goes in at one end of an oven, and comes out in the form of biscuits at the other end. As bread and biscuit bakers, Scottish tradesmen are recognised as being about the best in the world, and they have carried their methods into England and other countries where public bakeries are not so common as in Scotland. For some reason or other the baking of bread, apart from oatmeal cakes and scones, has never been an accomplishment of the Scottish housewife to anything like the extent of her English or American sister. Up till about thirty years ago the principal output of a bakery was wheaten loaves, cookies, flour rolls, biscuits, shortbread, currant loaves, and buns, and any ordinary baker could take a hand in the production of these. Since then, however, a public taste has sprung up for fancy tea cakes of various kinds, and there are now many Swiss, French, and German bakers domiciled in this country in the making of these foreign confections, which is a trade by itself.

Van Shed.

Front of Premises, Maxwell Place.

Section of Showroom.

JOHN WALLS, PAINTER, STIRLING.

The firm of John Walls is the second oldest painting business in Stirling, and was established in 1857. That is a long time ago—two years more than the half-century—but it does not seem so far off when we look upon the founder walking about amongst us still hale and hearty, and enjoying his respite from the labours of a lifetime. Mr John Walls, who only retired a few years ago, is, like many of the leading tradesmen of Stirling, not a native of the "City of the Rock." Dunfermline was his birthplace, and he comes of a family well-known in art circles 'n the capital of West Fife, where, it may be mentioned, Mr Walls' eldest son has been in business for himself for over twenty years.

After serving his apprenticeship in Dunfermline, Mr Walls spent some time in London and Edinburgh gathering experience in his trade, and then came to Stirling, where, after having a look round, he started business. One reason that induced him to do so was that he knew Mr Leonard Baker, the veteran Art Master of Stirling High School, who, like Mr Walls, retired a few years ago, but is also still with us enjoying release from the duties of his profession after many years' service. Mr Walls, it may further be stated, was one of Mr Baker's first pupils in the classes he conducted long ago in the Night School of Art, and Mr Walls derived much encouragement from him, and secured introductions which enabled him to start business with some prospect of succeeding. The town was a different place then, architecturally and otherwise, to what it is now, and though Mr Walls' first premises were in Murray Place, the shops in that street were not of the same class that they are to-day. Mr Walls set up for himself in what was then known as "Neddy" Peddie's fish shop, which was located in the ground flat of a five-storey building that stood at the corner of King Street and Murray Place, and afterwards became the site of Drummond's Tract Depot, and is now the British Linen Company's Bank. Nowadays there are two or three steps up to the bank entrance: at that time there was a step down into Mr Walls' shop. When the property was acquired for the purposes of the Tract Depot, Mr Walls removed to a shop that stood on the site of the property in Murray Place now occupied by Messrs Crowe & Rodgers, photographers, and there he remained for several years. Increasing business once more necessitated another change of premises, and this time

Friars Street was called upon to house his business. Here one, and latterly two, shops were occupied, the second one chiefly required to enable pictures to be shown. Of artistic bent himself, Mr Walls early got into touch with the artists resident in the district, and his premises became to be widely recognised as the principal centre in the town for the exhibition of the works produced by them. That connection still exists, and many fine paintings and engravings have been shown in the Maxwell Place property, to which Mr Walls removed his business nearly fifteen years ago, and where it is still carried on, though extension has been required there too, and was secured some years ago by the "taking in" of the two dwelling-houses above the shop. In connection with the picture branch of the business, Mr Walls was always entrusted with the packing and conveyance of loan paintings sent to Stirling Fine Art Exhibition by private gentlemen and by Corporations, and some very valuable works have been committed to his care. Once he was commissioned to convey to London a fine Raeburn, which sold in the Metropolis for a large sum, and to make assurance doubly sure, a trustworthy attendant travelled inside the van with the picture.

From the start of the business the decorative side of painting has been a feature in the trade of the firm, and many fine specimens of the artistic work of "John Walls, Stirling," are to be seen in the country mansions and public buildings in the district, whilst a wide connection has been established in the house painting and general branch of the trade. At an early period the firm was entrusted with the carrying out of a good deal of Government work in Stirling, whilst from Stirling to the Trossachs on the one side, and along the Forth and Clyde line to Loch Lomond and as far up as Inversnaid on the other, the firm has been commissioned to execute a great deal of work during the last half-century. At one time the painting contract for all the railway stations on the Forth and Clyde line was in the hands of Mr Walls, but for many years back the Railway Company has carried out this work itself. Picture framing and gilding has also been a special "line" of the firm for many years, and since the death of Mr Thomas Young, Baker Street, who was the last of the original framers and gilders in Stirling who made this their only branch of business, the firm of John Walls has

Part of Gilding and Framemaking Department.

One of the Paper Stores.

practically had the monopoly of it in this neighbourhood. To show the wide range of the firm's operations, the following list, by no means a full one, of county gentlemen's mansions, public buildings, and other establishments, where it has executed some fine decorative painting work, may be mentioned—Polmaise Castle, Bannockburn House, Ochtertyre, Stirling; Cromlix, Kilbryde Castle, and Argaty, Dunblane; Doune Lodge and Inverardoch, Doune; Rednock and Gartincaber, Thornhill; Boquhan and Arngomery, Kippen; Dunipace House, Gartmore House, Carbrook (Larbert), Darleith, Cardross; Ardgour, Argyllshire; Trossachs Hotel, Wemyss Bay Hydropathic; Holy Trinity Episcopal, St Mary's Roman Catholic, North Parish, Erskine U.F., and Allan Park U.F. Churches, Stirling. In connection with St Mary's Church, it may be interesting to relate that the painting work of the old R.C. Chapel in Irvine Place was the first job of the kind Mr Walls was entrusted with after starting business in Stirling, and the handsome new church for the same congregation, erected in Upper Bridge Street, the last contract of that nature that he executed before he retired.

When Mr Walls began business 52 years ago, the trade was very much different in many features to what it is at the present day. At that time there were only two painters in the town, and none in the country villages round about: now there are eight or ten in Stirling, and at least one in most of the larger villages. Except here and there, little decorative work was done forty years ago, everything being plain or oil painting or papering. What are known as "borders" in the trade were extensively used then, and a big trade was done in supplying wall paper to country people who came to Stirling to get it, and did the work themselves of pasting it on in their rooms.

House-painting is not a trade into which machinery can enter largely, or even beyond a small extent, but within the last forty years there have been great improvements which have made for better work and much more expedition in carrying out a job. Wall paper is now manufactured to any size, and where it has to be cut, a machine does this in a tithe of the time formerly occupied when hand scissors had to be used. At one time all paper had to be put on by hand, but now brushes are the implements employed for this work, and instead of the tedious scraping of old paint after acids had been requisitioned to

soften it, this work is now quickly performed by the use of the hot air blower, which enables an old coat of paint to be taken off and a new one put on in less than half the time previously required. Then in the olden days tradesmen occupied themselves in the slack winter season by grinding down their paint from the "raw material" by a laborious process, whereas the material needed is now supplied in tins by the manufacturers. The brushes in use are also much finer than was formerly the case, and altogether modern progress has developed many features that make for superior and much more expeditious workmanship.

Five years ago the business was taken over by Mr William M'Laren, Hamilton, who, whilst carrying it on in many respects on the lines of the founder, has, of course, also imprinted his own personality upon it in several directions. Though a young man yet—and will be for years to come —Mr M'Laren, besides having a hereditary connection with the painting trade, has had a practical experience in London, Edinburgh, and Dublin, which is bound to prove a valuable asset to him as the head of such an extensive and well reputed business as that of John Walls, Stirling. It is interesting to note that, though a native of Hamilton, Mr M'Laren has both a family and a trade connection with the "City of the Rock." He is the fourth generation of house painters in his family, the first being his great grandfather, Mr James Buchanan, who had a master painter's business in Baker Street, Stirling, in the early half of last century. Another link with that period exists in the person of Mr John Johnstone, foreman with the firm, his father having served his apprenticeship with Mr James Buchanan, the great grandfather of Mr M'Laren.

Under Mr M'Laren's regime, the amicable relationship that has always existed between the head of the firm and the employees is being maintained, and that master and men have a mutual consideration and regard for one another is shown by the fact of there never being any labour troubles to disturb the friendly atmosphere in which they work. Another object lesson in this direction is provided by the long period of service of the "hands." Seven of them have an average of 25 years each, which is a large proportion out of a list of 35 employees—this being the average number employed, though, of course, in the busy summer season the figures are much higher.

Section of Repair Shop.

GRAMPIAN MOTOR CO., LTD., CAUSEWAYHEAD.

Though this firm is the youngest dealt with in the present series of articles—the works at Causewayhead only having been erected in June, 1907—the business is an expanding one, and the premises are already becoming small enough for the trade carried on. Moreover, the Works have the distinction of being the only general engineering establishment in the district, the nearest industry of the same kind being as far away as Glasgow. The premises are well equipped with machinery of the latest type suitable for the complete overhaul and renewal of motor vehicles of any make, and in addition to this business, the firm undertake all classes of general engineering. This latter includes the repair of mill machinery, road rollers, pattern making, &c., and a specialty to which particular attention is given is in the construction of the "Flash" boiler, which is the type adopted in all steam motor cars and launches. Another specialty—and one which is exclusively manufactured by the firm—is the steam "Velox" disinfector. This apparatus has a simple but very effective method of dealing with microbes, insects, &c., such a heat being raised in a short time that their life is scalded out of them, whilst the blankets, sheets, and rugs to which they may be adhering, are completely dried and disinfected without being injured in any way. These disinfectors are constructed either as a stationary apparatus or on wheels, and the former kind have been introduced into many of the isolation hospitals of this country, whilst the War Office and the India Office have been supplied with a number of the apparatus in both forms. Whilst it is the case, as has already been stated, that the firm goes in for all kinds of general engineering work which enables them to keep a staff capable of undertaking any job placed in their hands, most of their trade is connected with the overhaul of motor cars. At the Grampian Works all the engineering parts of a car can be manufactured or supplied, and the enterprise shown in this direction has been justified, the firm having a connection in this line that extends all over the country. Difficulty is now being felt in accommodating the work entrusted to the Company in the busy season, and as the motor vehicle trade is increasing daily, it is only a matter of time ere the Works will have to be extended.

As the Grampian Company is practically an outcome of the motor car industry, it may not be without interest to give here a brief resume of that wonderful development which is rapidly revolutionising vehicular locomotion on the public roads. An English patent for a horseless carriage was taken out as far back as 1819, but to a Frenchman named Cagnot, belongs the credit of being the first to make a vehicle to actually run upon the road. This was a steam coach, of which there were various types in the early half of the last century, and very antiquated looking machines they appear to our eyes nowadays in the illustrations seen of them. In Great Britain, which has always proved herself more conservative than foreign nations to adopting new methods, the opposition of the road authorities and of the public, coupled with legislative enactments, effectively silenced all inventors in this direction for many years. The high speed combustion motor of Gottlieb Daimler revolutionised the whole subject of road traction in France in 1884, and since then the advance of the motor has been great in all civilised countries. In 1895, the first exhibition of motor cars in Britain took place at Tunbridge Wells, and how much the industry has progressed since then may be gathered from the fact that the engine of a first-class motor car fourteen years ago was only 4 horse power, whilst now racing vehicles of 100 horse power are built, and cars of from 20 to 70 h.p. are quite common. In many respects the motor car of the present day is a vast improvement on the vehicle of only half a dozen years ago, and particularly in the matter of speed, appearance, and general reliability. The sight of a broken-down car being dragged by a horse along the streets, to the amusement of unsympathetic onlookers, is now a rare occurrence, and it will soon be only a memory. Though kept behind for a long time in the domain of progress owing to the hostility of the authorities, Britain is fast catching up on her foreign rivals, and her manufacturers have now nothing to learn from them.

In conclusion, it may be remarked that the principals of the Grampian Motor and Engineering Company are all men in the prime of life, with, as the Yankees say, "no cobwebs" about them. Up to date in their ideas of business, no

High Pressure Steam Velox Disinfector.

conservative notions regarding industrial enterprise have a place in their vocabulary, and all are well equipped by education and training for the departments of which they have the oversight. The overhaul and repair of motor cars is mainly supervised by Mr W. B. M'Hardy, who had a long experience in the engineering department of the Fairfield Shipbuilding Company, Govan, and he is assisted by Mr John Simpson, formerly of Whins of Milton, Stirling, who had a valuable training in one of the principal marine engineering establishments in the country—Laird's of Birkenhead—and is also well-known for his knowledge and experience of steam cars. A third member of the firm is Mr Harold Barnwell, who was employed for several years in the designing department of the Fairfield Shipbuilding Company, and was also for a considerable time in the Argyll Motor Company's Works. The other director of the Company is Lieutenant-Colonel Oliver, late of that highly scientific branch of His Majesty's Service—the Royal Artillery—but who will be more familiar to the public of this district as the Commanding Officer at the Government Ordnance Stores, Forthside, Stirling, during the time of the South African War. The Grampian Engineering and Motor Company has, under the supervision of the gentlemen mentioned, successfully weathered the many difficulties inseparable from the starting of a new enterprise, and now that it has been firmly established on its legs, so to speak, we trust that this young firm will in years to come qualify for the distinction of being one of the oldest established industries in the district.

Part of Machine Shop.

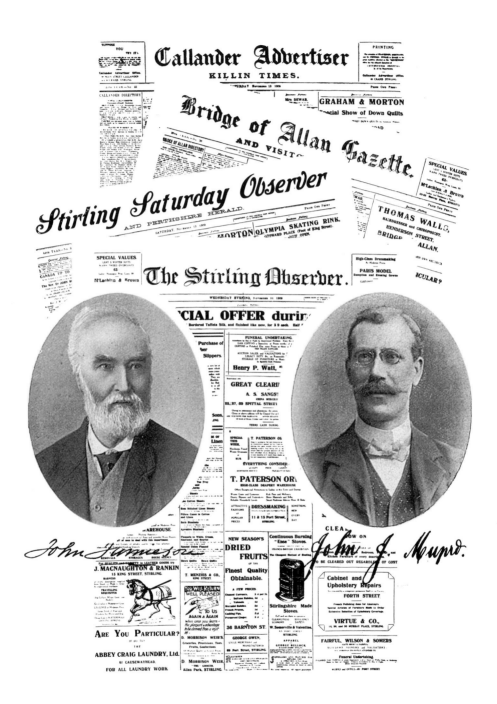

JOHN JAMIESON,

PRINTER, PUBLISHER, AND WHOLESALE STATIONER, STIRLING.

When the "Observer" was inaugurated it was printed in Baker Street, which was then, along with Broad Street and Bow Street, the business quarter of the town, but gradually the conditions altered, the old order passed away, and professional and commercial firms began to move downwards, with the "Observer" always in the forefront. The first number was published on 15th September, 1836, and whilst the paper was not half the size it is now, the price of a copy was 4d. The imprint bears the name of Ebenezer Johnstone, and there were only 24 advertisements in it. Now there are regularly between two and three hundred every week. Much less attention was apparently paid to local news in these days, prominence being given to Parliamentary intelligence and national events. The necessity for this was, of course, more urgent than is the case now. Evening papers were then an unknown quantity, and there were also few, if any, dailies outside London, and dependence had accordingly to be placed on weekly and bi-weekly journals for the supply of general news, but with the advance of printing and the cheapening of paper, all that is changed, and local newspapers nowadays find their mission in the chronicling of the happenings in their own districts, leaving the wider field for their daily contemporaries.

From its earliest days the "Observer" was recognised as the principal paper in the town, and the exponent of sensible and moderate views on all local topics; also a medium for reports that could be relied upon, and a fair criticism, that only dealt with the merits of the question at issue and left the personal alone, and we are glad to be able to think that it holds this reputation yet. Without troubling further with the details of the early days of the business, let it suffice to say that it was always increasing, and this necessitated changing to newer and more commodious premises. After leaving Baker Street, the "Observer" was issued next from Murray Place, from premises now occupied by Dean of Guild Steel and Robertson & Sons, and following on that was transferred to Upper Craigs, where three different buildings have been occupied at various periods. Since the business was located in the Craigs its greatest development has taken place. What was then known as Fotheringham's bottling store was taken over and occupied in 1865, and here the "Observer" enterprise was carried on with ever-increasing success until 1880, when another move had to be made. A commodious property was then erected on the other side of the street, and the prophecy was uttered by some friends that surely the new building would, by reason of its size, do away with the necessity of any more changing about. Not many years elapsed, however, before it became apparent that sooner or later removal to larger premises would again have to be faced if the business was to keep pace with modern requirements and the calls made upon it by the ever-increasing volume of trade, and the result was the handsome establishment in which the "Observer" now finds its home. Large as it is, some people already seem to have doubts that the new offices will serve as long as the building that has been vacated, but, be that as it may, it is to be hoped that like prosperity to that enjoyed in the past will attend the establishment, and that the due reward of the energy and enterprise displayed will be reaped.

Since 1873 the "Observer" has been published bi-weekly, and in 1884 the "Callander Advertiser" and "Bridge of Allan Gazette" were added, in order to provide local papers for these districts. In the same year the wholesale stationery branch was started, and this department has grown to very large dimensions for a town the size of Stirling.

Mr Ebenezer Johnstone was the head of the business for 24 years, then Mr Samuel Cowan possessed it for six years, Mr Robert Gray was proprietor for five years, and in 1871 Messrs Duncan & Jamieson took it over. Mr Duncan has been dead many years, and since then Mr Jamieson has been sole partner, his connection with the business having now lasted for 38 years.

Part of Machine Room.

Part of Caseroom.

He, however, retired from the active management in 1895, from which year his nephew—Mr John Jamieson Munro—has had the control. Mr Munro, like his uncle, has a thorough knowledge of the printing profession, and under his supervision the business has been enlarged and developed in several directions, until now it is equal to the best in the provinces in regard to up-to-date equipment for the execution of first-class general printing work. So far as the chief newspaper issued from the office—"The Stirling Observer"—is concerned, it maintains its reputation as the leading local organ in Stirling, and testimony to this fact is frequently received from readers both at home and abroad. Of recent years a feature has been made of illustrations in the pages of the paper, and the excellent fashion in which these are produced has earned commendation from many quarters in the printing trade, and also outside of it.

DESCRIPTION OF PREMISES.

For the purposes of the "Observer," a large double shop is utilised as the printing, advertising, and stationery office, whilst off it are rooms for the principal, and the editor and reporters, and also a small chamber where the files of the paper can be consulted. The office is fitted up with public telephone, private telephones, and a pneumatic tube for the conveyance of messages and the transport of literary and commercial communications to the type-setting and printing departments, which ensures getting promptly into touch with these parts of the building, and avoids the necessity of a considerable journey, which would otherwise have to be made on foot, with resultant delay and much loss of time. The printing department, where the various machines for this purpose are situated, has a floor area of 88 feet long by 50 feet broad, well lighted and ventilated, and providing excellent accommodation for the printing plant, part of which is shown in one of our illustrations. The motive power is electricity, individual motors driving each of the large machines. Besides economising the electric current by only using it when needed, this arrangement does away with the overhead shafting and belting which steam or gas motive power requires, and there is also an entire freedom from danger, and an absence of oil and dust, which are no mean advantages in any workshop, and particularly in a printing

office. Twelve electric motors are used in this department, giving an aggregate driving force of 50 horse-power. The printing plant provides facilities for the production of the four newspapers published from the office, in addition to a large general printing equipment, and the issuing of book work, colour printing, posters of all sizes, and illustrated work.

The type-setting room measures 60 feet long by 44 broad, and is carried on steel beams and columns, with a span roof on trussed steel principals. Accommodation is found on this floor for the large staff of compositors employed, whilst in a separate division is the linotype department, these machines also being driven by electricity. A hoist is used to convey goods and material between the printing establishment and the type-setting room.

The wholesale stationery department has an extensive showroom and ample storage accommodation for the very large stock of general and mercantile stationery, including notepaper and envelopes, inks, pens, pencils, stationery cabinets, picture postcards, account books, wrapping papers, and paper bags, and every kind of twines, etc.

Billposting is also allotted a separate department, and here are to be seen stocks of placards that are speedily to find a place on the "people's picture galleries." Specimens of printed posters and pictorial placards are likewise stocked for the use of customers when selecting something new for the hoardings.

INTERESTING COMPARISONS.

And now, to wind up, a few comparative notes may be of interest. In 1862—forty-seven years ago—the "Observer" employed seven "hands," now there are 44. Then there was only one printing machine, now there are 12; half-a-horse-power sufficed in 1862, now something like 50 h.p. is available, and that, as has been pointed out, all electric, causing the office to be reckoned the largest user of that power for current purposes that the municipality has.

OLD CONNECTIONS.

During its existence the "Stirling Observer" has had a long business connection with other local firms, and it is pleasing to note that, in addition to the Tract Depot, which has been on the books of the office since the beginning, Messrs

Section of Stationery Warehouse.

William Drummond & Sons, seedsmen; R. S.
Shearer & Son, booksellers; Thomas Menzies &
Co., drapers; Hugh Gavin & Sons, drapers;
Mathie, MacLuckie & Lupton, writers; William
Kinross & Sons, coachbuilders; the Gas-Lighting
Company; and others of the long-established firms
in town have been continuous customers, and have
accounts still open, not to speak of the public
offices, Town, Parish Council, etc.

LONG SERVICE EMPLOYEES.

And while these business relations have been
maintained for many years, another feature
worthy of note may be mentioned—that being the
long period of service in which many of the employees have been engaged. The 16 who were in
the office up to the date of Mr Jamieson's retiral
from the active management in 1894 have an
aggregate of 425 years, giving an average of about
$26\frac{1}{2}$ years each; and 9, who count more than 22
years' service, reach an aggregate of 288 years,
giving an average of 32. Few businesses, we
think, could produce a better record than that,
and it is a striking illustration of the pleasant
relations that have all along characterised the
connection between master and servant in the
office of the "Stirling Observer." Loyalty on
the one hand, and consideration on the other,
could only have made such a result possible.

Linotype Department.

Section of Printing Department.

Port Street Premises.

D. & J. MACEWEN & CO.,

FAMILY GROCERS AND WINE MERCHANTS, STIRLING.

This article deals with one of the oldest firms of grocers, wine, and general merchants in Scotland. When the firm was established the conditions of life for the great mass of the people were at a lower ebb than ever before in British history. Napoleon dominated Europe, and only waited an opportunity to carry out his long-cherished design of an invasion of Britain. At this period the old town of Stirling was gradually emancipating itself from the "Burgher" regime, under which trade within the walls could only be carried on under the closest restrictions and regulations. It is interesting to note that in 1794, according to an old record, "the principal professions of consequence" were represented as under :—Ministers, 8 ; writers, 17 ; physicians, 5 ; surgeons, 2 ; merchants, 30 ; shoemakers, 18 ; bakers, 13 ; weavers, 68 ; hammermen, 13 ; skinners, 2 ; butchers, 3 ; tailors, 15. The population was about 5000, and a considerable trade was done with the Continent, particularly Holland, in woollen goods. Besides being the centre of a wide and prosperous agricultural district, Stirling was the "depot" on which the inhabitants of a very extended area depended for their supplies. Broad Street was then the fashionable and business quarter in the town, and was the rendezvous for buyers and sellers from all parts of the country.

It was at such a time, and under such conditions, that the firm of D. & J. MacEwen opened their first place of business. For a quarter of a century it was the chief grocery establishment in the town, and in the firm's ledgers, so far back as 1807-08, are to be found the names of many of the leading families in central Scotland, whose descendants, in many cases, are customers of the firm to this day. The founders of the firm were Messrs Daniel and James MacEwen, who, some years later, were joined by Mr John MacEwen (originally a partner in the firm of Wright & MacEwen, writers), and father of the present senior partners. They were all men of great public spirit, and were universally esteemed for their integrity and business ability. Mr John MacEwen survived his brothers for many years, and was greatly respected, and is still remembered

for his great probity of character, kindliness of disposition, and courtesy of manner. Under his wise guidance the enterprise continued to prosper, and in the year 1848 the present senior partners, Mr Daniel and Mr John MacEwen, entered the business. In the interval, owing to the rapid extension of the town and the increase in their business, the Messrs MacEwen purchased the site of their present premises in Port Street, and erected a substantial property, which was taken down only a few years ago to make room for their present handsome property. The offices, which are large and commodious, contain a room for the staff of clerks, a private room for the partners, and sampling rooms for the various departments. The spirit cellar is situated immediately behind the shop and packing room, and contains a large and valuable stock. Large casks are reserved for the old and well known Whiskies always in demand, such as Burntisland, Cambus, Glen Grant, Lagavulin, Long John, Talisker, and "Sterlini" (the firm's special registered blend). "Sterlini" is supplied regularly to many of the leading provincial and London clubs, and is shipped in bond to India, Africa, and Canada. It is ten years old ; the produce of several of the most famous Highland malt distilleries, and possesses all the mellowness and character which age alone can give. It is matured in sherry wood, and is a healthful and invigorating stimulant. Quite recently a consignment was despatched to such an out-of-the-way place as Omdurman, in the very heart of the Soudan. The total floorage of the cellars extends to about 3000 square feet, the greater portion being used as the general storage cellar. The cellars are all provided with patent fire-proof doors, are well ventilated and scrupulously clean, and are lit with electric light throughout. Every bottle is washed, corked, and capsuled by machinery, and nothing is left undone to ensure the various liquors being sent out in perfect condition.

The front shop is large and suitably arranged for the display of fancy goods, while the marble provision shelves and counters, and mosaic floor, give a general impression of freshness and cleanli-

The Late Bailie John MacEwen.

Mr. Daniel MacEwen.

ness. Without undue extravagance, it is handsome and modern, and is fitted with all the latest labour-saving appliances.

The late Bailie John MacEwen laid the foundation of the firm's reputation as connoisseurs, and some of the wines bought by him, still in bins, are, for style and character, rarely to be met with. Fancy prices have on various occasions been offered for particular lots, but they have been retained exclusively for the firm's special trade. Surprise has often been expressed at it being found advisable to carry such large and valuable stocks. This, however, is rendered necessary by the changed habits of the wine-drinking classes. Formerly it was the custom of gentlemen of even moderate means to lay down "vintage" wines in their own cellars. The growing popularity of a lighter type of wine and of champagne and whisky, which do not require so much keeping, has done away with this practice, with the result that the wine merchant, to meet this demand, has to carry a larger stock ready for immediate consumption. This naturally has led to extreme competition, and for several years both provincial and city houses suffered from the "German invasion" of wine travellers and commission agents. But their promises, like the great majority of their wines, proved to be of comparatively little value, and those who were tempted to place their orders abroad have found it both wise and profitable to return to their own wine merchant.

There are four large flats devoted to the storage of groceries and provisions, and the total stock is turned over and replaced with fresh goods about nine times a year. Two large hoists are in continual operation for the raising and lowering of goods to and from the loading berths and the various floors.

The Seed and Grain Department consists of two flats, which were considered adequate at one time, but are now merely used for emergency orders. Almost from the inception of the firm a large seed and grain trade has been done, but this department, like the others, has undergone great changes during the past four decades. The whole district was at one time devoted to the cultivation of grain, but foreign competition gradually forced home farmers to change their policy and depend for a considerable portion of their revenue upon the raising and fattening of stock. The introduction of linseed cake and other concentrated foods revolutionised the

system of feeding, and created a new and important department in businesses such as this. What prepared foods have done for stock raising, prepared manures may be said to have done for grain and fodder growing. The introduction of Peruvian guano, and more recently, artifically prepared manures, materially improved the position of agriculturalists and assisted them in competing with the products of the virgin soil of the new world. The firm have been agents for many years for several of the best known manufacturers, and in the spring time dispose of large quantities to be used throughout various districts of the country. The machinery is driven by a 16-horse-power gas engine, recently supplemented by two 11-horse-power electric motors. The bulk of the grain, oilcake, and other feeding stuffs, as well as wool, is stored in Park Lane premises.

In order to more effectively develop the firm's business in Perthshire and the West Highlands, a branch was opened in Callander in the year 1857. This took place at an opportune time, for "The Wizard of the North" had thrown over that district the glamour of romance, and the quiet Highland village was being gradually transformed into a popular summer resort, with commodious hotels and modern villas. The introduction of railway facilities inaugurated a period of great progress throughout the whole of central Scotland, and to meet the ever increasing requirements of the business, new branches were opened at Bridge of Allan, Crieff, Killin, and Dunblane, and more recently at Fort William and Aberfoyle. The firm are also represented in Inverness under the name of MacDonald & Mackintosh, and the premises there have recently been remodelled and equipped with the latest labour-saving appliances.

The present partners are—

Mr John MacEwen, who retired from active business some years ago, after 40 years' service, but still counts amongst his friends many of the firm's most esteemed customers.

Mr Daniel MacEwen, senior, has been connected with the firm since his boyhood. He has all along taken the leading position in the general management of the business, and is largely responsible for the progressive and successful policy pursued during the latter half of the past century. He has always been interested in the larger questions affecting the trade and district. He was one of the witnesses who appeared before a Committee of the House of Commons in connection with the amalgamation of the Scottish Central and Caledonian Railways, and, along with others, was instrumental in obtaining a special schedule of rates applicable to Stirling. He also appeared as a witness before several Royal Commissions, including that on Grocers' Licenses in 1878, and the Royal Commission on the Liquor Licensing Laws in 1897. He is a Justice of Peace for the county of Perth, and a well-known churchman. He was for many years Chief Magistrate, and is Chairman of the School Board of Callander, where he resides, and has taken an active part in promoting the prosperity of that burgh.

Mr Robert M. MacEwen was also an active partner until his death three years ago. Mr Daniel MacEwen, jun., and Mr William MacEwen, who represent the younger generation of the family, joined the firm some years ago, and are now closely associated with their father in the control and general management of the business at headquarters and the branches. As can readily be understood, the turnover in the various departments amounts to a very large total, and it is interesting to know that notwithstanding the increased competition of city houses and "stores," and societies of every description,

it never stood at a higher figure than now. The customers of the firm include many of the nobility and county families of Scotland, and on three separate occasions they had the honour of supplying Her late Majesty Queen Victoria, viz. :—when residing at Invertrossachs, Inverlochy, and Ardveriekie Castle.

The centenary of the firm, five years ago, was made the occasion of one of the most interesting functions ever held in the business life of the town. Under the chairmanship of Sir John Ure Primrose, then Lord Provost of Glasgow, a representative assembly of over 250 gentlemen entertained the members of the firm to dinner in the Albert Hall, and on the following evening the members of the staff were entertained and presented Mr Daniel MacEwen, sen., with his portrait in oil, painted by Mr R. C. Crawford, the well-known Scottish portrait painter. To mark the occasion, an interesting booklet was issued giving the history of the firm, together with a series of tables showing the extraordinary changes in prices of many articles in daily use since 1804, as well as some quaint information regarding the business methods of the provincial grocer in the early decades of last century.

Front Shop Interior.

JOHN WALLS,

Painter and Decorator,

Gilder and

Picture Frame Maker,

3 and 5 MAXWELL PLACE

(Adjoining POST OFFICE),

STIRLING.

Contractor to H.M. Office of Works, for Stirling Castle and District.

Designs and Estimates submitted for House and Church Decoration.

Pictures Cleaned, Lined, and Restored :
Private Collections arranged and Hung.